The Politics and Performance of Mestizaje in Latin America

The term 'mestizaje' is generally translated as race mixture, with races typically understood as groups differentiated by skin color or other physical characteristics. Yet such understandings seem contradicted by contemporary understandings of race as a cultural construct, or idea, rather than as a biological entity. How might one then approach mestizaje in a way that is not definitionally predicated on 'race', or at least on a modernist formulation of race as phenotypically expressed biological difference? The contributors to this book provide explorations of this question in varied Latin American contexts (Mexico, Guatemala, Bolivia, Colombia and Peru), from the sixteenth century to the present. They treat 'mestizo acts' neither as expressions of preexisting social identities, nor as ideologies enforced from above, but as cultural performances enacted in the in-between spaces of social and political life. Moreover, they show how 'mestizo acts' not only express or reinforce social hierarchies, but institute or change them – seeking to prove – or to dismantle – genealogies of race, blood, sex and language in public and political ways.

The chapters in this book were originally published as a special issue of *Latin American and Caribbean Ethnic Studies*.

Paul K. Eiss is an Associate Professor of Anthropology and History at Carnegie Mellon, USA. In publications like *In the Name of El Pueblo: Place, Community, and the Politics of History in Yucatán* (2010), he explores labor, value, commodities, indigeneity, mestizaje, media, violence and the politics of historical memory.

Joanne Rappaport is Professor of Spanish and Portuguese at Georgetown University, USA. She is the author of *The Disappearing Mestizo: Configuring Difference in the Colonial New Kingdom of Granada* (2014) and *Intercultural Utopias: Public Intellectuals, Cultural Experimentation, and Ethnic Dialogue in Colombia* (2005) and coauthor (with Tom Cummins) of *Beyond the Lettered City: Indigenous Literacies in the Andes* (2011), *Cumbe Reborn: An Andean Ethnography of History* (1994) and *The Politics of Memory: Native Historical Interpretation in the Northern Andes* (1998).

The Politics and Performance of Mestizaje in Latin America
Mestizo Acts

Edited by
Paul K. Eiss
LACES Responsible Editor: Joanne Rappaport

Routledge
Taylor & Francis Group

LONDON AND NEW YORK

First published 2018 by Routledge

2 Park Square, Milton Park, Abingdon, Oxfordshire OX14 4RN
52 Vanderbilt Avenue, New York, NY 10017

Routledge is an imprint of the Taylor & Francis Group, an informa business

First issued in paperback 2019

British Library Cataloguing in Publication Data
A catalogue record for this book is available from the British Library

ISBN 13: 978-1-138-56433-6 (hbk)
ISBN 13: 978-0-367-89235-7 (pbk)

Typeset in MyriadPro
by diacriTech, Chennai

Publisher's Note
The publisher accepts responsibility for any inconsistencies that may have
arisen during the conversion of this book from journal articles to book chapters,
namely the possible inclusion of journal terminology.

Disclaimer
Every effort has been made to contact copyright holders for their permission to
reprint material in this book. The publishers would be grateful to hear from any
copyright holder who is not here acknowledged and will undertake to rectify
any errors or omissions in future editions of this book.

Contents

Citation Information

The chapters in this book were originally published in *Latin American and Caribbean Ethnic Studies*, volume 11, issue 3 (November 2016). When citing this material, please use the original page numbering for each article, as follows:

Introduction
Mestizo acts
Paul K. Eiss
Latin American and Caribbean Ethnic Studies, volume 11, issue 3 (November 2016)
pp. 213–221

Chapter 1
Indian allies and white antagonists: toward an alternative mestizaje *on Mexico's Costa Chica*
Laura A. Lewis
Latin American and Caribbean Ethnic Studies, volume 11, issue 3 (November 2016)
pp. 222–241

Chapter 2
Playing mestizo: festivity, language, and theatre in Yucatán, Mexico
Paul K. Eiss
Latin American and Caribbean Ethnic Studies, volume 11, issue 3 (November 2016)
pp. 242–265

Chapter 3
Foundational essays as 'mestizo-criollo acts': the Bolivian case
Javier Sanjinés C.
Latin American and Caribbean Ethnic Studies, volume 11, issue 3 (November 2016)
pp. 266–286

Chapter 4
Mestizaje as ethical disposition: indigenous rights in the neoliberal state
Deborah Poole
Latin American and Caribbean Ethnic Studies, volume 11, issue 3 (November 2016)
pp. 287–304

For any permission-related enquiries please visit:
http://www.tandfonline.com/page/help/permissions

Notes on Contributors

Paul K. Eiss is an Associate Professor of Anthropology and History at Carnegie Mellon University, USA. In publications like *In the Name of El Pueblo: Place, Community, and the Politics of History in Yucatán* (2010), he explores labor, value, commodities, indigeneity, mestizaje, media, violence and the politics of historical memory. Currently, he is at work on a study of practices and rhetoric of collective violence and collective self-defense in contemporary Mexico.

Laura A. Lewis is Professor of Anthropology at the University of Southampton, UK. In addition to numerous articles, she is the author of the books *Chocolate and Corn Flour: History, Race and Place in the Making of "Black" Mexico* (2012) and *Hall of Mirrors: Power, Witchcraft, and Caste in Colonial Mexico* (2003). She has received fellowships from the Guggenheim Foundation, the National Endowment for the Humanities and the Smithsonian Institution.

Deborah Poole is Professor of Anthropology at Johns Hopkins University, USA. Her most recent research examines cultural politics, expertise, decentralization and state form in Peru and Mexico.

Joanne Rappaport is Professor of Spanish and Portuguese at Georgetown University, USA. She is the author of *The Disappearing Mestizo: Configuring Difference in the Colonial New Kingdom of Granada* (2014) and *Intercultural Utopias: Public Intellectuals, Cultural Experimentation, and Ethnic Dialogue in Colombia* (2005) and coauthor (with Tom Cummins) of *Beyond the Lettered City: Indigenous Literacies in the Andes* (2011), *Cumbe Reborn: An Andean Ethnography of History* (1994) and *The Politics of Memory: Native Historical Interpretation in the Northern Andes* (1998).

Javier Sanjinés C. is Professor of Latin American Literature and Cultural Studies at the University of Michigan-Ann Arbor, USA. He obtained his PhD in Luso-Brazilian and Hispanic-American Literatures at the University of Minnesota (1988), and a postdoctoral Rockefeller Foundation Fellowship at the University of Chicago (1995), USA. He has published extensively on Bolivian Literature and Cultural Studies. He was a founding member of the Latin American Subaltern Studies Group.

Peter Wade is Professor of Social Anthropology at the University of Manchester, UK. He held a British Academy Wolfson Research Professorship 2013–2016. His latest book is *Degrees of Mixture, Degrees of Freedom: Genomics, Multiculturalism, and Race in Latin America* (2017) and he is currently co-directing the project "Latin American Antiracism in a 'Post-Racial' Age" (https://www.lapora.sociology.cam.ac.uk/).

John M. Watanabe received his PhD in Social Anthropology from Harvard University, USA, in 1984 and he is currently associate professor of Anthropology at Dartmouth College, USA. He has done anthropological research on Mam Maya identity in Guatemala since 1978. He is currently in a project on the history of interactions between Mam and Ladino communities and the Guatemalan state in southern Huehuetenango during the nineteenth century, based on administrative and land tenure records from the General Archive of Central America.

Introduction: Mestizo acts

Paul K. Eiss

ABSTRACT

How is one to approach mestizaje in a way that is not definitionally predicated on 'race,' or at least, on a modernist formulation of race as phenotypically expressed biological difference? The contributors to this volume provide explorations of this question in varied national contexts (Mexico, Guatemala, Bolivia, Colombia, Peru), from the16th century to the present. They treat 'mestizo acts' neither as expressions of preexisting social identities, nor as ideologies enforced from above, but as cultural performances enacted in the in-between spaces of social and political life. Moreover, they show how 'mestizo acts' not only express or reinforce social hierarchies, but institute or change them – seeking to prove – or to dismantle – genealogies of race, blood, sex, and language in public and political ways.

The spectacular opening ceremony of the 2016 Olympics in Río de Janeiro began with a series of enactments of the encounters of peoples of indigenous, Portuguese, African, Middle Eastern, and Asian origin throughout Brazil's history. Those multifarious encounters, however, culminated in the drawn out catwalk of a single figure – supermodel Gisele Bündchen – who crossed the vast stage to the strains of 'The Girl from Ipanema.' After viewing it all, psychologist Letícia Bahia asked: 'What does it say about a mixed-race country, boasting about its pride over miscegenation, to choose a supermodel who is white, ultraskinny, blond and blue-eyed to represent the women of Brazil?' (cited in Romero 2016).

The topic of *mestizaje* or *mestiçagem* – i.e. race mixture – is one that lies at the core of Latin America's past and of the ways that past has been rendered into national historical narratives like the one that opened the 2016 Olympics. It is also a topic that has been studied abundantly by scholars of Latin American studies across disciplines. The general outlines of the history of mestizaje seem clear. While in the wake of conquest, the Spanish initially sought to establish separations between the *república de españoles* and the *república de indios*, contact and sexual relations between European and indigenous populations, whether forced or consensual, soon produced a population of mixed descent. With the arrival of African slaves ethnic mixture became more complex. Over the course of colonial rule, populations of mixed lineage came to outnumber both Spanish and indigenous populations in many regions. Ensuing processes of cultural exchange, the story goes, led to linguistic, religious, and cultural mixing, as well as important political consequences, beginning with the breakdown of the notional system of separate republics. A caste system emerged founded upon a taxonomic lexicon of racial titles derived from the complex panorama of interracial unions involving persons of mixed European, indigenous, and African heritage: one memorably depicted in the interracial family portraits of Mexico's 18th-century *casta* paintings (Esteva Fabregat 1995; Mörner 1967).

In the history of postcolonial Latin America, mestizaje continued to figure centrally – and in ways that were more explicitly public and political. By the time of independence in the early 19th century, elites in Mexico, Central America, and the Andes came to regard their nations' mixed heritage, and indigenous pasts, as inescapable – even foundational (Earle 2007). In sharp distinction from their segregationist North American analogues, they viewed racial and cultural mixing as offering a basis for the construction of distinctive national identities. Mixing – often conceived as a process of 'whitening,' as may have been echoed in the 2016 Olympics ceremonies in Río – became a dominant political discourse, an 'ideology of mixture that extends the illusion of defined "racial" identities as it simultaneously portends the erosion of ethnic hierarchies' (Poole 2016). Thus, indigenous or African-descended populations, conceived as racially inferior and culturally isolated, were to be assimilated in bio-racial, social, and cultural terms (Graham 2006; Skidmore 1993; Wade 2010). In the wake of the Mexican Revolution and over the course of the 20th century such ideas, and the related phenomenon of 'indigenism' (*indigenismo*), became central to revolutionary and populist projects of social reform and nation making and modernist mestizo aesthetics (Alonso 2004; Gotkowitz 2011; Knight 1990; Miller 2004). In Mexico, in particular, social and cultural programs were aimed at the redemption of indigenous populations, and their transformation from impoverished 'Indians' and 'proto citizens' (Dawson 2004, xx) into mestizo citizens – what José Vasconcelos in 1925 famously termed a 'cosmic race' (Knight 1990; Vasconcelos 1997); rhetorics of mestizaje have underpinned cross-border Chicana/o ethnic, cultural, political, and religious identities as well (Anzaldúa 2007; Pérez-Torres 2006). Across contemporary Latin America, scholars have demonstrated the continued salience of ideologies of mestizaje and mixed 'ethnoracial' identifications – for instance, in studies of 'mestizo genomics' (Wade et al. 2014) and the workings of 'pigmentocracy' (Sue 2013; Telles and Project on Ethnicity and Race in Latin America 2014).

The scholarship on mestizaje across Latin America is so vast as to defy summary, though several scholars have provided useful comparative discussions of the literature in monographs and review essays (de Castro 2002; Mallon 1996; Mangan 2014; Martinez-Echazabal 1998; Miller 2004; Rahier 2003). While earlier studies of mestizaje were predicated on a conception of race difference as biologically or phenotypically defined, more recently scholars of race and mestizaje have tended to eschew biologically defined conceptions of race, instead approaching racial categorizations – and hence race-mixing – as social and cultural constructs. In Stolcke's memorable formulation, 'Los mestizos no nacen, se hacen' ('mestizos are not born, they are made') (Stolcke 2008, 19). Recent studies have provided welcome complications of earlier accountings of mestizaje's colonial and postcolonial history, highlighting the ideological and political dimensions of perceptions surrounding race difference and race mixture. They analyze how forms of cultural admixture attendant on mestizaje are conditioned by relations of class, gender, and sexuality, and dynamics of nationalism and state formation. Thus, they tend to analyze mixture and discourses of mixture not as a generic, singular mestizaje but in the plural, as mestizajes: i.e. as regionally and historically specific formations of mestizo or mixed racial identity (Appelbaum, Macpherson, and Rosemblatt 2003; Cope 1994; Fisher and O'Hara 2009; Gotkowitz 2011; Loveman 2014).

In a 1996 review that still retains its utility, Florencia Mallon (1996) argued that scholarship on mestizaje tended to fall into two currents of interpretation. The first follows Stutzman's analysis of mestizaje as an 'all inclusive ideology of exclusion' – a discourse of social control that maintains hierarchies of race and class even as it seems to offer escape from them (Stutzman 1981; see also Gould 1998). The second interprets mestizaje as a 'liberating force that breaks open colonial and neocolonial categories of ethnicity and race … [and] … rejects the need to belong as defined by those in power' (Mallon 1996, 171) – a kind of mestizaje Hale has called 'mestizaje from below' (2005, 25). There are significant differences between these two currents; postcolonial celebrations of mestizaje, as an expression of hybridity and escape from racial hierarchies, have been met with criticism for the adoption of discourses that to some remain inseparably attached to the 'racialism' and 'essentialism' (Martinez-Echazabal 1998, 22, 30, 37) of European racial thought (Rahier 2003). But on one point, there seems to be agreement between studies of mestizaje in colonial and postcolonial contexts, whether interpreted 'from above' or 'from below': mestizaje is about race.

The articles in this collection question this seemingly straightforward assumption. They suggest that to view mestizaje as fundamentally 'about' race, at least according to its modern biological or ethnoracial formulation, may be both partial and anachronistic. Recent studies of medieval and early modern Iberian conceptions of racial difference, particularly in the context of the emergence of the doctrine of *limpieza de sangre* (purity of blood), have challenged any expectation that race in medieval contexts conform to modernist conceptions of race; i.e. to the 'application of 18th- and 19th-century vocabularies of biological classification to human populations differentiated by skin color' (Nirenberg 2009, 235). In contrast, Iberian racialism emerged out of a different equation of culture and nature, involving complex judgments about lineage, descent, religion, social honor, and blood purity, as well as physical characteristics. Iberian conceptions of *raza, casta,* and *linaje* (race, caste, and lineage) closely aligned conceptions of human difference with ideas derived from animal breeding and husbandry (Goode 2009; Hering Torres, Martínez, and Nirenberg 2012; Nirenberg 2009). Martínez has argued that building upon those ideological precedents, the ideas and doubts surrounding *limpieza de sangre* produced a 'Spanish society obsessed with genealogy' (2008, 1). Imported to the colonies and particularly to Mexico, such ideas were transformed into the caste system, with its complex taxonomic categories and genealogical procedures for distinguishing individuals and populations by gradations of mixture and purity (Hering Torres, Martínez, and Nirenberg 2012; Martínez 2008). Yet recent scholarship throws into question even notions of stable *casta* identifications and of a caste 'system' per se (Katzew 2004; Restall 2009). Historical analysis of *casta* as a fluid, changeable, and situational signifier has led to characterization of Mexico's 'caste system' as an 'integrated system of relations and dispositions rather than a series of distinct stations' (Lewis 2012, 106).

Consideration of the lineage of the term 'mestizo' takes such points further. Used in Spain as early as the 13th century, 'mestizo' referred to a variety of forms of mixture – of religions, languages, moral standings, class and status groupings, nationality, and other qualities thought transmitted in blood – long in advance of the bio-racial usages that have characterized the more recent deployments of that term as a category of identity. In a study of the New Kingdom of Granada, Joanne Rappaport has argued that 'mestizo' operated metaphorically; ascriptions of mestizo status were 'floating signifiers that can only be interpreted situationally' (2014, 172) in the context of complicated sociopolitical struggles within which certain individuals were ephemerally, if consequentially, marked as mestizo, only to eventually 'disappear' (Rappaport 2014) into other social groupings. To reconsider the significance of 'mestizo' in light of such work is to question whether the racial meaning generally accorded to the term might be a late spin on the term, one that occludes the complexity of the term's meaning in the colonial period and perhaps afterward.

The genealogy of 'mestizaje' is equally complicated – even if today it may be 'nearly impossible to think of *mestizaje* as anything other than biologized race mixture inflected with segregationist or assimilationist state policies and multiracial identity politics' (Watanabe 2016). In published sources (disproportionately representing views of privileged men of letters), the term seems to have come into general use in Latin America in the 19th century, but for much of that century does not seem to have been used only – or even principally – to connote human bio-racial mixture.[1] The majority of its appearances over the course of the 19th century were in the context of animal husbandry: discussions of qualities of breeds of cattle, sheep and the like, and the consequences of their interbreeding, as either diminishing the purity or quality of particular breeds (*razas*); or creating new breeds combining the superior qualities of their ancestral lines and sometimes, in a Lamarckian spirit, the heritable influences of environment and geography. A second, though less common, use of mestizaje was to refer to the consequences of the political mixture of distinct groups in the postcolonial Latin American republics. Though Simón Bolívar did not seem to have employed the term mestizaje, his reference, in the famous 1819 address at Angostura, to Latin Americans as a 'mixed species' (Miller 2004, 8), set the stage for later, more explicit references to mestizaje by politicians and intellectuals from the mid-19th century forward (see, for instance, Samper 1861).

Only in the late 19th century, following the rise of European and North American racial science, would mestizaje become a term of general use to characterize the mixture of discrete races defined by differences of biology (skin color, cranial morphology, etc.) rather than the murkier complexities of lineage. European discussions of 'polygenism' (i.e. different origins of distinct races) versus 'monogenism,' and ethnological and physical anthropological analyses of different races and their characteristics brought the issue of mixture to the fore. Thinkers like Spencer, de Gobineau, Agassiz, and Le Bon held forth on the deleterious consequences of 'miscegenation,' which in their view fostered vice, sterility, criminality, and political instability – rebellion and disorder – especially in Latin America, which they often cited. Such racial discourse was widely received in Latin America by the century's end; some intellectuals contributed to the growing corpus of scientific racism by documenting imputed deficits of indigenous and African-descended populations, and especially of mixed race populations (Hale 1989).

However, the same period saw the emergence of countercurrents of what Basave Benítez (1992) has called 'mestizophilic' political discourse to challenge Euro-American miscegenation theories, albeit typically in favor of a kind of mixture that could form new national bodies politic by breeding out indigenous or African-descended populations through European immigration, intermarriage, or social reforms. Such ideologies of national mixture emerged not only in Latin America, where they were championed by Justo Sierra, José Martí, Franz Tamayo, Andrés Molina Enriquez, José Vasconcelos, Ricardo Rojas, and others but also in Spain, where race scientists, anthropologists, and advocated for a conception of Spanish *raza* that was defined as the outcome of a 'fusionary process' (Goode 2009, 9). But while present-day scholars of European, including Spanish, racial ideology often tend to distinguish 'medieval' from 'modern' conceptions of race (Nirenberg 2009), in Latin America, the racial languages of caste, blood, lineage, pedigree, and descent – and analogization of human intermixture with the interbreeding of animals – retained considerable force into the 20th century. This may be the case even in versions of mestizaje that scholars have characterized as hegemonic expressions of bio-racial ideology. Considered in such terms, José Vasconcelos' 1925 paean to the 'cosmic race' is less a foundational text than a culminating one – one that bears the mark of multiple genealogies of race thinking, ranging from the discourse of *casta* and lineage, to analogies with animal husbandry and agricultural grafting (Alonso 2004), to Latin American political 'mestizofilia,' to modern bio-racial discourse.

The tangled genealogies of 'mestizo' and 'mestizaje' present several questions to those who presume to study them. How is one to approach 'mestizo,' or other mixed categories of identification, in a way that is not definitionally predicated on 'race,' or at least, on a modernist formulation of race as phenotypically expressed biological difference? And once 'mestizo' has been so questioned, whither mestizaje, with its own complicated lineage? In short, how might we take mestizaje – Latin America's 'signature racial and cultural ideal' (Poole 2016) – beyond race?

The contributors to this volume provide no easy answers. They are, moreover, quite diverse in approach and focus, deploying the methods of anthropology, history, and literary studies in the analysis of multiple categories of identification (*ladino, moreno, mestizo, cholo*) in varied national and regional contexts (Mexico, Guatemala, Bolivia, Colombia, Peru), from the 16th century to the present. A comparative review by Matthew Nielsen introduces yet other cases. Yet, all begin from a critical approach to race: what might be called a 'genealogical materialism' (West cited in Martínez 2008, 3) that situates mestizaje in the specific historical, cultural, regional, and political conjunctures that give it meaning. They treat mestizaje neither as an expression of a preexisting social identity nor as an ideology enforced from above, but rather as provisional and situated 'acts of naming and acts of claiming' (Poole 2016) that are performed or embodied in the in-between spaces of social life – 'actively reconstructing' indigeneity and blackness, as well as mestizo-ness (Wade 2005, 245, 250). Finally, they interrogate forms of mestizaje as 'acts' in the political or legal sense – i.e. as momentous political interventions. As such, 'mestizo acts' not only enforce but also institute or change social realities; they seek to prove – or dismantle – genealogies of race, blood, sex, and language in public and political ways.

The first three contributors to this collection consider three categories of mixed identity in as many regions: 'ladino' in Guatemala (Watanabe), 'moreno' in Guerrero (Lewis), and 'mestizo' in Yucatán (Eiss). In a study of *ladino* categories and claims in the colonial kingdom of Guatemala, John Watanabe demonstrates that the terminology emerged not as a mixed race label, but rather as the product of a competitive 'descent ideology' that elided such heritage by 'foregrounding Spanish Catholic affiliations and loyalties, regardless of birth.' Laura Lewis follows with a historical ethnography of *moreno* identifications among Afro-descended communities on Guerrero's Costa Chica; she shows how that nomenclature conveys mixed black and Indian heritage, while specifically excluding whites from the region's mix. Moving to Yucatán, Paul Eiss provides a historical and cultural reading of the significance of 'mestizo' in a region where Maya-speaking populations have been predominant; Eiss traces three 'genealogies' of Yucatecan mestizo identifications, as expressed through festivity, language, and theatre. Taken as a group, these cases demonstrate how mixed identifications are not merely *ex post facto* categorizations of prior interracial, reproductive mixture. Rather, they are genealogical claims that selectively amalgamate some lineages not only of 'blood' and family descent but also of religion, language, land claims, and language – even as they exclude others. Through a performative approach to 'ladino,' 'moreno,' and 'mestizo,' they demonstrate how mixed-ness is expressed, enacted, or denied, via a variety of cultural signifiers that are performed in social life. Finally, they explore how forms of expression that are culturally demarcated *as* performance genres (i.e. the dances and ritual combats of saints' festivals on the Costa Chica or the skits of Yucatecan *teatro regional*) become arenas where mixed identifications are not only expressed but also actively produced in ways that alternately confirm, contest, and diverge from national hegemonic constructions.

The remaining three articles in this collection shift their attention to national rhetorics and practices of mestizaje. Javier Sanjinés examines 'mestizo-criollo acts' – and the hidden presence of the European *homo sylvestris* or wild man – in the work of two foundational contributors to early 20th-century Bolivian discussions of the so-called Indian problem: Alcides Arguedas and Franz Tamayo. Deborah Poole explores recent Peruvian controversies surrounding the 2015 publication of a database identifying indigenous people. Those debates, she argues, have been colored by an 'ethos of suspicion' surrounding claims to racial identity, and a normative conception of mestizaje that is bolstered by the presumably 'post-ideological' mechanisms of neoliberal governance. The collection concludes with Peter Wade's consideration of the relationship between mestizaje, liberalism, and multiculturalism in Colombia. Even after multiculturalism has eclipsed mestizaje as a hegemonic political discourse, patterns of violence and displacement experienced by Afro-Colombian populations have reproduced prior formulations of mestizaje as assimilation and 'ethnocide.' Considered together, the three articles portray political mestizajes as genealogical acts, writ large: acts that authoritatively enunciate a series of connections, proofs, and claims; even as they commit critical elisions, erasures and disclaimers. There are notable distinctions between the mestizajes examined here: between mestizaje as a process of uncontrolled, barbarous intermixture – i.e. *encholamiento* (choloization), in Sanjinés' Bolivian case – or as an ideologically controlled process of national domestication; and between an explicit national politics of mestizaje, and the implicit mestizajes of neoliberal governance and patterns of violence and displacement. Despite such distinctions, these three articles all feature mestizaje as mestizo act: not just as ideological expression or representational construct but also as an act that institutes or constitutes national bodies through the operations of law, policy, science, or violence.

By approaching mixed identifications and mestizaje neither in terms of identity nor ideology, but as mestizo *acts*, all the contributors to this collection demonstrate how mestizaje is *about* race, yet also *beyond* race. They avoid assimilating mixed identifications like 'ladino,' 'moreno,' and 'mestizo' to modern conceptions of bio-race – whether conceived as 'natural' or as socially constructed. Instead, such mixed identifications, whether in colonial or postcolonial contexts, are revealed to be complicated genealogical claims or performances in which rhetorics of blood, color, or lineage are inextricably entangled with class, language, dress, religion and sexuality, and grounded in the specificities of place, geography, and region. The contributions to this collection also suggest the importance of not drawing sharp conceptual distinctions between the domesticated mestizaje of political elites, and counterhegemonic alternatives voiced from below. Mestizaje, whether in its explicit ideological expressions or its implicit normative forms, appears here as a concept whose genealogy is always mixed, impure. It is a product of the exploitation, hierarchies, and hegemonic ideologies of colonial and postcolonial orders, and yet at the same time of the long and varied history of how those very orders have been appropriated, redeployed, and sometimes flipped, both by subaltern and elite actors. The mestizo acts depicted here collectively make the case – against the conceptual domestication of mestizaje under a modernist conception of bio-race – that mestizaje is always about joining things that seem incommensurate. To borrow a Bolivian point of reference, *mestizaje* is *encholado*. To purify mestizaje of its complicated genealogy, to reduce its tangled lineages and histories to a single one, would be to miss the point.

Note

1. This characterization of the meanings of the term *mestizaje* is largely based on searches and survey of all digitized Spanish language sources available in the Hathi Trust database, as well as Google Books, both accessed in July 2015.

References

Alonso, A. M. 2004. "Conforming Disconformity: 'Mestizaje,' Hybridity, and the Aesthetics of Mexican Nationalism." *Cultural Anthropology* 19 (4): 459–490. doi:10.1525/can.2004.19.issue-4.

Anzaldúa, G. 2007. *Borderlands/La Frontera: The New Mestiza*. San Francisco: Aunt Lute.

Appelbaum, N. P., A. S. Macpherson, and K. A. Rosemblatt, eds. 2003. *Race and Nation in Modern Latin America*. Chapel Hill: University of North Carolina Press.

Basave Benítez, A. F. 1992. *México mestizo: Análisis del nacionalismo mexicano en torno a la mestizofilia de Andrés Molina Enríquez*. México, D.F.: Fondo de Cultura Económica.

Cope, R. D. 1994. *The Limits of Racial Domination: Plebeian Society in Colonial Mexico City, 1660-1720*. Madison: University of Wisconsin Press.

Dawson, A. S. 2004. *Indian and Nation in Revolutionary Mexico*. Tucson: University of Arizona Press.

de Castro, J. E. 2002. *Mestizo Nations: Culture, Race, and Conformity in Latin American Literature*. Tucson: University of Arizona Press.

Earle, R. 2007. *The Return of the Native: Indians and Myth-Making in Spanish America, 1810-1930*. Durham, NC: Duke University Press.

Esteva Fabregat, C. 1995. *Mestizaje in Ibero-America*. Tucson: University of Arizona Press.

Fisher, A. B., and M. D. O'Hara, eds. 2009. *Imperial Subjects: Race and Identity in Colonial Latin America*. Durham, NC: Duke University Press.

Goode, J. 2009. *Impurity of Blood: Defining Race in Spain, 1870-1930*. Baton Rouge: Louisiana State University Press.

Gotkowitz, L., ed. 2011. *Histories of Race and Racism: The Andes and Mesoamerica from Colonial Times to the Present*. Durham, NC: Duke University Press.

Gould, J. L. 1998. *To Die in this Way: Nicaraguan Indians and the Myth of Mestizaje, 1880-1965*. Durham, NC: Duke University Press.

Graham, R. 2006. *The Idea of Race in Latin America: 1870-1940*. Austin: University of Texas Press.

Hale, C. R. 1989. "Political and Social Ideas." In *Latin America: Economy and Society, 1870-1930*, edited by L. Bethell, 357–442. Cambridge: Cambridge University Press.

Hale, C. R. 2005. "Neoliberal Multiculturalism." *PoLAR: Political and Legal Anthropology Review* 28 (1): 10–19. doi:10.1525/pol.2005.28.issue-1.

Hering Torres, M. S., M. E. Martínez, and D. Nirenberg, eds. 2012. *Race and Blood in the Iberian World*. Munich: Verlag.

Katzew, I. 2004. *Casta Painting: Images of Race in Eighteenth-Century Mexico*. New Haven: Yale University Press.

Knight, A. 1990. "Racism, Revolution, and Indigenismo in Mexico, 1910-1940." In *The Idea of Race in Latin America, 1870-1940*, edited by R. Graham, 71–113. Austin: University of Texas Press.

Lewis, L. A. 2012. "Between 'Casta' and 'Raza': The Example of Colonial Mexico." In *Race and Blood in the Iberian World*, edited by M. S. Hering Torres, M. E. Martínez, and D. Nirenberg, 99–123. Munich: Verlag.

Loveman, M. 2014. *National Colors: Racial Classification and the State in Latin America*. Oxford: Oxford University Press.

Mallon, F. E. 1996. "Constructing Mestizaje in Latin America: Authenticity, Marginality, and Gender in the Claiming of Ethnic Identities." *Journal of Latin American Anthropology* 2 (1): 170–181. doi:10.1525/jlca.1996.2.1.170.

Mangan, J. E. 2014. "Mestizos." *Oxford Bibliographies*. Accessed November 9 2015. http://www.oxfordbibliographies.com/display/id/obo-9780199730414-0240.

Martínez, M. E. 2008. *Genealogical Fictions: Limpieza de Sangre, Religion, and Gender in Colonial Mexico*. Stanford, CA: Stanford University Press.

Martinez-Echazabal, L. 1998. "Mestizaje and the Discourse of National/Cultural Identity in Latin America, 1845-1959." *Latin American Perspectives* 25 (3): 21–42. doi:10.1177/0094582X9802500302.

Miller, M. G. 2004. *Rise and Fall of the Cosmic Race: The Cult of Mestizaje in Latin America*. Austin: University of Texas Press.

Mörner, M. 1967. *Race Mixture in the History of Latin America*. Boston: Little, Brown.

Nirenberg, D. 2009. "Was There Race before Modernity? The Example of 'Jewish' Blood in Late Medieval Spain." In *The Origins of Racism in the West*, edited by M. Eliav-Feldon, B. Isaac, and J. Ziegler, 232–264. Cambridge: Cambridge University Press.

Pérez-Torres, R. 2006. *Critical Uses of Race in Chicano Culture*. Minneapolis: University of Minnesota Press.

Poole, D. 2016. "Mestizaje as Ethical Disposition: Indigenous Rights in the Neoliberal State." *Latin American and Caribbean Ethnic Studies* 11 (3): 287–304. doi:10.1080/17442222.2016.1219082.

Rahier, J. M. 2003. "Introduction: Mestizaje, Mulataje, Mestiçagem in Latin American Ideologies of National Identities." *Journal of Latin American Anthropology* 8 (1): 40–50. doi:10.1525/jlca.2003.8.1.40.

Rappaport, J. 2014. *The Disappearing Mestizo: Configuring Difference in the Colonial New Kingdom of Granada*. Durham, NC: Duke University Press.

Restall, M. 2009. *The Black Middle: Africans, Mayas, and Spaniards in Colonial Yucatan*. Stanford, CA: Stanford University Press.

Romero, S. 2016. "A Gilded Olympics Begin with the Opening Ceremony in Gritty Rio." *New York Times*, August 5.

Samper, J. M. 1861. *Ensayo Sobre Las Revoluciones Políticas y La Condición Social de Las Repúblicas Colombianas (Hispano-Americanas)*. Paris: Imprenta de E. Thunot y Ca.

Skidmore, T. E. 1993. *Black into White: Race and Nationality in Brazilian Thought*. Durham, NC: Duke University Press.

Stolcke, V. 2008. "Los mestizos no nacen, se hacen." In *Identidades ambivalentes en América Latina (siglos XVI-XXI)*, edited by V. Stolcke and A. Coello, 19–58. Barcelona: Ediciones Bellaterra.

Stutzman, R. 1981. "El Mestizaje: An All-Inclusive Ideology of Exclusion." In *Cultural Transformations and Ethnicity in Modern Ecuador*, edited by N. E. Whitten Jr. Urbana: University of Illinois Press.

Sue, C. A. 2013. *Land of the Cosmic Race: Race Mixture, Racism, and Blackness in Mexico*. Oxford: Oxford University Press.

Telles, E. E., and Project on Ethnicity and Race in Latin America. 2014. *Pigmentocracies: Ethnicity, Race, and Color in Latin America*. Chapel Hill: University of North Carolina Press.

Vasconcelos, J. 1997. *The Cosmic Race: La raza cosmica (Race in the Americas)*. Baltimore: Johns Hopkins University Press.

Wade, P. 2005. "Rethinking Mestizaje: Ideology and Lived Experience." *Journal of Latin American Studies* 37 (2): 239–257. doi:10.1017/S0022216X05008990.

Wade, P. 2010. *Race and Ethnicity in Latin America (Anthropology, Culture and Society)*. 2cd ed. London: Pluto Press.

Wade, P., C. L. Beltrán, E. Restrepo, and R. Ventura Santos, eds. 2014. *Mestizo Genomics: Race Mixture, Nation, and Science in Latin America*. Durham, NC: Duke University Press.

Watanabe, J.M. 2016. "Racing to the Top: Descent Ideologies and Why Ladinos Never Meant to Be Mestizos in Colonial Guatemala." *Latin American and Caribbean Ethnic Studies* 11 (3): 305–322. doi:10.1080/17442222.2016.1219083.

Indian allies and white antagonists: toward an alternative *mestizaje* on Mexico's Costa Chica

Laura A. Lewis

ABSTRACT

San Nicolás Tolentino, Guerrero, Mexico, is a 'mixed' black-Indian agricultural community on the coastal belt of Mexico's southern Pacific coast, the Costa Chica. This article examines local expressions of race in San Nicolás in relation to Mexico's national ideology of mestizaje (race mixing), which excludes blackness but is foundational to Mexican racial identities. San Nicolás's black-Indians are strongly nationalistic while expressing a collective or regional identity different from those of peoples they identify as Indians and as whites. Such collective expression produces an alternative model of mestizaje, here explored through local agrarian history and several village festivals. It is argued that this alternative model favors Indians and distances whites, thereby challenging dominant forms of Mexican mestizaje.

Every year in late July, towns and cities in Mexico celebrate the Apostle Santiago (St. James). On the Costa Chica of Guerrero in the agricultural village of San Nicolás Tolentino, a highlight of the festival occurs when crossbars are erected in front of the Church. Here over two days, six roosters and a cat are hanged – the roosters by their feet and the cat by its hindquarters. For each hanging, dozens of young men on horseback gallop back and forth below the animals, repeatedly seizing the roosters' heads and an old coin pressed into a medallion hung from the cat's neck. The animals eventually die. Whoever kills a rooster gets to eat it, and whoever secures the medallion wins a cash prize. As far as I know, and according to what San Nicoladenses told me during my fieldwork from the late 1990s to mid-2000s, San Nicolás is the only place in the region where this is practiced.

Santiago is the patron and warrior saint of Spain who is said to have led Spaniards battling Moors during the Reconquest of the Iberian Peninsula. Conquest plays featuring Santiago are documented from the earliest days of Spain's Mexican colony. During these plays, missionaries forced defeated Indians to dress as 'Moors' and to celebrate their victimizer, under whose banner Spain had also conquered Mexico (Trexler 1984, 582). In the New World, the saint who aided Spain in Iberia, Santiago the Moor slayer (*Matamoros*), became Santiago the Indian slayer (*Mataindios*), a symbol of conquest. Astride a white steed alien to the Americas, Santiago's powerful image entered local belief systems and fiesta cycles, and Spaniards bestowed his name on cities and towns throughout the land. Near San Nicolás, these towns and cities include Santiago Ometepec, Santiago Collantes, Santiago Jamiltepec, Santiago Pinotepa Nacional, Santiago Llano Grande, and Santiago Tepextla. San Nicolás is an exception on the Costa Chica, and it is also the only town there named for San Nicolás of Tolentino.

The village of San Nicolás (population 3500) is located on the Costa Chica's coastal belt in a historically black area of Mexico's southern Pacific Coast. In the late 16th century, its fertile soils attracted Spanish conquistadors as landowners and ranchers. They brought with them mostly male black and mulatto slaves and servants to an area already home to indigenous Triques, Amuzgos, Mixtecs, and Nahuas. Subsequently, two 'ethnic' zones developed, a distinction that still holds today: the highlands are largely indigenous – indeed, they became a region of refuge for Indians during the colonial period – while the coastal belt became a mixed zone of Spaniards, African descended people, and Indians drawn into the colonial ambit. San Nicolás is in this mixed zone, about 15 km from the ocean.

Colonial censuses and judicial records refer to mulattoes (*mulatos*) and/or blacks (*negros*) in San Nicolás and its vicinity and even to some ancestral names of San Nicolás's current residents. Today, however, 'mulatto' has disappeared from San Nicoladenses' vocabulary. While they still use 'black,' it is generally limited to certain contexts: ancestors, as an insult or form of ribbing for particularly dark-skinned people, as a distancing mechanism for African descent people elsewhere on the coast (Lewis 2004), and as an indication of how outsiders refer to them. Their preferred and more accurate term is *moreno* (also Amaral Lugo 2005; Hoffmann 2014, 82). In English *moreno* means 'dark-skinned,' but to San Nicoladenses, it is less a skin color than a reference to their mixed black-Indian (*indio negro* or *negro indio*) heritage. In describing this heritage, they use biological terms to claim membership in a race (*raza*)[1] whose blood (*sangre*) is no longer pure (*limpia*) after centuries of black/Indian mixing.[2] 'The founders of [San Nicolás] were already crossed (*cruzados*),' Don Margarito said. 'They were not legitimate, legitimate blacks. Indians were already here. Race was well-preserved before and now it's not.' 'Now the people from here are mixed with Indians,' said Ernesto. He is married to Susana, an Indian from Tacubaya in the municipality of Tehuantepec, Oaxaca. Rosa's mother, Doña Mirna, is from Jamiltepec, northeast of the Costa Chican city of Pinotepa Nacional, Oaxaca. She grew up speaking Mixtec. Because Rosa and one of her siblings lived for a time in their mother's natal town, they also spoke Mixtec when they were young. Don Domingo was born in 1923 in San Antonio Ocotlán, also north of Pinotepa Nacional, to an indigenous Amuzgo woman from there and a *moreno* man from San Nicolás. One of his father's grandmothers was Zapotec, and she raised him in San Nicolás after his parents separated. Thus, Don Domingo is Indian on both his mother's and his father's side. 'Our race,' Don Margarito emphasized, 'is *moreno*/Indian or Indian/*moreno*. Now it's even mixed in Indian villages. Among blacks there are Indian blacks and among Amuzgos [there are those] with Indian hair but the color of a black,' such as Judit's grandfather, a 'little Indian' from Ometepec who spoke Spanish but wore Indian clothes, a man with straight hair but *moreno* skin. Don Margarito described one of his grandmothers as a black Indian and his own *raza* as black Indian. 'Now everyone is mixed.'

Moreno indexes a collective or regional identity (see also Hoffmann 2006, 2014). Here I examine it as a field of meanings expressed through historical narratives and cultural production. *Morenos* differentiate themselves from neighboring and distant peoples they refer to as Indians and as whites.[3] Indians are generally poorer, with 'traditional' communities found mostly in the uplands, particularly around Ometepec, Guerrero, an Amuzgo region, and Pinotepa Nacional, Oaxaca, a Mixtec one. The less assimilated they seem to be, the more 'Indian' they are such that monolingual indigenous language speakers are referred to as 'Indian Indians.'[4] San Nicoladenses label as 'white' (*blanco*) people who would be known as mestizo in national parlance. Local whites are old landowning families and government officials – including those in the nearby city of Ometepec, a Royalist stronghold during the Independence Wars and counter-Revolutionary during the Revolution. More generally, whites are 'the rich,' and those who traditionally dominate the region's cities, as well as its commerce, agriculture and politics.

While San Nicolás has a number of Indian resident families who, like most *morenos*, are small farmers and whose arrival is discussed below, it has had no white residents except for schoolteachers, the occasional doctor, anthropologists, evangelicals and military personnel, since the mid-1950s, when several white traders (*comerciantes*) from Ometepec were murdered. 'There aren't any legitimate whites here now,' said Don Domingo. 'White cattle ranchers were here but they left. Today's whites are in Ometepec. The governor, he's white; the municipal president, he's white. Whites are more interested in money than in humanity.' *Morenos* ally with Indians in the scorn they sense from whites, who are said to not want either to be educated, who cheat them out of their crops and money, and who benefit from government protection. On a more intimate level, while whites do not allow their children to marry 'a dark-skinned or a poor person,' said Don Domingo, '[Indians and blacks] marry each other, so it's as if everyone is of the same race. People in San Nicolás don't care,' he added. Sirina agreed while introducing me to a new word: *champurrado*, a corn flour based chocolate *atole*, which she used to describe the union of her 'chocolate' *moreno* son and a 'corn flour' Indian. 'It doesn't matter to me if my son marries an Indian woman or a *morena*,' she said, 'The important thing is that he loves her.' Don Domingo would concur, 'If the kids love each other, it's all right,' he said. And then he concluded, 'So blacks and Indians are separate from whites.'

Here I take up such separation to examine black-Indianness in relation to Mexico's national ideology of *mestizaje* (race mixing), which is foundational to Mexicans' racial identities as mestizos. As a national ideology, *mestizaje* was most fully developed by the early 20th century Mexican theorist José Vasconcelos (1924), whose 'cosmic race,' though not without precedent, became the template for a range of similar race mixing ideologies throughout Latin America (Miller 2004). Among its features is the biological and aesthetic fusion of white, black, and Indian as a superior race. Yet to Vasconcelos, not only would the 'black race' vanish over time, but white and Indian were not equal. Instead, he privileged whitening (*blanqueamiento*) through continual mixture as pro-gress and evolutionary promise, while the pre-Columbian Indian of the past served an ideological function as the heroic and ancient backbone of a contemporary Mexicanness, rendering all but invisible its indigenous citizens (Alonso 2004; Bonfil Batalla 1990; Friedlander 1975; see also Gould 1998; Stutzman 1981). What I would term a mestizo *mestizaje* thus represents what Ana Alonso calls an 'internal colonialism' (2004, 479) as it assimilates indigenous peoples to a Western ideal that exists in tension with a view of the Mexican character as primarily derived from the Indian peoples of the past.

Vasconcelos's cosmic race, along with the 'folkloric nationalism' of what were still top-down but more heavily indigenist and revolutionary ideals (*indigenismo*) (Knight 1990, 82), excluded the African descended people whose ancestors were brought to Mexico mostly during the 16th and 17th centuries (Lewis 2012; Stepan 1991; Sue 2012).[5] Today, as Christina Sue notes, 'blackness does not exist in the collective imaginings of the [Mexican] nation' (2012, 17; see also; Banks 2006). Mexico does not recognize its African descended citizens through a national census;[6] nor is their history told in school text-books. Because of this, because of anti-black racism, and because of ongoing biological and cultural mixing especially with Indians, San Nicolás's *morenos* generally also do not construct blackness, however framed, as a robust part of their heritage.[7] They do, however, center Indians in their village festivals and in their history. Such Indo-centrism in part draws on *moreno* understandings of Mexican mestizo *mestizaje* ideology, which holds Indianness as key to national identity (Lewis 2000, 2001, 2012). Yet the *moreno* version of *mestizaje* also subverts the mestizo version because it actively excludes whites and whiteness from Mexicanness.[8] In doing so, it challenges and reconfigures the national *mestizaje* paradigm without diluting San Nicoladenses' fervent nationalism.

My discussion of *moreno* expressions of *mestizaje* draws on many years of field and archival research to identify some of what Odile Hoffmann calls the 'local and territor-ialized realities' (2006, 109) that anchor *moreno* experiences.[9] I focus on agrarian history and on contemporary festival performances, as collective understandings of the past find expression through pageantry. These understandings I read as enactments of racialized identities formed out of historical accretions and consciousness. As rituals, festival performances are 'large worlds writ small' (Van Young 1994, 349). They commu-nicate local ideas of history as well as local visions of fundamental aspects of national identities (Rowe and Schelling 1991, 56–57). Here those visions engage Indians as allies and whites as antagonists while communicating messages about Mexican national identity. Agrarian history displays some of the contemporary and historical engage-ments with Indians and whites that seem to have shaped San Nicoladenses' imaginative lives, including as enacted through festivals.

Agrarian histories

Contemporary coastal belt *moreno* culture is a variety of cowboy culture. It originated in the late 16th century when the Spanish Crown rewarded conquistadors deemed to have 'pacified' the Indians of the region with land for cattle ranching and rights to Indian tribute and labor (Lewis 2012; Motta Sánchez 2006; Widmer 1990). Although the mid-16th century New Laws curtailed Spanish access to that labor, Spaniards continued to force Indians to pan gold and to work land Spaniards often stole or acquired through trickery. When Don Tristán de Luna y Arellano, perhaps the best known of the early conquistadors, died, his son inherited his land. His son then sold this land to his brother-in-law, Don Mateo Anaus y Mauleón, an 'insatiable *hacendado*' who extended his dominion throughout the region (Aguirre Beltrán [1958] 1985, 43–44, 46–47). Anaus y

Mauleón might have been the Spaniard referred to only as 'Mariscal' (Marshall) in the records, who owned a vast hacienda just north of San Nicolás called Los Cortijos, which remained in Mariscal family hands until the mid-19th century. Late 18th century records show that the majority of its employees were blacks and mulattoes (Motta Sánchez 2006, 125). Indeed, by this time, the vast majority of non-Indian coastal residents were black and mulatto. By 1791, San Nicolás had about 126 families, most identified as 'mulatto natives' (*mulatos naturales*)[10] (AGN Padrones 18; Gerhard 1993, 151). It is identified as an *estancia* (ranch outpost) under the tutelage of perhaps another Mariscal, this one 'de Castilla,' a generic reference to a Spaniard, and perhaps a descendent of Mauleón (AGN Padrones 18).[11] One hundred years later, the village included over one thousand residents (Aguirre Beltrán [1958] 1985, 62; Moedano Navarro 1986, 557).

The site where San Nicolás now stands was therefore a ranch and farming outpost for a succession of Spanish and then white ranchers throughout the 18th and 19th centuries. Although the names of some are lost, that San Nicoladenses worked for them is indicated not just by the documentation but also by the fact that throughout the Independence Wars of the early 19th century, its residents, along with other *morenos* in the region, fought on the side of the Spanish Crown and their own bosses (Lewis 2012, Ch. 1; Jacobs 1982; Moedano Navarro 1986, 553; Ravelo Lecuana 1990; Widmer 1990, 189). A similar pattern prevailed during the Revolutionary Wars, when many San Nicoladenses supported landowners rather than Emiliano Zapata and his Liberation Army of the South (Lewis 2012, Ch. 1; Ravelo Lecuana 1990, 259–60, 264). Although this changed as Mexico's Post-Revolutionary government implemented Agrarian Reform in the following decades, during the 19th and early 20th centuries and through white patronage and hegemony, colonialist social and political domination prevailed on the Costa Chica.

During the colonial period, Indians were prohibited from riding horses and were, in any event, deemed ineffective cowboys. In contrast, blacks and mulattoes were regarded as such superb horsemen that even slaves routinely rode horses (Motta Sánchez 2006, 121, 124–25). Due to black and mulatto equestrian expertise, ranchers employed them as cowboys. They were also assigned to the *pardo*[12] militias established by the Crown in the late 17th century under the command of Spanish district officials and designed in part to subdue Indian uprisings (Lewis 2003, 97–98; Motta Sánchez 2006, 125; Vinson 2001, 51; Widmer 1990, 189). In both roles, they acted as extensions of Spanish authority.[13]

During the first century of conquest, coastal belt Indian villages declined due to European illnesses, overwork, ethnocide, town reorganization, and flight from Spaniards, their cattle, and their black and mulatto slaves and employees. Judges were also inclined to ignore colonial protection laws in order to make Indian land and labor available to Spanish landowners. Many Indians fled to the nearby hills of the Sierra Madre del Sur mountain range. Yet Indian community holdings and subsistence activities reached into the humid and fertile lowlands prized by Spaniards for cattle and for small-scale cotton cultivation. Indians consequently came into extensive and extended contact with non-Indians, including with the blacks and mulattoes often directed to collect tribute from their communities and oversee their labor for Spaniards. As early as the 1580s, the Costa Chica's Indians petitioned colonial courts to rein in the Spaniards' marauding cattle, which trampled their *milpas* (corn plots) and therefore destroyed their livelihoods. They also lodged complaints against blacks and mulattoes under Spanish control (AGN Tierras 48.6; Aguirre Beltrán [1958] 1985, 59, 65; Widmer 1990, 127–131).

Parallel to this structural enmity, however, the daily lives of blacks, mulattoes and Indians were marked by cooperation. Indians taught blacks and mulattoes agricultural techniques for small plots of land, new forms of supernaturalism and curing using local herbs, and how to build shelters with local materials (Aguirre Beltrán 1963, 101; Widmer 1990, 18, 140). Blacks, mulattoes, and Indians also cooperated as, for instance, black and mulatto men cultivated cotton while Indian women wove it into the thread that Spanish landowners sent to Puebla for textile production.[14] By about 1700, many traditional coastal belt Indian villages had become what Rolf Widmer terms 'Afro-indigenous' as Indian women willingly and unwillingly partnered with the black and mulatto men who constituted the non-Indian majority on the coast (Widmer 1990, 131; Gerhard 1993, 151; Quiroz Malca 2004).

On the colonial Costa Chica 'mulatto' was the most common caste term. The sparse extant judicial documents dealing with the region do not contain genealogical information, but in central Mexico mulatto could refer to the offspring of a black and a Spaniard or of a black and an Indian (Lewis 2003, 74–78; Martínez 2009, 32, 281 n. 35).[15] Indeed, most of the mulattoes the conquistadors brought to the coast were probably black-Indian (Motta Sánchez 2006, 121).[16] By the 17th century, the word *pardo* also identified black-Indian mixture, and by the middle of the 18th century, *moreno* entered the vocabulary. It is unclear why but in the famous 18th century caste paintings, *moreno* identified a variant of mulatto or black-Indian mixture. While black-Indianness is therefore as old as the colony itself, mulatto and *pardo* are no longer used today while *moreno* has become the preferred local term for mixed black and Indian ancestry. While *moreno* is also a color term, as Sue (2012, 38) notes for Veracruz, for San Nicoladenses, *moreno* skin color signifies that they are not black by virtue of their Indian admixture.[17]

The colonial coastal belt saw little central government oversight. Spaniards considered the climate inhospitable, and most did not settle there. The few that did (largely in the cooler Ometepec) tended to hold minor official positions, which helped them to protect their own interests by, for instance, harboring slaves fleeing Mexico City and Puebla's sugar plantations, who would then work for them in return for protection (Moedano Navarro 1986; Widmer 1990, 138–139). In fact, settlements that likely included some runaways alongside the black and mulatto descendants of Mauleón's cowboys and servants eventually arose in San Nicolás and nearby (Aguirre Beltrán [1958] 1985, 48; Manzano Añorve 1991, 18–20; see also; Widmer 1990, 139).

San Nicoladenses are mostly unfamiliar with the Atlantic slave trade that brought Africans to Mexico and generally deny that any of their ancestors could have been slaves.[18] But while this part of the Costa Chica never saw a maroon settlement per se (Lewis 2012; Motta Sánchez 2006), San Nicoladenses do tell stories about the historical coastal wreck of a foreign slave ship that released runaways, who are always said to be from elsewhere. According to San Nicoladenses, the ship's emancipated human cargo settled among people who already 'owned' the area. These owners were mixed, but they 'accepted [the others] as their family,' said Don Domingo. 'They were slaves,' Judit said of the people who escaped, 'but once they escaped they were guaranteed their liberty.' Today in San Nicolás and elsewhere on the coast, maroonage is something of a trope if not a fact. It characterizes the way San Nicoladenses understand slavery, which, like blackness itself, is always temporally and spatially distanced, and the way they under-stand Mexico as a 'free' place where slaves were liberated as soon as they came aground. Indeed, maroonage and freedom are perhaps the themes most characterizing *morenos'* sense of themselves as 'black.'

Few historians dwell on the coastal belt's 18th century history because there is little documentation. However, with respect to San Nicolás, this history is key because it is alive in San Nicoladenses' narratives, though they never assign an accurate date. Those narratives give context to an important link between Indians and African descended people, especially with respect to San Nicolás's agrarian history. During a search in the Mexican National Archives in Mexico City, I found documentation for a story San Nicoladenses told me. This involves a coastal belt Indian *cacica* (noble woman) named Doña María Ambrosia de Vargas, who passed away in 1755 owning some 50,000 hectares of land near San Nicolás (AGN Tierras 472.2 1726-28, 3668.3 1755). San Nicoladenses believe that in her will she donated some of her land to their ancestors because she was grateful they had carried her in a hammock to a healer when she fell ill (Hernández Moreno 1996; Manzano Añorve 1991, 22–23; Valdez 1998, 64–65). According to Don Domingo, 'the *cacica* was the boss around here. San Nicolás was a small settlement, but when she left land to the people, everyone united to found the village.[19] The people were her servants; the Petatán and Noyola families [two of San Nicolás's founding families whose names are still among the most prominent in the community] were her servants.' On another occasion, he told me that '[San Nicolás] was a small settlement [*ranchería*]. A *cacica* named María Ambrosia de Vargas owned these lands at the time and had a cattle ranch. The people of San Nicolás were her cowboys. Then she left … she was an Indian. She donated her land to San Nicolás, to [the towns of] Maldonado, Cuaji and Huehuetán.'

The Vargas documentation tells a story different from what San Nicoladenses like Don Domingo believe. Doña María was an Indian *cacica* and she did donate land, but not to San Nicolás. The documentation instead states that on her deathbed and without heirs, she bequeathed her holdings to the 'mulatto natives' (*mulatos naturales*)[20] of the coastal belt town of Huehuetán who worked for her and to the 'Indian poor' of Ometepec. It is possible that Huehuetán subsequently rented some of that land to San Nicolás (Manzano Añorve 1991). But there is no proof of this and San Nicoladenses deny it, claiming instead to have owned land willed directly to them by Doña María. As they tell it, they then loaned this land in the 19th century to the white U.S. landowner Charles 'Carlos' A. Miller.

By the 1910 Revolution, Carlos was one of the most prominent local whites. His hundreds of thousands of hectares in holdings included the ranching outpost of San Nicolás, whose residents worked for him in agriculture and as cowboys. Carlos was a mechanical engineer who originally came to Mexico in the 1860s at the behest of General Juan Alvarez, who owned a small estate between Acapulco and Chilpancingo and had gone to the United States to purchase a turbine from the company for which Carlos worked. One job led to another until Carlos found himself in Cuajinicuilapa, San Nicolás's municipal seat, to fix a broken cotton-felling machine for a man named Daniel Reguera, a member of a prominent white landowning family from Ometepec.

Carlos married Daniel's daughter Laura. They had two sons, Guillermo and Germán. The former became a judge for the State of Guerrero. The latter took over his father's company, Carlos Miller and Sons (Aguirre Beltrán [1958] 1985, 41–51; Manzano Añorve 1991, 33). It appears that Carlos in part acquired his land from the long line of Spanish and then white owners of Los Cortijos, referenced above (Aguirre Beltrán [1958] 1985; Motta Sánchez 2006).[21] Yet Germán claimed into the late 20th century that Carlos had purchased the bulk of it from Doña María Ambrosia de Vargas's descendants, though we know she had no heirs.

In contrast to Germán, San Nicoladenses insist that they already owned a portion of Carlos's land because Doña María had given it to them. They say they 'loaned' it to Carlos to enclose for cotton cultivation. Following the Revolution and during Agrarian Reform in the 1930s, San Nicoladenses fought to recover this portion of Carlos's land but Germán consistently blocked them while insisting that they had 'invaded' land rightfully his, and he forged documents to that affect (Manzano Añorve 1991, 37, 109). In the 1980s, one elderly man credited Germán with 30 years of agrarian problems in San Nicolás as the 'rich' with government backing fought the poor over land boundaries. 'Germán was responsible for the violence,' he said. Germán engaged in extensive intimidation by arming his *moreno* cowboys and using them as henchmen to intimidate peasants; he had an engineer sent to measure the land assassinated; and he made people fear that taking 'his' land was illegal (Manzano Añorve 1991, 103).

On 30 June 1933, the Mexican government granted San Nicolás 9840 hectares for its *ejido*, which was carved out of the 30,000 hectares still controlled by the Miller family (Gobierno del Estado de Guerrero 1933, 7–8). Yet with the help of Germán's brother Guillermo, the State judge, through the following decades Guerrero's white elites blocked the aspirations of San Nicoladenses as well as those of other coastal belt *morenos* (Manzano Añorve 1991, 102). In the 1930s and beyond, agrarian conflict took the lives of many local activists, including that of the man San Nicoladenses refer to as the 'father of the *ejido*' for valiantly fighting to recover land stolen by whites. This man, Porfirio Pastrana, was assassinated in San Nicolás on 27 August 1937 'by federal forces accompanied by servants of the American (sic) landowner Germán Miller … whose crimes against the agrarian activists of this region have long been known' (AGN Dirección General de Gobernación 2.012.8[9]26474:40).

As the conflict over San Nicolás's land went on, it included more struggles with other people *morenos* identify as whites. This is because in the 1950s, the Guerreran state government sold some of the Miller family lands to encourage mestizo immigration to the coastal belt. Together with Germán, these so-called 'colonists' (*colonos*), as they are also known, attempted to gain or to retain San Nicolás's territory during violent struggles. In the mid-1960s, part of the Panamerican Highway – Federal Highway 200 – was completed down the coastal belt. With the new road came Mixtec Indians from the Costa Chica's northwest upland region of Ayutla de los Libres, who were searching for arable land. Because San Nicoladenses were still battling Germán Miller and white colonists when migrants arrived, and because some of the town's land lay fallow, they were given land to till and plots for houses. Settling in San Nicolás, they became a buffer between white outsiders and the *moreno* community. Today the Indians constitute about five per cent of San Nicolás's population but San Nicoladenses still have unsettled boundaries with white colonists: 'this problem of regularizing the land will never end,' Antonio told me, '[The colonists] are white.' San Nicolás's Indian residents, like those who have always lived among African descended people on the coast, continue to marry their *moreno* neighbors, giving birth to a new generation of mixed *moreno* Indians. There is no special racial label for this young generation. 'They're just called "crossed" (*cruzados*),' Amelia told me.

A *moreno* saint and an indian warrior

In the 18th, 19th, and early 20th centuries, seasonal goat herding activities by Indians most certainly connected the coastal belt of the Costa Chica to Guerrero's Nahua uplands Montaña region 300 kilometers to the north (Martínez Rescalvo and Obregón Téllez 1991, 263–68; Widmer 1990, 131–34). The few Nahuas remaining on the coast today are still referred to as shepherds, although they no longer herd (Valdez 1998, 59). San Nicoladenses do not have regular contact with these coastal Nahuas, who live north of Ometepec and are 'descendants of the families of the stock-tenders' (Valdez 1998, 94–95) ('there's another "shepherd race" up there – they have a different language,' Don Elidio said). But the 'authentic' statue of San Nicolás's patron saint – San Nicolás of Tolentino – lives in the Nahua Indian village of Zitlala in those uplands. 'He's *moreno* like us,' San Nicoladenses say of the saint. 'He's really big, he's *moreno*, he has kinky hair.' They speak of his birth as the 'son of an Indian and a black' and of his upbringing in San Nicolás, where he is referred to as 'Papa Nico,' an endearing kinship term that uses the informal *papá* as well as a diminutive, Nico. Their tales about how the saint came to be in Zitlala focus on a Spanish priest who stole him from them because he was skeptical that the village was worthy of such a saint (see Dehouve 1995; Sánchez Andraka 1983). 'It was a Spanish priest,' Doña Consuelo confirmed. 'He said that San Nicolás [the village] didn't deserve such a miraculous saint. "I'm going to take him," the priest said.' As the priest was nearing what was likely the Augustinian bishopric in Chilapa, the saint 'decided' on his own to stay among Zitlala's Indians. The saint 'planted himself;' he 'made himself heavy;' 'he wanted to stay there.' So Zitlalans built his church and the priest could no longer lift him. 'No one says anything about the saint living among Indians,' said Doña Consuelo. When pilgrims from San Nicolás visit, 'the Indians make a lot of food and are really welcoming.'

During the saint's three-day September festival, San Nicolás's *morenos* travel to Indian Zitlala and the saint leaves Zitlala to visit San Nicolás. San Nicoladenses who go to Zitlala and those in San Nicolás greeting the saint stage the *toro de petate* (lit. straw mat bull) dance in homage to the saint's ranch childhood. This centers on the figures of Don Pancho and La Minga, a male and female couple who don white masks to represent the Spanish owners and bosses of the land San Nicoladenses' ancestors worked. The dancers who accompany them represent their employees, ranch hands, and cowboys, the latter sporting colorful hats capped with 'ponytails' (*coletas*). As the dancers perform, Pancho playfully but aggressively chases women and girls with a lasso, while Minga thrusts a white baby doll she carries at the crowds who gather around, begging them to cuddle it but turning against them if they do.

Two days after this festival concludes, San Nicoladenses celebrate Independence Day with a dance/performance called La América or Los Apaches (The Apaches). During it, young men take on roles as *gachupines*, which is a derogatory colonial word for Spaniards. Meanwhile, a young woman plays the central character: an Indian woman known as La América. She is escorted by a number of male Apache warriors. 'It's a fierce

Indian,' said Don Guillermo of the Apaches. 'They fought the Spaniards with arrows and didn't compromise.'

Mexican dances featuring antagonistic groups of Indians and Spaniards typically reenact the Conquest. Common throughout Latin America, including on the Costa Chica, where *La Danza de la Conquista* is performed in nearby mestizo and indigenous towns (Bonfiglioli 2000), such dances developed out of the 16th century theater that missionaries introduced to evangelize Indians as they instructed them through role-playing to be Christians (Trexler 1984). Typically, these dances therefore reenact the defeat of Indians by Spaniards. While there appears to be no full record of them, when performed by Indians, they might contain what Max Harris describes as hidden transcripts, for instance in Mexico the resurrection of the conquest figures Moctezuma and Cuauhtemóc (Harris 1997). In mestizo versions, in contrast, there might be 'no redress against the Spanish victory' in a place imagined as Spanish, as William Rowe and Vivian Schelling note of a Peruvian version (1991, 57). While La América takes the form of a conquest play insofar as its participants act out antagonistic roles as Spaniards and Indians, San Nicolás does not perform La Conquista per se. Nor is there any sign of Spanish victory in La América. Instead, in a performance and process heavily steeped in nationalist symbolism, it maps reconquest rather than conquest as Indians defeat Spaniards in order to take territory *back*. They therefore gain Independence by freeing Mexico from its Spanish captors, expelling them from territory that belongs to Indians. La América is 'from here,' San Nicoladenses told me; here we 'honor Indians.'

The young *morena* who plays La América cannot be too pale or too dark, or have hair that is too straight or too tightly curled. Her eldest daughter would never be La América, Sirina told me, because her hair was too kinky (*cuculuste*) and one has to be able to put one's hair in corkscrew curls or waves (*olas*), which even straight-haired Indians cannot do without a perm because their hair will not hold a curl. La América's elaborate float on a pickup truck is adorned with a painted Indian warrior, while her outfit consists of an ornate feathered headdress and several costumes that include a green, white, and red gown in the colors of the Mexican flag. This was adorned the year I saw it with a sequined eagle and serpent – Aztec symbols and the central emblem of the Mexican flag. La América's protectors, the Apaches, whoop in their red tunics and small, feathered headdresses, which, later in the festival, are replaced with small Mexican flags. With bows and blunted arrows, they prepare to fight a street battle with the *gachupines*, who hold shortened hand-launched firecrackers representing firearms.

The *gachupines* wear no special clothing. Nor do they dance. In fact, there is a general lack of interest in elaborating the Spanish characters while the ritual importance of Indians is indexed by their detailed costume, their dance, and the crowd's intense focus on and identification with them (see Harris 1997). When the Apaches defeat the *gachupines*, as they inevitably do, everyone returns to town hall, where La Reina, the Spanish Queen, *la gachupina* who no girl really wants to play because she is white and because she is ignored, has been sitting neglected while the action takes place outside. As La América enters with her Apache protectors to cheers of 'Viva México,' the crown and scepter are taken from La Reina. Simultaneously, La América takes a large Mexican flag and tears down 'the chains of slavery,' crepe paper chains in green, red, and white, hanging from the ceiling of town hall. 'Why Indians?' I once asked. 'Well,' Don Domingo told me, 'they fought while blacks did not.'

In La América, then, whites are therefore written out of the nation as Indians (re)take it. Both aspects of the performance are important because they point to the ways in which whites and Indians are more discursively excluded and embraced by the local community. The character of La América, moreover, suggests a *feminized* Indian nation. She might even symbolically secure the historical figure of the *cacica* Doña Maria Ambrosia, whose alleged gift of land San Nicoladenses fought to recover. In La América, then, Indians reclaim Mexico to give *morenos* their liberty in a nation that San Nicoladenses always point out is 'free' (*libre*). Because the village's patron saint, San Nicolás of Tolentino, is *also* indebted to Indians for their graciousness in allowing him to stay in their territory when he escapes a Spanish priest, Indians and liberation are more discursively contrasted to whiteness and captivity or control in the ritual life of the village. We might even say that while the 'government' is white and male, the nation is Indian and female. I have elsewhere suggested that the patron saint's escape parallels that of a runaway slave who finds shelter among Indians (Lewis 2001, 2012, Ch. 3). Stories of maroonage, of Doña María Ambrosia, and the even more recent history of Indians from Ayutla securing village land from white encroachment all indicate that in the historical register as well as in the ritual one, San Nicoladenses owe debts to Indians. 'The authentic Mexican is Indian,' Margarita once told me. Manuel told me basically the same thing: 'The flag, the money, an eagle, a *nopal* … if you are Indian, well, the flag is yours.' In this vein, San Nicoladenses refer to themselves as *criollos* and to Indians as *naturales*. Both words mean 'native,' but *criollo* indicates that one is born in a place, while *natural* indicates that one is *of* a place. In addition to implying a more primordial character than *criollo*, *natural* therefore privileges the national belonging of Indians.

Santiago: conquest or reconquest?

I now return to the festival with which I opened this article, that of Santiago. Santiago is not the village's patron saint and he is white/Spanish, unlike the two other figures I have discussed – San Nicolás of Tolentino (*moreno*) and La América (Indian). It is perhaps not surprising that instead of townspeople honoring Santiago by, perhaps, suffering humiliating defeat under his horse's hooves or by otherwise enacting a world 'safe for Hispanicism' (Trexler 1984, 208), Santiago's festival in San Nicolás appears to point to another triumph over whiteness as it repeats the pattern of white expulsion found in the other festival performances, in historical narratives and in the social identities of San Nicolás's *morenos*.

Santiago's statue is normally mounted on a white steed and holds a sword in its upraised hand. At the festival's start, this sword is replaced with a harmless and colorful ribbon. The statue rests on an altar cloth depicting two other horses, whose noses are calmly sniffing flowers rather than subduing the Moors or Indians that otherwise characterize Santiago's iconography. Thus, a symbol of conquest becomes one of tranquility, if not of surrender.

During the festival, young men and women lead processions on horseback and take on military-like support roles as captains, flag-bearers, and commissioned officers. The young women don cowboy hats and voluminous long skirts colorfully embroidered and sequined with flowers, stars, and fanciful scenes that their female relatives and ritual kin have spent months producing by hand. The young men wear capes adorned with national motifs, such as Mexico's patron saint, the Virgin of Guadalupe, and the country's national colors. Thus, even though the festival is not a national one, the nation still makes an appearance.

In another possible nod to San Nicolás's ranch history, as well as to the equestrian theme of conquest, the participants gallop for miles escorting the *santiaguito* (a youth representing the saint) to the nearby *moreno* villages of Maldonado and Montecillos, where the revelers are plied with food and drink as they consolidate a network of inter-village reciprocity. For weeks before the festival, these employees host dances to which the whole village is invited. The expenses are enormous. In the high temperatures and humidity of late July, occasionally a horse that has galloped for miles collapses and dies from heat exhaustion. Santiago himself is said to cause such an event as punishment for the horse owner's lack of devotion and unwillingness to part with the substantial funds necessary to make the festival a success. Because of this, when Sirina's husband badly cut his foot one year after the family declined to host Santiago because of the expense, Sirina believed they were being punished by the saint. Since no one is ever accused of lacking devotion to San Nicolás (although the elderly might say that the young do not know enough about him), the unusual and burdensome punishments caused by Santiago bear some attention, for they suggest this Spanish saint can be punitive.

Carnival has not been held in San Nicolás since the 1950s, when, I was told, 'whites stopped it because they saw the customs of the blacks as very bad, really dumb,' Don Domingo said. 'They were rich and the rich gave the commands …we had no schedule; they wanted to go to bed.' However, several Carnivalesque elements survive in the Santiago festival, including the appearance of *mojigangas*, women dancers who sexually jest while wearing just one special adornment: white-faced masks. Another Carnivalesque feature is *La Tortuga* or The Turtle Dance, which is wildly popular among African descent peoples on the Costa Chica. Anita González points out that fertility is one of this dance's themes. She would likely describe San Nicolás's version as 'raunchy' due to its overt sexual innuendo (González 2010, 78, 83). Indeed, in San Nicolás, where public modesty is highly valued, especially for women (Lewis 2004), this is among the bawdiest of popular dances as the Turtle – a man dressed in a hoop skirt – uses a club or a stick in a playful yet aggressive way as a phallus thrust from the recesses of his 'shell' at the women who dance with him, mimicking just for a second sexual acts.

Yet rather than depicting broad cultural traits such as what González considers to be the generally 'rebellious' nature of 'Afro-Mexicans,' I would suggest that the dance is really about who *morenos* are *not* rather than about who they are, for in San Nicolás the turtle figure also wears a white mask, which merges his character with the Pancho at the center of the festival for San Nicolás, the saint. Here again gender bears some attention. This is not just because Pancho and the Turtle are male. It is also because in the context of both festivals, masculinity combines with sexual aggression and is marked as white. *Morenos* attribute violence in their community to historical conflicts over land and to Spanish cultural influences – especially to Spanish male ones. Festival characters – particularly The Turtle and Pancho – therefore recall not just the whiteness and maleness of the bosses and owners of the past. They also seem to represent the fact that in the village until not long ago, young (virgin) women were sometimes kidnapped and raped by young men on horseback as a prelude to marriages generally unwanted by the victims (see Lewis 2012, Chs. 4 and 6). This devastating and violent practice of 'abduction' (*rapto*) is said to have originated in the Spanish male practice of seizing black and Indian women by force. 'The custom of abduction is Spanish,' Don Margarito said. 'If Spaniards liked the Indian and black women, they would grab them. What could [the women] do?'

Further to this, San Nicoladenses told me that Santiago was 'not from here' (not from San Nicolás). 'This (festival) is Spanish,' Doña Adelfa said. This claim might be contrasted to La América, which honors Indians and 'is from here,' so it is said. In addition, like La América, San Nicolás the saint is 'from here.' Not only is the village named after him. He was born and raised there, the son of an Indian and a black. I believe these distinctions are important because although the three main characters – a white (Santiago), an Indian (La América), and a *moreno* (San Nicolás) – are of different 'races,' the performances in their festivals suggest similar processes at work. In La América, the Indians in the guise of La América and the Apaches are victorious over Spaniards. Similarly, San Nicolás defies the will of a Spanish priest in order to live in Zitlala, where Indians welcome him and feed his 'children' once a year during his festival days. That the Spanish Santiago is said to be 'not from here' while the other two are suggests that his presence in San Nicolás triggers a certain amount of ambivalence because the same story is told: Spanishness/whiteness is precisely what needs to be overcome. Although the Indian-as-liberator theme is not prominent, Santiago's festival also transcends whiteness as '*moreno*-ness' sees itself in opposition, even when the public transcript would indicate that a white saint is being honored.

In analyzing the Santiago festival near the Afro-Puerto Rican city of Loíza, Max Harris argues that there this saint is also an ambiguous figure whose festival performances point to a hidden transcript that speaks to local interests and meanings. Here the saint – especially in his incarnation as a white adult male – encourages subversion, as devotion to him speaks to his 'ambiguous role in Spanish mythology' (Harris 2001, 360; see also, 2000, 129–131). Such ambiguity was indicated at the beginning of this article: Santiago is both Mataindios and Matamoros. In his latter role he protects, while in his former he massacres. In San Nicolás, his festival opens with the distribution of tamales made by local women to all comers at Town Hall. It ends with the sacrifice of the cat, usually in front of the Church. As the festival begins, then, people emphasize abundance: everyone's bellies will be full at the start of a season when their wellbeing depends on the rain for crops and grazing. Moreover, the tamales are stuffed with beef, chicken, and pork in a region where beef, especially, is a luxury item but must also be at the center of every small and large ritual occasion. Once the tamales are distributed, the families of the sponsors and the women who have cooked feel a sense of relief that they have met their debts. '*Salvé*,' they say, 'I managed it.' Feasting on meat continues until the early morning hours and no one goes hungry. Santiago thus provides as he did in his incarnation as the Old World Matamoros.

But taken in the context of the festival's Carnivalesque features, Santiago's whiteness is also parodied, as other qualities are drawn on but not celebrated. Indeed, in San Nicolás, those qualities – depicted not just with mocking white masks but also through sexual innuendo and symbols of aggression, including Santiago's sword – seem to become catalysts for their own neutralization. Thus, for instance, the sword is lowered. The Santiago image is therefore publicly feted but hidden in the days of his fiesta is what appears to be his defeat, or at least the defeat of qualities that San Nicoladenses ascribe to Spaniards.

It was startling to see the sacrifice of the animals I described at the beginning of this article. When I asked what they represented and why they were hanged, most people said, 'it's tradition,' which is what they say about many things. 'It's only done in San Nicolás,' they added. But then I was told that the cat always had to be male. And Don Margarito mentioned that what happened to it 'was like the Inquisition. You know,' he said, 'decapitation and paying a fine.' 'Cats are very proud,' he went on to explain. And then he told me that all of the animals 'represent Spanish haughtiness' (el orgullo español). Could it therefore be that during Santiago's festival, young men slaying animals said to be haughty are once again defeating 'whites' using the equestrian skills their ancestors long ago learned as slaves and servants of Spaniards? At the risk of over-interpreting, might the destruction of the animals represent the elimination of 'white-ness' in the village? And with that elimination the defeat of threats to local wellbeing, including traditional power hierarchies as represented by 'Spanish' conquistadors and landowners, whose qualities are mocked in myriad ways throughout the annual festival cycle? Somewhat ironically, then, the festival for the white saint Santiago is perhaps another illustration of a moreno version of a national ideology that emphasizes white banishment rather than white authority. 'Very few whites have come and gone [from San Nicolás] without problems,' Don Domingo once explained. We have already seen whites banished in La América and in the festival for San Nicolás. White banishment also speaks to an agrarian past during which many morenos – including the 'father' of the community's ejido, Porfirio Pastrana – died at the hands of whites. By slaying prideful roosters and a cat, which are all males, morenos are effectively neutralizing qualities associated with the arrogant overlords of local history.

Like La América, the Santiago festival is filled with national symbols such as the Virgin of Guadalupe, the colors of the Mexican flag and, indeed, flags themselves. But while La América uses a Mexican flag to tear down the chains of slavery, in Santiago's festival the central emblem of that flag – an eagle perched on a cactus holding a serpent with its talon and its beak to mythologically represent the nation's Aztec roots – is curiously absent. Instead, the area at the flag's center, where this emblem would otherwise be, is blank. When I asked about this omission, Sirina told me, 'the ancestors didn't give an explanation.' But, she said, long ago the eagle wanted to land in San Nicolás but the ancestors feared that if it grabbed a serpent in its mouth, the serpent would 'eat everything up.' 'They were so ignorant,' she said. 'We would have been so rich.' Her reference to wealth recalls the ways in which San Nicolás's morenos describe Indians – represented here by the eagle that did not land – as the 'owners' of the country. The roles Indians have played in their lives, both historically and symbolically, indeed suggest that the wealth of the land belongs to Indians. The absence of the eagle and the serpent on the flag during a festival said to be Spanish might possibly therefore suggest that the nation is not Spanish (white), and therefore the flag must be unfinished for the duration of the festival. While whites might be the government (the state), the nation belongs to La América, and the moreno version of what is alleged to be a mestizo nation not only heavily favors Indians, it does not include whites at all.

Mexico's patron Virgin of Guadalupe is nationally considered to be a mestiza: the altered white Virgin who miraculously appeared to an Indian and then aided the Spanish project of conversion. Like the Virgin of Guadalupe, San Nicolás of Tolentino is mixed, but he is the *moreno* son of a black and an Indian. Among some of San Nicolás's *morenos*, the Virgin of Guadalupe, like their own patronymic saint, is considered *moreno* too, 'like the people of San Nicolás,' said Sirina. San Nicoladenses might thus mold the national Virgin in their own image rather than recalibrate their identities to fit hers. At least some local understandings of her therefore also test dominant national symbols of what being Mexican means. Such an interpretation would fit with the discourses and practices I have described here as San Nicoladenses refract their understandings of their own history with both the whites and the Indians that constitute the mestizo version of *mestizaje*.

Conclusion: toward an alternative *mestizaje*

Mexican racial history is rooted in a colonial past in which typologies that included mixture developed under the rubric of what was known as caste (*casta*). Norman Whitten observes that beginning in the early colonial era, 'one category that flummoxed the powerful ... was that of the indigenous-descended-African descended mixture' (2007, 365). As he observes, in the Spanish thought of the day, the progeny of indigenous and African descended people were *mixed* but not *hybridized* because by the criteria of 'early modern breeding conceptualizations' hybridization would imply the presence of a 'domesticating' Spanish, Christian, or 'civilized' element (Whitten 2007, 358–359). The lack of a unique and established colonial classification for 'uncivilized' black-Indians from the early days of the colony was reflected in the shifting terrain of terms that ranged from *mulato* to *pardo* to *zambo* to *moreno* for the only major mixed caste category that contained no white anchor, nor a future promise of whiteness through breeding. In this respect, Vasconcelos' *mestizaje* formulation did not just write blackness out of Mexico. It also ignored black-Indianness or what Whitten calls *zumbaje* after the term *zambo* or *zambaigo*. While mestizo *mestizaje* models such as that of Vasconcelos are critiqued for exclusions that rest on holding out whitening as evolutionary promise and, more broadly, for promoting 'myths' of Latin American racial democracy that divert attention from inequalities (Daniel et al. 2014, 22), they nevertheless continue to dominate scholarly debates about mixing, whether such mixing is seen as hegemonic or as liberating. In this respect and in the way that white is always present, one might argue that mestizo *mestizaje* is itself a dominant race paradigm.[22]

If mestizo *mestizaje* might be read as a variation on white hegemony, however, it would be difficult to read the *moreno* form of *mestizaje* as anything other than counter-hegemonic. My phrase *moreno mestizaje* may even be oxymoronic if, as Whitten (2007) argues, *mestizaje* as hybridization cannot exist without whiteness. In this respect, the two forms of mixing could not be further apart and therefore are not equal sorts of what Walter Mignolo terms 'border thinking,' by which he means challenges to Eurocentric knowledge produced from a subaltern perspective (2002, 71, 2012). Instead, *moreno mestizaje* operates from a position that is simultaneously inside and outside. It is both a local Western history and a non-Western local history (Mignolo 2012, xxii) that draws on 'Western' mestizo *mestizaje* and introduces a 'non-Western' logic emergent from a colonial experience that was itself marginalized, including through the myth that blacks and Indians were natural enemies.[23] Countering this myth is ample documentation that – despite silences and partial stories – draws a picture of simultaneous Indian-black antagonisms and alliances with complex and often powerful spaces of social and cultural communication (Lewis 2003, 2012). The documentation from the Costa Chica suggests that colonial labor needs for racial Others – small farmers, cowboys, textile workers and miners – which brought black and mulatto males in great numbers to the coast, resulted in new peoples. They were sometimes called *mulatos*, other times *pardos*, other times *morenos* and still other times black-Indians, but the very lack of definition is meaningful. These *morenos* first displaced those known as Indians from coastal belt villages and later displaced those known as whites from large landed estates. *Moreno* San Nicoladenses' historical experiences in this respect might not have been a singular one on the coast, but it has been little examined. Here I have tried to capture some of that experience and attend to it in conversation with the mestizo *mestizaje* paradigm meaningful to the broader Mexican sense of belonging and therefore to San Nicolás's *morenos*, whose local histories and cultural productions speak to a particularly Mexican alterity.

Notes

1. Of course, *raza* has other meanings, including 'people' or 'community,' depending on the context. But when San Nicoladenses refer to *morenos* as a *raza*, they speak in terms of blood.
2. There is some evidence that individuals who self-identify as black (*negro*) on the Costa Chica also see themselves as the product of mixture (Martínez Casas 2013).
3. Non-*moreno* peoples in turn see themselves as distinct from *morenos*.
4. More on race and color terms can be found in Lewis (2012, Ch 2).
5. Less well known are African descended people in Coahuila and Michoacán.
6. As of this writing, the Mexican government has conducted a survey. However, the data is not yet released and I do not know how racial questions were formulated nor in what contexts they were asked.
7. The Costa Chica's African descended population is not a monolithic group in terms of its experience and identity. For instance, some urban Afromexicans (a term they prefer) from Cuajinicuilapa and elsewhere on the coast, especially Oaxaca, have become involved in cultural promotion and social movements organized around a 'black' or 'Afro' identity (Lara 2014). But this is generally not the case for San Nicoladenses, who are among the uninterested (Lewis 2012, Chs. 4 and 5). On similar issues in Veracruz, see Christina Sue (2012).
8. As Peter Wade points out, 'mixture reconstitutes origins' (2004, 362; see also; Alonso 2004). *Moreno* subversion of the mestizo paradigm does not negate this reconstitution. But it does destabilize its national form.
9. As Hoffmann argues, and as I have argued elsewhere, the theoretical frameworks scholars have employed to analyze local cultural patterns as evidence of 'Afro' Diasporic or essentialized in the language of race and genetics do not accord with the historical record, with current approaches to identities as constructed, or with the local experiences and consciousness of African descended peoples (Hoffmann 2006, 2007, 2014; Lewis 2012).
10. On the question of mulattoes identified as *naturales*, a designation otherwise only applied to Indians, see note 20.
11. Aguirre Beltrán calls 'de Castilla' an 'inherited title' ([1958] 1985, 48). See also Motta Sánchez (2006, 125, 146 on the Mariscal line).

12. Like *mulato, pardo* also referred to mixed black-Indians (Love 1971).
13. On the colonial roles of blacks and mulattoes, see Lewis (2003, Ch 3 for the colonial period in general) and Lewis (2012, Ch. 1 for the Costa Chica in particular).
14. *Morenas* in San Nicolás still learn to embroider from Indian women, especially from Amuzgos.
15. While the terms *lobo* and *zambahigo* also existed, they were not often used in Mexico (Martínez 2009, 32).
16. It is also possible that most of these mulattoes were free rather than enslaved, as legal status followed the mother and most black-Indian mulattoes would have had Indian mothers.
17. The complexities of the term *moreno* might be traced to its historical instability. In some quarters, it is a catchall for a 'coffee-colored' person and/or a euphemism for 'black' (see Sue 2012, 38–39), though Sue does not address why her informants might use the two terms as separate categories, as in 'I see the whole world the same, everyone, *morenos*, blacks, whites' (Sue 2012, 31). As I discuss elsewhere, San Nicoladenses' use of *moreno* becomes particularly clear not just when they discuss their ancestry but also when they compare themselves to African Americans, whom they consider to be 'blacker' and *not* mixed (Lewis 2012).
18. With respect to the slave trade, San Nicoladenses are not unlike other Mexicans, given that the history of the trade is not taught in schools and that blacks are invisible in national discourse (Weltman-Cisneros and Mendez Tello 2013).
19. Don Domingo believed this to have taken place right after Independence. The historical record indicates that San Nicolás was identified as an *estancia* or a *cuadrilla* (settlement) until 1883, when it became an official town (*pueblo*) (AGEG-AHE, AP 607).
20. Despite extensive work in the archives on the colonial caste system (see Lewis 2003), I have never elsewhere seen mulattoes described as *naturales*, a term that even today *moreno* San Nicoladenses reserve for Indians. It might be that these mulattoes were considered in some ways 'indigenous' by Doña María's representatives and by the authorities adjudicating her land. This does not mean that they were Indian in the strict sense of the term as it was used. But they were free (the label 'slave' [*esclavo*] never appears), they were peasants, they were not outsiders, and they presumably had family members who were classified as Indian.
21. General Antonio López de Santa María was also a landowner in the region. According to Manzano Añorve (1991, 21), Santa María's rather than Doña María's holdings eventually passed to Carlos Miller. It is possible that the lands held by the Mariscal line went first to Santa María and then to Miller, but we do not know because the Millers long ago covered their paper trail.
22. While I do not have the space here to address *mulataje* (black/white mixing), Whitten (2007) argues that it too is hegemonic for its insistence on whiteness as one part of any mixed race identity.
23. For insight into this issue on the historical and contemporary Costa Chica, see Flanet (1977), Vinson (2000), and Widmer (1990).

References

Archival Sources

AGN (Archivo General de la Nación). Dirección General de Gobernación 2.012.8 (9) 26474, box 102, 1937.
AGN (Archivo General de la Nación). Tierras, volume 48, dossier 6, 1583.
AGN (Archivo General de la Nación). Tierras, volume 472, dossier 2, 1726-28.
AGN (Archivo General de la Nación). Tierras, volume 3668, dossier 3, 1755.

AGN (Archivo General de la Nación). Padrones, volume 18, 209–306, 1791.

AGEG–AHE, AP (Archivo General del Estado de Guerrero, Archivo Histórico del Estado, Archivo Paucic), volume 607, Analisis de Comunidades Guerrero.

Published Sources

Aguirre Beltrán, G. 1963. *Medicina y magia: El proceso de aculturación en la estructura colonial.* Mexico City: Instituto Nacional Indigenista.

Aguirre Beltrán, G. [1958] 1985. *Cuijla: Esbozo etnográfico de un pueblo negro.* Mexico City: Secretaria de Educación Publica.

Alonso, A. M. 2004. "Conforming Disconformity: '*Mestizaje*,' Hybridity, and the Aesthetics of Mexican Nationalism." *Cultural Anthropology* 19 (4): 459–490. doi:10.1525/can.2004.19.issue-4

Amaral Lugo, A. 2005. "*Morenos, Negros*, and *Afromestizos*: Debating Race and Identity on Mexico's Costa Chica." *BA thesis*, University of California, Los Angeles.

Banks, T. L. 2006. "*Mestizaje* and the Mexican *Mestizo* Self: No Hay Sangre *Negra*, So There Is No Blackness." *Southern California Interdisciplinary Law Journal* 15 (199): 199–234.

Bonfiglioli, C. 2000. "La danza de la conquista en México en la Costa Chica: Fragmentos de historia oral." *Revista Casa del Tiempo* July–August: n/p.

Bonfil Batalla, G. 1990. *México profundo*. Mexico City: Grijalbo

Daniel, G. R., L. Kina, W. M. Dariotis, and C. Fojas. 2014. "Emerging Paradigms in Critical Mixed Race Studies." *Journal of Critical Mixed Race Studies* 1 (1): 6–65.

Dehouve, D. 1995. "L'apparition d'une mémoire afro-indienne dans le Mexique colonial: Les tribulations d'un saint sur la route d'Acapulco." *Mémoirs en devenir: Amérique Latine, xvi-xx siècles*, 113–135. Bourdeaux: Maison des Pays Ibériques.

Flanet, V. 1977. *Viviré si Dios quiere: Un estudio de la violencia en la mixteca de la costa*. Mexico City: Instituto Nacional Indigenista

Friedlander, J. 1975. *Being Indian in Hueyapan: A Study of Forced Identity in Contemporary Mexico*. New York: St. Martin's Press.

Gerhard, P. 1993. *A Guide to the Historical Geography of New Spain*. 2nd ed. Oklahoma: University of Oklahoma Press.

Gobierno del Estado de Guerrero. 1933. *Periódico Oficial*, January 17.

González, A. 2010. *Afro-Mexico: Dancing Between Myth and Reality*. Austin: University of Texas Press.

Gould, J. L. 1998. *To Die in This Way: Nicaraguan Indians and the Myth of Mestizaje*. Durham, NC: Duke University Press.

Harris, M. 1997. "The Return of Moctezuma: Oaxaca's '*Danza de la Pluma*' and New Mexico's '*Danza de los Matachines.*'" *Drama Review* 41 (1): 106–134. 10.2307/1146575

Harris, M. 2000. *Aztecs, Moors, and Christians: Festivals of Reconquest in Mexico and Spain*. Austin: University of Texas Press.

Harris, M. 2001. "Masking the Site: The Fiestas de Santiago Apóstol in Loíza, Puerto Rico." *The Journal of American Folklore* 114 (453/Summer): 358–369.

Hernández Moreno, T. 1996. "Una historia de poder regional." *Amate: Arte, Cultura y Sociedad de Guerrero* 5: 20–24.

Hoffmann, O. 2006. "Negros y afromestizos en México: Viejas y nuevas lecturas de un mundo olvidado." *Revista Mexicana de Sociología* 68 (1): 103–135.

Hoffmann, O. 2007. "Las narrativas de la diferencia étnico-racial en la Cosa Chica, México: Una perspectiva geográfica." In *Los retos de la diferencia: Los actores de la multiculturalidad entre México y Colombia*, edited by O. Hoffmann and M. T. Rodríguez, 363–397. Mexico City: La Casa Chata.

Hoffmann, O. 2014. "The Renaissance of Afro-Mexican Studies." In *Blackness and Mestizaje in Mexico and Central America*, edited by O. Hoffmann and E. Cunin, 81–116. Trenton, NJ: Africa World Press

Jacobs, I. 1982. *Ranchero Revolt: The Mexican Revolution in Guerrero*. Austin: University of Texas Press.

Knight, A. 1990. "Racism, Revolution, and *Indigenismo*: Mexico, 1910–1940." In *The Idea of Race in Latin America, 1870–1940*, edited by R. Graham, 71–113. Austin: University of Texas Press.

Lara, G. 2014. "An Ethno-Political Trend on the Costa Chica, Mexico (1980–2000)." In *Blackness and Mestizaje in Mexico and Central America*, edited by O. Hoffmann and E. Cunin, 117–138. Trenton, NJ: Africa World Press.

Lewis, L. A. 2000. "Blacks, Black Indians, Afromexicans: The Dynamics of Race, Nation, and Identity in a Mexican *Moreno* Community (Guerrero)." *American Ethnologist* 27 (4): 898–926. 10.1525/ae.2000.27.4.898

Lewis, L. A. 2001. "Of Ships and Saints: History, Memory, and Place in the Making of *Moreno* Mexican Identity." *Cultural Anthropology* 16 (1): 62–82. 10.1525/can.2001.16.issue-1

Lewis, L. A. 2003. *Hall of Mirrors: Power, Witchcraft, and Caste in Colonial Mexico*. Durham, NC: Duke University Press.

Lewis, L. A. 2004. "Modesty and Modernity: Photography, Race, and Representation on Mexico's Costa Chica (Guerrero)." *Identities: Global Studies in Culture and Power* 11 (4): 471–499. 10.1080/10702890490883830

Lewis, L. A. 2012. *Chocolate and Corn Flour: History, Race, and Place in the Making of "Black" Mexico*. Durham, NC: Duke University Press.

Love, E. F. 1971. "Marriage Patterns of Persons of African Descent in a Colonial Mexico City Parish." *The Hispanic American Historical Review* 51 (1): 79–91. 10.2307/2512614

Manzano Añorve, M. A. 1991. *Cuajinicuilapa, Guerrero: Historia oral (1900–1940)*. Mexico City: Ediciones Artesa.

Martínez, M. E. 2009. "The Language, Genealogy, and Classification of 'Race' in Colonial Mexico." In *Race and Classification: The Case of Mexican America*, edited by I. Katzew and S. D. Smith, 25–42 Stanford: Stanford University Press.

Martínez Casas, R. 2013. "The Ideology of *Mestizaje* and Identity on the Costa Chica." Paper presented at the biannual meeting of Ethnicity, Race, and Indigenous Peoples Conference, Latin American Studies Association (ERIP-LASA), Oaxaca, October 24.

Martínez Rescalvo, M., and J. R. Obregón Téllez. 1991. *La montaña de Guerrero: Economia, historia y sociedad*. Mexico City: Instituto Nacional Indigenísta, Universidad Autónoma de Guerrero.

Miller, M. G. 2004. *Rise and Fall of the Cosmic Race: The Cult of Mestizaje in Latin America*. Austin: University of Texas Press.

Mignolo, W. 2002. "The Geopolitics of Knowledge and the Colonial Difference." *South Atlantic Quarterly* 101 (1): 57–96. 10.1215/00382876-101-1-57

Mignolo, W. 2012. *Local Histories/Global Designs: Coloniality, Subaltern Knowledges and Border Thinking*. 2nd ed. Princeton: Princeton University Press.

Moedano Navarro, G. 1986. "Notas etnográficas sobre la población negra de la Costa Chica." In *Primer coloquio de arqueología y etnohistoria del estado de Guerrero*, edited by R. Cervantes-Delgado, 551–560. Mexico City: Instituto Nacional de Antropologia e Historia, Gobierno del Estado de Guerrero.

Motta Sánchez, J. A. 2006. "Tras la heteroidentificación: El 'movimiento negro' costachiquense y la selección de marbetes étnicos." *Dimensión Antropológica* 13 (38): 115–150.

Quiroz Malca, H. 2004. "La migración de los afromexicanos y algunos de sus efectos culturales locales: Una moneda de dos caras." In *Migrantes indígenas y afromestizos de Guerrero*, edited by C. G. Barroso, 244–270. Acapulco: Editorial Cultural Universitaria.

Ravelo Lecuana, R. 1990. *La revolución zapatista en Guerrero*. Chilpancingo: Universidad Autónoma de Guerrero.

Rowe, W., and V. Schelling. 1991. *Memory and Modernity: Popular Culture in Latin America*. New York: Verso.

Sánchez Andraka, J. 1983. *Zitlala: Por el mágico mundo indígena guerrerense*. 1 vol. Chilpancingo: Fondo de Apoyo Editorial del Gobierno del Estado de Guerrero.

Stepan, N. L. 1991. *"The Hour of Eugenics:" Race, Gender, and Nation in Latin America*. Ithaca, NY: Cornell University Press

Stutzman, R. 1981. *"El Mestizaje*: An All-Inclusive Ideology of Exclusion." In *Cultural Transformations and Ethnicity in Modern Ecuador*, edited by N. Whitten, 45–94. Urbana: University of Illinois Press.

Sue, C. 2012. *Land of the Cosmic Race: Race Mixture, Racism and Blackness in Mexico*. Oxford: Oxford University Press.

Trexler, R. 1984. "We Think, They Act: Clerical Readings of Missionary Theatre in Sixteenth-Century New Spain." In *Understanding Popular Culture: Europe from the Middle Ages to the Nineteenth Century*, edited by S. L. Kaplan, 189–227. Berlin: Mouton.

Valdez, N. 1998. *Ethnicity, Class, and the Indigenous Struggle for Land in Guerrero, Mexico*. New York: Garland Press.

Van Young, E. 1994. "Conclusion: The State as Vampire – Hegemonic Projects, Public Ritual, and Popular Culture." In *Rituals of Rule, Rituals of Resistance: Public Celebrations and Popular Culture in Mexico*, edited by W. H. Beezley, C. E. Martin, and W. E. French, 343–374. Wilmington, DE: Scholarly Resources Books.

Vasconcelos, J. 1924. *La raza cósmica: Misión de la raza iberoamericana*. Paris: Agencia Mundial de Librería.

Vinson III, B. 2000. "The Racial Profile of a Rural Mexican Province in the 'Costa Chica': Igualapa in 1791." *The Americas* 57 (2): 269–282. 10.1353/tam.2000.0022

Vinson III, B. 2001. *Bearing Arms for His Majesty: The Free-Colored Militia in Colonial Mexico*. Stanford: Stanford University Press.

Wade, P. 2004. "Images of Latin American Mestizaje and the Politics of Comparison." *Bulletin of Latin American Research* 23 (3): 355–366. 10.1111/blar.2004.23.issue-3

Weltman-Cisneros, T., and C. D. Mendez Tello. 2013. "Negros-Afromexicanos: Recognitionand the Politics of Identity in Contemporary Mexico." *Journal of Pan-African Studies* 6 (1): 140–156.

Whitten Jr., N. E. 2007. "The *Longue Durée* of Racial Fixity and the Transformative Conjunctures of Racial Blending." *The Journal of Latin American and Caribbean Anthropology* 12 (2): 356–383 10.1525/jlat.2007.12.2.356

Widmer, R. 1990. *Conquista y despertar de las costas de la Mar del Sur (1521–1684)*. Mexico City: Consejo Nacional para la Cultura y las Artes.

Playing mestizo: festivity, language, and theatre in Yucatán, Mexico

Paul K. Eiss

ABSTRACT

This article takes Yucatán's 'Monument to Mestizaje' as the entry point to an analysis of mestizo culture in Yucatán in the 19th and 20th centuries. Providing three genealogies of mestizaje in Yucatán – focused on festivity, language, and theatre – this article takes a historical and performative approach; it focuses neither on the workings of 'mestizo' social identity nor on ideologies of mestizaje, but on the performance of mestizo acts in particular historical contexts and in politically charged ways. In festive dances, the speaking of 'mixed' Maya, and racial impersonations performed on stages of theatre or politics, Yucatecans enact mestizaje in ways that sometimes ratify hegemonic racial discourses, but other times leave them in pieces.

An unlikely figure watches over the Paseo de Montejo, a wide boulevard in Mérida named after the conqueror of Yucatán. Atop a base meant to evoke the architecture of the Maya pyramids stands a sculptural group collectively titled the 'Monument to Mestizaje.' A bearded Spaniard identified as Gonzalo Guerrero stands dressed as a Maya warrior, spear aloft. Seated behind him is his Maya wife nursing a naked infant; a naked boy plays with a Spanish helmet. Guerrero's story is well known. In 1511, in advance of Hernán Cortés' conquest of Tenochtitlán, a group of conquistadors shipwrecked on the coast of Yucatán and was captured by Maya warriors. While several of his companions were killed, Guerrero survived and prospered. He rose as a warrior in the service of a Maya lord, marrying his daughter, with whom he had several children. Eventually, Cortés sent friar Gerónimo Aguilar on a mission to retrieve Guerrero, but Guerrero – now dressed as a Maya warrior, with facial tattoos and piercings – demurred. Guerrero shared his knowledge of Spanish military tactics with the Maya, leading a series of campaigns against Spanish forces, until meeting his end in 1536, in a battle in Honduras.

Spanish chroniclers viewed Guerrero unkindly. But from the 1970s forward, Mexican authors and artists recuperated him as a mythic hero: father of the 'first' mestizos not only of Mexico but also of the Americas (Adorno 2007; Mueller 2001).[1] The monument erected in 1993 was the last of several castings of a work finished by sculptor Raúl Ayala

Arellano in 1974. What messages do such monuments convey about *mestizaje* in postrevolutionary Mexico, whose governing classes have claimed legitimacy in discourse that is both indigenist and '*mesticist?*' (Alonso 2004, 462–468; Knight 1990; Lomnitz 2001, 50–54; Lund 2012). They are about *mestizaje* as a bio-racial process – here figured as mixed-race children – and about ensuing cultural assimilation; the boys are literally naked of cultural markers. In these masculinist depictions, woman serves as mere vessel for the making of the new race. Indeed, Mérida's monument – like a similar monument in Mexico City, which credits Hernán Cortés with fathering the 'first' mestizo with his native interpreter, la Malinche – mirrors the multiracial families of Mexico's 18th-century *casta* paintings: men in front gesture toward standing boys, with women seated passively behind.

But while the messages of the Mérida and Mexico City monuments might seem to converge neatly, to embrace Guerrero's perspective – or more precisely, a Yucatecan regional perspective – on *mestizaje* is to decenter accounts that privilege the perspectives of national elites and power holders. It is to consider what *mestizaje* might look like from the margins. In Yucatán, populations of indigenous descent historically have been in the majority, playing a predominant role in a kind of *mestizaje* that has been as much about 'going Indian' – Guerrero's path – as about whitening or loss of indigeneity. In Yucatán, we may find a kind of *mestizaje* different from, and prior to, the versions expressed by figures like Manuel Gamio (1916) and José Vasconcelos (1925) – one that may have shaped, intersected with, or in some ways diverged from the hegemonic mestizo nationalism of the postrevolutionary Mexico.

What if we flipped Guerrero's monument, to find an entirely different message about *mestizaje* from the one its makers intended? We might dismiss Guerrero's children as 'first' mestizos, for they were fully socialized into the Maya world into which they were born. What if we took Guerrero – alongside La Malinche (cf. Anzaldúa 2012) – as the 'first' mestizo? To do so would be to discard the assumption that bio-racial *mestizaje* is 'first,' to consider the possibility that other things were 'first' – taking on other clothes, speaking other languages, and negotiating the middle ground between peoples, languages, worlds. To entertain such possibilities would be to question whether *mestizaje* is fundamentally about race as biologically defined. It would pose a challenge to much scholarship on *mestizaje* in Latin America, which has been characterized by a bifurcation into studies of mestizo-ness in terms of hybrid racial identity, expressed from below, and studies that consider *mestizaje* as a hybridizing, whitening, or assimilationist racial ideology, imposed from above.[2]

To indulge this alternative mythology of Guerrero as 'first' mestizo is, finally, to raise the suggestion that *mestizaje* might be, above all else, a put on. Here, while building upon scholarly literature on the workings of ethnic and social identity and identity discourses in Yucatán, from the classic studies of Redfield and Villa Rojas (Redfield 1941; Redfield and Villa Rojas 1934) to more recent historical and ethnographic work (Loewe 2010; see also Gabbert 2004; Hervik 1999), this study is historical, genealogical, and above all performative. My focus is neither on patterns of mestizo social identity nor on the workings of ideologies of *mestizaje*, but on mutable, historically embedded, and politically charged mestizo acts.

Beginning with Guerrero's costumed and tattooed figure, *mestizaje* from a Yucatecan standpoint is thus in the first instance neither about engendering offspring nor even about *being* mestizo, but about *becoming* mestizo. It is not so much about the osmotic mixing of traits of blood and culture, but about public acts and political action. It emerges neither from above nor from below, but in the spaces and places in-between. In Yucatán, *mestizaje* is about *looking* mestizo, *speaking* mestizo, and *playing* mestizo.

Looking mestizo

The Yucatecan public festivity called the *vaquería* – and *jarana* music and dances associated with it – is performed in varied contexts: in pueblos, towns, and cities, on important holidays; in political events and shows for tourists. Accompanying commentary typically depicts the *vaquería* as the defining expression of Yucatecan – in distinction from Mexican – mestizo culture, combining elements of Spanish and Maya origin. Special costumes are worn by '*vaqueros*' and '*vaqueras*,' notably the *terno*, a development of the Maya *huipil*, with more elaborate embroidery and lacework. Stomping dances in 6/8 time and waltzes are considered to be of Spanish origin; most are performed without any touching between males and females, who hold hands aloft or linked by a handkerchief. There might be dances around a pole festooned with ribbons; sometimes cries of '*bomba*' interrupt the dancing and music for competitive jesting in rhymed couplets (Loewe 2010; Pérez Sabido 1983; Pinkus Rendón 2010). In pueblos of Western Yucatán where I did ethnographic fieldwork, *vaquerías* were major public events, staged during fiestas that honored principal saints. Maya speakers typically referred to such an event as a *cha'an*: a word that translates as 'looking.' Indeed, such festive dances always drew crowds that looked on in fascination.

How, where, and when did this genre of festivity emerge, and how did it come to be considered emblematic of *mestizaje*? Such questions require consideration of the workings of social identity and festivity in the wake of conquest. Though the Spanish introduced profound changes in Maya society, and subjected it to an exploitative colonial regime, in numerical terms their presence was modest. By 1570, the population of Yucatán was still overwhelmingly indigenous, with one Spaniard, and one African slave, for every 500 Maya. Indigenous *repúblicas* retained substantial lands, resources, and autonomy. Maya leaders, called *batab* in Maya (or *cacique*, an imported term) exercised prerogatives and powers. For the first two centuries of colonial rule, the world remained separated between a tiny Spanish world that included mixed populations in subordinate roles, and a vast indigenous majority, occupying the countryside as well as the outer peripheries of towns and urban areas (Farriss 1984; Restall 1997, 2009).

The terms of ethnic and social categorization reflected that divide. Spaniards used words like *indígena* and *indio* to refer to Maya populations, and referred to mixed race populations collectively as *castas*, and more specifically by presumed descent as *mestizos, mulatos*, or *pardos*. Maya speakers rarely referred to themselves as *indígenas* or *indios*, identifying instead by place of residence, as members of an indigenous republic (*cah*), or by status as commoner (*macehual*, a borrowing from Nahua). A Spaniard was a *ts'ul* (Maya for foreigner), or *kastelan winik*, derived from 'Castilian' and *winik*, the word for 'man.' Terms used to refer to people of mixed descent included *xak'a'an winik* ('mixed man'), *k'ank'an* ('yellow yellow'), or *sak ek'* ('white black') (Barrera Vásquez 1980; Gabbert 2004; Restall 2009).[3] As Joanne Rappaport (2014) has argued in the case of colonial Nueva Granada, however, references to mixed categories in Yucatán may not have reflected the existence of mixed race people as discrete social groups but situational, transitory, and metaphorical judgments about who looked mixed, in a world where social identity was defined by *calidad* – an amalgam of color, descent, station, wealth, occupation, residence, and dress, among other factors.

Public festivity remained an important arena for social and religious life after conquest, as it had been before. Writing in the mid-16th century, Franciscan friar Diego de Landa noted the proclivity of the Maya to honor 'demons' on particular dates by drinking and engaging in large-scale feasts and celebrations (de Landa 2011). Among the various Maya equivalents for 'fiesta' listed in early Franciscan dictionaries was *mank'inal*, literally in Maya an 'occasion of passing of days' (Barrera Vásquez 1980). The majority of preconquest festivities, however, were suppressed as institutions of Christian origin were established in indigenous communities. Indigenous *cofradías* not only promoted veneration of saints but also managed communal properties and large-scale festivities involving the distribution of food and drink, dancing, and offerings of food and drink to saints and deceased ancestors (Farriss 1984; Rugeley 2001b). Maya musical instruments, especially the wooden drum called the *tunk'ul*, continued to sound.[4] Indeed, the majority of the Maya terms that are translated as 'fiesta' in 16th- and 17th-century Franciscan dictionaries evoke the saints' fiestas of the *cofradías*: tsiktsil k'in, for a day dedicated to offering reverences; *ta'kunbil* or *kanan* as words signifying guarding or taking care.

Toward the middle of the 18th century, colonial Yucatán underwent major social changes, among them the decline and collapse of the two-estate system. Urban and rural population levels rose sharply, leading to increasing pressure on land and demand for agricultural products. In the late 18th century, Spain's Bourbon rulers enacted a series of measures that encouraged the privatization of indigenous communal properties, including those of the *cofradías*, and restricted the prerogatives and powers of indigenous caciques. While even in the wake of independence, the cacique remained a necessary man for labor drafts policing, as well as the collection of taxes and church fees, in 1868 the position was finally eliminated (Dutt 2014; Patch 1994; Rugeley 1996).

As consequential as the decline of the *repúblicas* was the rise of another institution, the rural *hacienda*, both as a form of agricultural production and as a regime of racial, class, and gender domination. As the number and size of the haciendas expanded so did their labor needs. In response to threats, enticements, or the pressures of need, indigenous workers left their pueblos of residence, eventually becoming indebted hacienda peons or *sirvientes* who were legally bound to service. Public whippings were commonplace and deemed necessary for the motivation of indigenous laborers presumed disposed to laziness and indifference. Female hacienda residents were subjected to forced marriages and sexual exploitation by owners and overseers.

These changes also brought mixed-race populations in the countryside, as workers and artisans of Spanish and mixed descent established smaller farms and ranches. While some worked on the haciendas, others settled in pueblos and towns, working as artisans, butchers, and shopkeepers. By the end of the colonial period, mixed populations accounted for roughly 20 per cent of the population of the rural northwest. While the wealthiest *hacendados* lived in Mérida as absentee landlords, poorer Spaniards and people of color became integrated into the pueblos, marrying into indigenous households. Terry Rugeley has demonstrated how *cofradías* in cities, towns, and haciendas incorporated persons of diverse social classes, and of African, indigenous, Spanish, and mixed descent (Heller 2007, 191; Rugeley 2001b, 144). In short, within a generation or two, most working *vecinos* lived in Maya households and cultural worlds, often speaking Maya as their first language.

With these developments, a system in which social status was defined by membership in corporate ethnic groups ceded place to a class system. Social and racial distinctions were made by markers of wealth, especially clothes, whether of the barefoot or sandal-wearing *indio* or of the well-heeled *gente de vestido*. Spanish speakers, and especially those of privilege, tended to divide the world between Yucatecos, or *blancos* (whites), and *indios or indígenas*. The term mestizo, which throughout the colonial period had referred to a person of Spanish and indigenous descent, now became a generic descriptor; as Matthew Restall observes, 'toward the end of the colonial period it began to expand and take on the meaning once held by *"casta"* (that is, a mixed-race person of any kind)' (Restall 2009, 107; see also; Patch 1994). For their part, Maya speakers tended to describe their world as one divided between ts'ul (for a person of wealth and often lighter skin color), and *macehual*, or commoner. Those in the middle, whom those of Spanish descent might label mestizos, now often were classed as *vecinoil*, a hybrid term (Gabbert 2004; Rugeley 1996).

This was the context in which the *vaquería* emerged as an invented mestizo tradition. The *vaquería* seems to have been connected to the region's haciendas and ranches, not least via the word '*vaquería*,' which refers to a time of festivities after the work associated with branding recently weaned cattle. In 1843, the American explorer, diplomat, and travel writer John Lloyd Stephens witnessed a dance on one hacienda, whose mayordomo 'got up a dance of the Indians' for his visitor's entertainment. To the sound of violins and the tunk'ul, women and men lined up on opposite sides of a corridor and by turns performed a slow dance, with couples holding opposite corners of a handkerchief (Stephens [1843] 1963, Vol. 1, 81).

The *vaquería* was celebrated more elaborately in pueblos and towns. In one, which Stephens described as the 'most backward and thoroughly Indian of any village we had visited,' he noted that indigenous *cofradías* nonetheless incorporated *vecinos* in dominant roles (Stephens [1843] 1963, 228). A religious procession ended at the house of a patron, where seats were occupied by 'whites and Mestiza women' (230). Once vecinos were done dancing *jaranas*, 'Indians' streamed in to take their places (231). In the large town of Ticul, Stephens witnessed the daughters and sons of the principal landowning families playing the roles of vaqueros and vaqueras, in the 'báyle[sic] de las Mestizas:'

> ... a fancy ball, in which the señoritas of the village appeared as las Mestizas, or in the costume of Mestiza women: loose white frock, with red worked border around the neck and shirt, a man´s black hat, a blue scarf over the shoulder, gold necklace and bracelets. The young men figured as vaqueros, or major domos [sic], in shirt and pantaloons of pink striped muslin, yellow buckskin shoes, and low, roundcrowned, hard-platted straw hat ... The place was open to all who chose to enter, and the floor was covered with Indian women and children, and real Mestizoes[sic] in cotton shirts, drawers, and sandals; the barrier, too, was lined with a dense mass of Indians and Mestizoes, looking on good-humouredly at this personification of themselves and their way. (Stephens [1843] 1963, Vol. 2, 63, 65)[5]

What might such an event have been called by participants? In one mid-19th-century dictionary new Maya equivalents appear for fiesta: *cha'an*, and *cha'anil*, both terms signifying 'looking' (Pío Pérez 1866–1877, 65). In a change from colonial era terms relating to the care of saints, the usage made public spectacle central to festivity and reflective of emergent forms of public social interaction on pueblo and hacienda. To be festive was to stage a *vaquería*; for propertied elites to take a leading role on the dance floor was to 'look' mestizo, impersonating the rural working class (those Stephens called 'Indians' and 'real mestizoes') in a way that simultaneously set themselves apart.

But Stephens toured Yucatán on the verge of the Yucatán Caste War, an event that altered the region's social geography, ethnic and class hierarchies, and cultural politics. In 1847, a rebellion swept much of the peninsula, particularly involving indigenous populations of the south and east. The rebels almost took Mérida, before being beaten back by Yucatecan forces – whose base of support lay in the northwest (Dumont 1997; Rugeley 2009). Despite the participation of indigenous and mestizo populations on both sides of the conflict, Yucatecan men of letters interpreted it as a race war pitting indigenous 'savages' or 'barbarians' against the 'whites' (*blancos*), and their mestizo allies.

The violence of the Caste War seems to have hardened conceptions of essential racial difference, at least among Yucatecan elites. Lettered Yucatecans increasingly applied bio-racial schema to the population of the state, which they tended to divide into three distinct groups – '*blanco*,' '*mestizo*,' and '*indio*.' In 1857, novelist and historian Justo Sierra O'Reilly ascribed the origins of the war to intractable racial antagonisms based on 'diversity of skin color' (Sierra O'Reilly [1848–1851] 1994, 24). Centuries of living together, he wrote, had not led to intermarriage and 'social identification,' but rather to a race hate that had erected an 'insurmountable wall' (104–105). Onetime governor Eligio Ancona declared the 'mestizo race' a blood ally of Yucatecan whites, one that always embraced 'the cause of civilization … scarcely adopting anything other than its costume from its maternal progenitors' (Ancona 1878, 171). In fact, he explained,

> in Yucatán the term white is used to refer not only to those who have pure European blood running in their veins, but to those who have any quantity of European blood mixed with indigenous blood. Thus, especially in the war, our population was and is divided into two portions: the Indians and the whites. The former are the descendants of the Mayas, who haven't mixed their blood with anyone else, and the latter individuals of all the other races who inhabit the peninsula (Ancona 1889, 13).[6]

Such views emerged in conversation with discussions of race, and race mixing, at the national and transnational levels. In Mexico, as in other Latin American nations of the late 19th century (Earle 2007), the attitudes of political leaders and intellectuals toward indigenous populations were schizophrenic. Under the regime of Porfirio Díaz for instance – himself of mixed descent – Aztec leaders like Cuauhtémoc were literally monumentalized, taking statuesque form on Mexico City's principal boulevard, the *Paseo de La Reforma*, in the 1870s (Tenenbaum 1994). Yet at the same time, Porfirian politicians and intellectuals derided contemporary indigenous populations – like Maya populations in Yucatán – as racially degraded remnants that presented obstacles to national development.

In this context, race mixture was perceived with ambivalence. European and US racial theorists like Count Arthur de Gobineau, Louis Agassiz, and Hippolyte Taine, posited the biological superiority of peoples of European descent, and decried miscegenation as a route to degeneration; Herbert Spencer and Gustave Le Bon linked race mixture to Latin American political instability, and physical anthropologists and criminologists attributed violent and criminal tendencies to the offspring of mixture (Hale 1989). While some Mexican intellectuals embraced such views, others advanced what Agustín Basave Benítez has called 'mestizophilic' postures (Basave Benítez 1992). Most notable among them was Sierra O'Reilly's son, Liberal politician and man of letters Justo Sierra, whose newspaper La *Libertad* as early as 1879 advocated for *mestizaje* as a process by which backward indigenous populations would be assimilated into the nation, 'eventually producing a new natural grouping that could be called genuinely Mexican' (La *Libertad*, México City, November 12, 1879). The mestizophilic views of such figures as Sierra, Francisco Pimentel, and Andrés Molina Enríquez diverged sharply from European accounts of race mixing as degeneration, while converging with elite Yucatecan renderings of *mestizaje* as a process of whitening whereby racial differences might be eliminated to the nation's benefit.

By the 1870s, however, the political and economic context of such discussions of *mestizaje* had changed. Díaz's presidency paved the way to the establishment of a law and order state throughout Mexico, combining export-driven economic development with authoritarian political consolidation. In Yucatán, increased international demand for henequen, a cactus-like plant used to produce fiber for cordage, led to an export-driven agricultural boom and the expansion of indebted servitude. With the movement of an increasing portion of the indigenous working population to the haciendas came a corresponding shift in the geography of ascribed social identity. Eastern Yucatán, largely occupied by subsistence farmers, continued to be a zone of indigeneity, while the modernizing west was perceived as a zone of *mestizaje* – even though most hacienda workers and pueblo residents continued to be working class Maya speakers.

The rise of henequen monoculture fueled the consolidation of power not only among the largest henequen hacendados and magnates but also among local landowning elites in Yucatán's rural towns. On festive occasions, local landowners offered exuberant, public tributes to a new era of progress in which tradition and modernity were seamlessly joined. National holidays occasioned elaborately staged *vaquerías* in the capital and in towns and pueblos. While earlier in the 19th century such *vaquerías* did not receive much notice, now they were widely advertised on national holidays, religious holidays, and saints' days, as well as for political events and celebrations of public works. The display of young females of the privileged classes – suitably garbed as 'mestiza' – was the focus of such *vaquerías*, which both Yucatecan and non-Yucatecan onlookers viewed as exceptional spectacles of popular morality, hygiene, and civic virtue. In 1890, one Mexico City visitor commented extensively on a Yucatecan baile de mestizos, viewing it as evidence that 'The [Yucatecan] pueblo is well educated, industrious, and clean, professes respect for the law and an understanding of honor. Perhaps it is to this that the Yucatán peninsula owes its wealth and progress …' (M. Larrañaga y Portugal 1890, cited in Trujillo 1946, 333).

In such events the uses of the *vaquería* changed, as Yucatecan social and political elites made the impersonation of mestizos and mestizas central to regional statecraft.

The politics of the festive state (cf. Guss 2000) stopped neither at town-level political events nor at the state governor's office. In February 1906, Porfirio Díaz visited Yucatán for annual Carnival festivities, during which a parade wended its way along Mérida's avenues, including the Paseo de Montejo. The whole event exalted Yucatán's Maya past: floats and costumes bore young men and women of the wealthiest families in ancient Maya getup as archers, priests, warriors, dancers, and 'sacrificers.' Parade sections dedicated to 'conquest' and 'Spanish domination' followed, as well as a 'goddess of Liberty' holding aloft fragments of chains – the broken fetters of slavery.

While the parade was the most dramatic of the proceedings, an event of equal symbolic importance had preceded it that morning, when Díaz and his retinue traveled to Hacienda Chunchucmil to attend *vaquería* featuring mestizas of Chunchucmil – their faces cosmetically whitened. While Carnival summoned forth the ancient Maya to embody the glories of Yucatán's Maya past, the 'vaqueras' on Chunchucmil impersonated the Yucatecan pueblo, both present and future, as consummately mestizo. Accompanying Díaz was Rafael de Zayas Enriquez, a Porfirian politician and man of letters who had earlier published works of criminal psychology in which he favorably cited Le Bon and others regarding the immoral, criminal, and violent tendencies of the offspring of 'races that are diverse in their customs and social institutions' (de Zayas Enríquez 1891). Yet on Chunchucmil, he was charmed; he gazed as the mestizas danced to their 'strange music' – a 'mix of Arab, African, and Maya' elements, their physical beauty offering 'irrefutable proof' of the 'convenience of racial mixing' (de Zayas Enríquez 1908, 341).

Once a rustic fiesta performed on cattle ranches, and then a public spectacle for local landowners, the *vaquería* had completed its transformation. The form of the festivity had not changed so much, nor had its content. What had changed was its context, transforming the *cha'an* – the act of looking mestizo – from a cowboy fiesta into a spectacle fit for a king. Within a few years, though, the 'king' was ousted from power, amid the factional struggles that inaugurated the Mexican revolution. An era of infighting, rebellion, and civil war followed at the national level and in Yucatán. In September 1914, Constitutionalist revolutionary leader Venustiano Carranza ordered the abolition of indebted servitude on Yucatán's haciendas. In March, he appointed Sonoran General Salvador Alvarado as governor; Alvarado proceeded to enact a panoply of social reforms (labor, land, education, etc.) affecting all domains of life (Joseph 1988; Wells and Joseph 1996).

Despite such radical changes, Yucatán's political festivities not only continued but also expanded under revolutionary rule. As an outsider, Alvarado sought to legitimize himself by donning regional garb and taking part in mestizo festivities staged around his official appearances. During the revolutionary and postrevolutionary periods, Yucatecan politicians, and their governments, adopted mestizo dance, festivity, and costuming whole cloth to ratify their regional legitimacy and their claim to political rule. Mesticismo, as much as the indigenismo (cf. Fallaw 2008) to which it was integrally linked, provided a regionalist cultural idiom that underwrote Yucatecan postrevolutionary statecraft, securing political legitimacy in mixture and its performance.

Yucatán's *mestizaje* provided inspiration to emergent theorists of *mestizaje* at the national level. While Vasconcelos dismissed Yucatán's mestizo festivities in La *raza cósmica*, stating that 'Yucatán's famous, pseudonative dances, ... in reality are old

Spanish dances' (1925, 185), anthropologist Manuel Gamio visited the state and was impressed. He made Yucatán a centerpiece of *Forjando patria* as a region where the 'conquered indigenous race and the invading Spanish race have mixed together more harmoniously, and extensively, than any other region of the Republic' (1916, 18). Gamio's description of Yucatecan *mestizaje*, however, was not about costuming or festivity, nor was it couched in the kind of cultural argument he is generally credited with bringing to the anthropological discussion of race in Mexico (Lund 2012, 87). Rather, in Yucatán, the 'first and most solid basis of nationalism' was the 'happy fusion of races' in biological terms. Yucatán enjoyed 'racial homogeneity, a unification of the physical type,' evidenced in 'pronounced brachycephalism' (shortness and broadheadedness): an identifying characteristic of all Yucatecans (Gamio 1916, 19).

For Gamio, though, language was second only to race in Yucatán's happy fusion. According to him, the entire population spoke either Spanish (in urban contexts) or Maya (in rural contexts), or both, meaning that there was not only more biological homogeneity but also more linguistic unity than in most other parts of Mexico; 'all the state's inhabitants can communicate with each other with one language or the other. This is not true of any other region of the Republic' (Gamio 1916). Gamio was in a sense right, but for the wrong reasons. He misrecognized what Yucatecan intellectuals long had perceived as a fundamental characteristic of Yucatán's *mestizaje*. It wasn't about speaking Spanish *or* Maya; it was about speaking mestizo.

Speaking mestizo

Soon after the Constitutionalists took power, Carranza turned his attention to Yucatán, determined to gain legitimacy and enact limited social reforms, while stabilizing the hacienda labor regime. At his order, on 11 September 1914, a decree was issued ending indigenous indebted servitude and annulling the debts of hacienda laborers. In order to disseminate the decree among Maya speakers, the government commissioned a Yucatecan expert, Santiago Pacheco Cruz, to translate the decree into Maya (Pacheco Cruz 1953).

While communicating the decree's basic provisions, Pacheco Cruz's Maya version often diverged in meaning from the original Spanish version, typically where terminology relating to modern concepts, political institutions, or titles lacked clear Maya equivalents. Thus, '*derecho*,' for 'right,' was translated into *tucul*, a Maya term denoting idea or intention. Searching in old dictionaries for Maya terms that might match to modern institutions and concepts, he revived words long in disuse or combined existing words to invent new ones. Nonetheless, the translator recognized that the translation's purity might make it dysfunctional at a communicative level. In an addendum, he instructed agents disseminating the pure Maya decree to workers to explain its meaning to them in 'modern, or mesticized Maya, which they understand best' (Pacheco Cruz 1914b, 12).

What is one to make of such a text, or of Pacheco Cruz himself? How did nonindigenous Yucatecans like him come to be involved in the production of Maya writings? Where did notions of 'pure' and 'mestizo' Maya come from, and what was their relationship to each other?

Here, we must return to the early colonial period to consider the role of Franciscan friars in the study of Maya. Schooled by missionaries in reading and writing using Latinate script, Maya scribes produced a plethora of Maya writings in the fulfillment of their charge as officials of the indigenous republics (Restall 1997). At the same time, Franciscan linguists produced an abundance of texts in Maya from the 16th through 18th centuries – lexicons, dictionaries, and grammars, and doctrinal, catechistic, and sermon literature. They sought to devise theologically consistent schema for the translation of Christian religious concepts into a Maya lexicon. Thus, according to William Hanks, Maya was not replaced, but rather reshaped, under Spanish rule. Preexisting Maya terms were charged with new meanings, as Spanish concepts and practices were joined to Maya expressions, and Spanish signifieds were joined to Maya signifiers (Hanks 2010, xvii, 2–4, 16).

Notwithstanding such deep interventions into Maya language, some Franciscans discouraged admixture of Spanish language into liturgy. In his widely disseminated *Arte del Idioma Maya* (1746), Pedro Beltrán de Santa Rosa María criticized languages 'spoken vulgarly,' with admixture of colloquialisms and loan words. He extolled the 'grace' and concision of Maya as a perfect, divinely given language whose purity was necessary for communicating the gospel (Beltrán de Santa Rosa [1746] 1859; Berkley 1998). By the early 19th century, a spate of religious texts, from prayers to sermons and catechistic literature, had been printed and published in Maya and were widely used by the clergy in their ministrations to Maya speakers.[7]

But such 'pure' Maya texts contrasted strongly with the kind of Maya spoken throughout much of Northwestern Yucatán: what some speakers called *xak'a'an*, or 'mixed,' Maya. It was characterized by a more extensive and dynamic intermixture of Maya with Spanish – not just the occasional Spanish loan word, but large numbers of them, as well as Spanish–Maya hybrid terms and phrasing. Mixed Maya served as *lingua franca* of the haciendas and pueblos of the northwest; it found expression in the quotidian speech of pueblo dwellers whatever their descent. It was the way songs were rendered in the *vaquería*, with alternating Maya and Castilian verses and interjections. But 'mixed Maya' remained a spoken language, one largely untranscribed in printed, literary, or archival sources.[8]

Commentary on mixed Maya, however, was published in abundance, with observers from Yucatán and abroad drawing ideologically loaded conclusions about linguistic admixture. Observers characterized contemporary Maya as laden with 'barbarisms' introduced from African languages (Baeza cited in Rugeley 2001a, 21) or, in the words of onetime state governor Santiago Méndez, as 'adulterated' by Spanish due to 'almost constant intercourse with whites and mestizos' (Méndez [1870] 1921, 192). Some associated linguistic admixture with social debasement; hence, the mid-19th-century travel writer B. A. Norman considered Maya to have been so 'Castilianized' that 'the original is nearly lost to those who are now held in vassalage' (Norman 1843, 69).

Such observations sharpened from the 1860s forward, as amateur Yucatecan scholars became advocates of the study and documentation of Maya language and culture. Men of letters like the amateur linguist and collector Juan Pío Pérez and bishop Crescencio Carrillo Ancona, authored and published a new wave of secular Maya texts as part of a romantic international movement toward the 'discovery' of Maya antiquities and recuperation of the glories of the ancients. But there seemed little to extol in the situation of contemporary indigenous populations, which starkly contrasted with the nobility of their forbears. Nowhere was this more evident than in the contrast between 'pure' Maya and the speech of the northwestern haciendas and pueblos, which Carrillo y Ancona described as a 'Maya corrupted by Hispanisms, the mesticized Maya that the most vulgar people speak, which we don't know whether to consider barbarized Spanish, or sadly, degenerated Maya' ([1870] 1937, 153). The *mayistas* embraced a purist linguistic ideology, decrying the language of contemporary speakers as an audible portent of their impending racial extinction (Palma y Palma 1901; Rejón García 1905, 19; Zavala 1896).

Linguistic mixing also went the other way. Yucatán had long been considered a place where those of Hispanic descent, even elites, adopted Maya language. During his travels in the area of the town of Ticul Stephens noted that 'Many of the white people could not speak Spanish, and the conversation was almost exclusively in the Maya language' (Stephens [1843] 1963, Vol. 1, 231). To Yucatecan observers, though, such admixture need not efface ethnic distinctions; Justo Sierra O'Reilly, for instance, faulted Stephens for being confused by the fact that in the countryside whites and indios both spoke Maya and wore the same costume, and thus coming to the 'absurd' and 'ridiculous' conclusion that everyone he met was an Indian (Stephens 1848, 110).[9]

Others, however, drew opposite conclusions. In 1861, while arguing for the recognition of Campeche as a federal state, jurist Tomás Aznar Barbachano denounced Yucatecans 'born of the crossing of the races,' who had acquired indigenous 'customs, habits and character' (Aznar Barbachano and Carbó 1861, 4). 'In the interior,' he railed, 'they can be seen speaking the Maya language, unable to understand Spanish, living out of their hammocks, dressing and eating like the Indian, and even acquiring the slothfulness and shiftiness that seem to be intrinsic to that unfortunate race …' (Aznar Barbachano and Carbó 1861). Even in elite homes in Mérida, Spanish was spoken 'with the accent and phrasings that are typical of Maya.' Thus, children were 'infiltrated, from the first moments of their lives … [with] indigenous feelings, language, and customs …' 'It is,' Aznar Barbachano concluded, seemingly conjuring the specter of Guerrero, 'as if the Spaniards had come to Yucatán in order to be conquered by the Indians' (Aznar Barbachano and Carbó 1861). Whether from the standpoint of *mayista* purism, or elite fears of racial contagion, by the late 19th century 'mixed Maya' was widely perceived as a vehicle of degradation. It was in the domain of language, rather than biological race, that Yucatecans converged with the mestizophobia of racial theorists in Europe, the United States, and elsewhere, who held miscegenation as a route to racial degeneration.

Such texts set the context of Santiago Pacheco Cruz's own investigations into Maya. In 1912, he published a language instruction manual consisting of brief grammatical explanations, Maya phrases with Spanish translations, and practical translation exercises. But the *Compendio* presented an explicit linguistic politics as well, with interjected pleas for the preservation of 'legitimate' Maya language against the forces working inexorably for its destruction through its transmutation into 'mesticized' Maya. Passionately dismissing modern speakers as 'Hispanicized,' Pacheco Cruz considered the Maya language to be mortally wounded by *mestizaje*: 'There is no hope of salvation for this patient, who is [now] in his final agonies …' (Pacheco Cruz 1912, 122).[10]

With the issuance of the 1914 liberation decree, though, Pacheco Cruz found his opportunity to advance the cause of 'legitimate' Maya. More than a measure aimed at liberating workers, Pacheco Cruz's translation seemed intended to liberate Maya from its presumed adulteration and decay. It presented pure Maya as a language of law and political institution: as an ur-text for a revolution that might stake new claims over Maya, as a theological language of power. Yet in the addendum calling for the oral explication of the decree into mixed Maya, Pacheco Cruz seems to have recognized that the law's effectiveness was predicated on oral transmission. Here, the Revolution demanded that its agents, among them Santiago Pacheco Cruz, speak mestizo (Pacheco Cruz 1914b).

Indeed, in ensuing years the government's language politics evolved in ways that sidelined 'pure' Maya and recuperated mixed Maya from ignominy. From 1915 forward, Governor Alvarado's overriding concern was not only for how revolutionary laws and decrees might define policy but also to secure the transformation of the indigenous population into a revolutionary citizenry. Alvarado (1915) created an 'Office of Information and Propaganda,' charging a corps of 15 Maya-speaking 'propaganda agents' with publicizing Constitutionalist decrees and laws not as mere regulations but rather as 'teachings' conveyed through 'sincere and persuasive words.' To achieve their mission, the agents – including the first one appointed, Santiago Pacheco Cruz – were enjoined to speak what Alvarado described as a 'plain language within the intellectual comprehension of the workers and peons of the haciendas' – presumably mixed Maya (Alvarado 1915).

In official discourse, linguistic *mestizaje* rose in prominence, not only for ideological reasons but also as a medium of political communication and state formation. The Yucatecan Socialist party rose to prominence by 1917, incorporating emancipatory rhetoric within a more radical slate of demands, including the eventual breakup and redistribution of hacienda lands, and formation of Socialist 'resistance leagues' on haciendas. Led by the light-skinned, green-eyed, Maya-speaking firebrand Felipe Carrillo Puerto, the Socialists claimed popular legitimacy through symbols and gestures that alternately conveyed Maya-ness, and *mestizaje*: through Maya motifs and designs that adorned government buildings, through large-scale mestizo festivities accompanying official events, and mixed Maya speeches delivered by Socialist organizers.

In no domain were indigenismo and mesticismo so tightly conjoined as that of language. Such tendencies are best demonstrated in later works of Santiago Pacheco Cruz, who continued to publish Maya texts under the Socialist government. In 1923, he published a pamphlet entitled 'Defanaticizing Letters …' – an epistolic text consisting of eight letters presumably sent by 'Zez Chí,' an 'Indian' who seemed to be a Socialist party official, to his friend 'Juel,' who had recently joined the Socialist Party but was unschooled in its tenets. More remarkable than the content of the letters was their language: neither 'pure' Maya, nor the intercalation of Spanish words where Maya equivalents did not exist, nor the singsong mixed Maya of *vaquería* songs. Rather, Pacheco Cruz (1923) incorporated Spanish into Maya phrasing and grammatical structures in subtler ways that followed the practice of contemporary speakers, in what may well be the first fairly accurate published rendering of mixed or mestizo Maya as a spoken tongue.

While a coup overthrew the Socialist government in 1924, in the mid to late 1930s, Mexican President Lázaro Cárdenas once again made Yucatán a staging area for experimental social and educational reforms under federal auspices. An agrarian reform definitively broke up henequen haciendas, distributing the majority of their lands to the control of collectives called *ejidos*. Again Pacheco Cruz was employed to author a number of short works in mixed Maya – skits intended for performance among or by indigenous populations for propaganda purposes (against alcoholism and Catholic 'fanaticism,' in favor of literacy, education, unionization, etc.). Moreover, Pacheco Cruz was commissioned to translate Article 123 of the Mexican Constitution, concerning workers' rights. He did so in mixed Maya, adding extensive explications to make terminology accessible to speakers. Never again, in such official translations, did Pacheco Cruz proffer 'pure' Maya as a language of law or state. Now, even federal law would be voiced in 'mestizo' Maya, as an institutionalized language of political communication (Pacheco Cruz 1937, 1940).

Decades later, in 1969, an elderly Pacheco Cruz published his last work: the *Hahil tzolbichunil tan mayab* – 'True Dictionary of the Maya Language.' It was the first of its kind: a Maya-Maya dictionary of Maya words defined in Maya, rather than translated into Spanish. In a prologue the *mayista* José Díaz Bolio saluted Pacheco Cruz for his achievement: 'Everything in here is said in Maya, and this is the first time that has been the case' (Bolio in Pacheco Cruz 1969, viii). But while the definitions were indeed in Maya, they were filled with interjections of Spanish words, in brackets, where the meaning of a 'pure' Maya word might have been opaque. There were, moreover, long discursive commentaries in Spanish interspersed in some definitions, distinguishing 'mestizo' usages or practices – even those denoted with seemingly Maya terms – from those the author considered genuinely indigenous. It was as if the dictionary were meant not only as a guide for contemporary Maya speakers or writers but also as a means to sort out what was really Maya from the mesticized Maya language that Pacheco Cruz – in spite of himself – had such an important role in disseminating.

Moreover, the dictionary became a means for its author to lexically identify himself in terms of purity and mixture. Reminiscing on the origins of his fluency in Maya, he invoked the most intimate of metaphors: 'I suckled on it' (Pacheco Cruz 1969, xiii). Growing up on a hacienda where his father worked as a mayordomo, he had 'mixed, even as an infant, with the humble "servants" … listening to how they conversed, pronouncing the language in its pure form and without Castilian admixture … so I had to learn it that way. That is why I say I suckled on it, and that is how I developed such deep affections and attachments, which I continue to feel, to this day, for every indigenous person' (xiii–xiv). But language was not enough to fix his own identity. 'I am proud to say,' he declared, 'that the blood in my veins is 80 per cent Indian, and 20 per cent Moorish' (xiv).

Hahil tzolbichunil foregrounded the deepest contradictions in Pacheco Cruz's own identity: his 'suckling' on pure Maya, and the way it had drawn him, like Guerrero, near to the Maya in the most intimate of bonds. Yet, such words were only a preface to the rhetoric of blood quantum: the most convincing of put-ons. Here, Pacheco Cruz's pure indigenous heritage – suckled on speech – was preempted by a mestizo identity, mixed and fixed in blood. To speak of blood and language, in their pure and mixed forms, was to open a paradoxical meditation that left not only language but also race, suspended between truth and simulation: and between *being* mestizo and *playing* mestizo.

Playing mestizo

In 1875, a play entitled opened in Mérida: *El rábano por las hojas: una fiesta en Hunucmá* (*The Radish by the Leaves: a Fiesta in Hunucmá*). In the musical farce, a young man from a well-connected family in Mérida endeavors to seduce a betrothed, working class mestiza in the rural town of Hunucmá. Since the young woman could not 'reach [his] level, due to social position, costume, and customs,' the young man proposes with a friend to 'lower [them]selves to her level, by adopting her [i.e. mestizo] attire, and dancing the *jaranita*' at a fiesta in Hunucmá (García Montero 1901, 4). After some dances, accompanied by songs in Maya and Spanish, the two men are discovered by the woman's betrothed, a local official who denounces them:

> not content with taking advantage of mestizas in Mérida, the little gentlemen come to the pueblos of the state, seeking more conquests, to pervert and sully them. Not content with mixing up el pueblo in the farces called elections and swindling them, they come here to adulate them, joining in their dances and even wearing their clothes, in order to insinuate themselves more easily among the mestizas. (García Montero 1901, 8)

> Under the 'pretext' of 'civilizing el pueblo,' he announced, such 'little gentlemen … corrupt it iniquitously' (García Montero 1901, 8–9).

To play mestizo was to cross boundaries of class and social privilege, precisely by assuming the costume, festive practices, and mixed Maya language of Yucatán's mestizos. But while some might perform such roles legitimately, others, like the young men, did so as deceptive fakery. Where might the boundary be drawn between 'pure' mestizo acts, and merely mixing-it-up, in a put-on with insidious consequences?

Precedents for such mestizo performances run deep. Diego de Landa documented a variety of Maya performance genres he considered analogous to Spanish theatrical performances. The Maya of his time, he wrote, performed 'farces' with such skill that Spaniards employed them for their amusement, and especially for their imitations of the Spaniards themselves. A century later bishop Pedro Sánchez de Aguilar advised readers of his 1639 idolatry investigation to 'learn the language of the Indians very well, and their phrases and way of speaking, so that they might understand the sharp and jocular comments of their comedians' (Sánchez de Aguilar [1639] 1937, 110, 149). The Franciscans tried to supplant such farces with more wholesome entertainments, like short Maya-language plays that accorded with Christian piety and celebrated, rather than ridiculed, the presence and deeds of the Spaniards. The one surviving example, the *Auto o misterio de La adoración de los pastores*, is a somewhat comedic work of uncertain date that dramatizes events following the birth of Jesus (Ancona 1878–1880, 532–533; Gamboa Garibaldi 1946; Ponce 1873, 403; *Registro Yucateco* 1845, Vol. 2, 218).

Maya and Christian precedents notwithstanding, it was once again in the emergent social and cultural world of the hacienda that Yucatecan populations began playing mestizo. By the mid-19th century, the performance of 'pastoral skits' (*representaciones pastoriles*) frequently accompanied *vaquería* festivities in rural Yucatán. The farces often depicted imperious officials of the indigenous republics, and the subjugation of indigenous hacienda workers. Yucatecan politician and author Manuel Barbachano y Tarrazo (1986) witnessed a pueblo skit in which the 'amo' of a hacienda figured, as well as a *chiquerero* (calf herder), an indigenous 'fiscal,' and young women and men of prominent families in mestizo garb, who played the role of the servants of the hacienda. After the 'mestizas' approached him to complain about their husbands' misbehavior, the amo ordered the fiscal to enact punishment. The monolingual Barbachano was entertained: 'Oh! Yes, in effect, they whipped and scolded [the vaqueros]. It was a reenactment of what is done with the servants on the haciendas. What caused the most laughter? The commentaries made by the chiquerero. What a shame that they only spoke in Maya language' (64–66).

The most extensive description of such a performance is provided by John Lloyd Stephens ([1843] 1963, Vol. 2), who beheld an astonishing spectacle during Ticul's festivities. The skit featured vaqueros and mestizas, as well as several men playing officers of the *república de indígenas*:

> They wore long, loose dirty camisas hanging off one shoulder, and with the sleeves below the knees; calzoncillos, or drawers, to match, held up by a long cotton sash, the ends of which dangled below the knees; sandals, slouching straw hats, with brims ten or twelve inches wide, and long locks of horse hair hanging behind their ears. One of them wore awry over his shoulder a mantle of faded blue cotton cloth, said to be an heirloom descended from an ancient cacique, and each flourished a leather whip with eight or ten lashes. (Stephens [1843] 1963, 65)

While young men and women of Ticul's principal families played vaqueros and mestizas, they refused to personify indigenous officials, employing low-born men for those parts. The 'cacique,' Stephens noted, was a pig butcher who only during the fiesta was put on 'equal terms with those who, in his daily walks, were to him as beings of another sphere' (Stephens [1843] 1963).

For the duration of the skit those terms were tilted the other way. Disheveled 'Indian' officers ruled with 'absolute and unlimited authority' over 'vaqueros' and especially mestizas, whom they had a 'right to whip … if they pleased' (Stephens [1843] 1963, 66). 'A crowd followed wherever they moved,' Stephens noted, 'and all the time … they threw everything into laughter and confusion …' They assaulted a 'respectable gentleman of high office;' hoisting him up and 'pulling apart the skirts of his coat, [they] belaboured him with a mock vigour and earnestness that convulsed the whole company with laughter.' The 'cacique' noticed Stephens and strode up 'lash raised in the air' to deliver a 'loud harangue in Maya.' 'All knew that I did not understand a word,' Stephens recalled, 'and the laugh was strong against me' (Stephens [1843] 1963). But Stephens responded with orations in English and Greek that stunned his challenger, who then 'called [him] "amigo," and made a covenant not to speak in any language but Castilian' (67).

No longer just a spectator, Stephens had joined the action. But then the center of attention shifted away from him. There were dances of vaqueros and mestizas, one of whom attracted the cacique's attentions. He spread his mantle at her feet, tore off his shirt, and even the sash that held up his shorts, holding up his sagging drawers as he danced, leaving everyone 'convulsed with laughter.' Then the mestizas danced while vaqueros and *fiscales* voiced a 'hacienda song' in alternating Maya and Spanish. During ensuing feasting, Stephens thanked a mestiza for bringing him food, but the 'cacique' rushed over to stop him. It was as if in thanking her, Stephens had stepped out of character. The 'cacique' would have none of it; he seized Stephens' hat and pulled it down over his eyes, 'saying that we were all Indians together.' In entering the action, and engaging in the free play of languages and dramatis personae, Stephens had become 'Indian.' When he stepped out of that role the 'cacique,' with his hat trick, took action to restore the performance.

As such accounts demonstrate, the ontology of the *representaciones pastoriles*, like the rest of the *vaquería*, had shifted. Festive performance had become a public act of *mestizaje*, one that constituted a new cross-class, cross-ethnic, cross-gender, cross-linguistic public through the action of playing or looking mestizo. These mestizo performances were also acts of memory, conjuring figures from the past, if only to exorcise them in the end with mockery and laughter (cf. Roach 1996; Taylor 2003). To some, the cacique and the *fiscales* – as dirty, disheveled clowns – might have evoked the denigration and elimination of the indigenous republics and their leaders, but at the same time – via the whips, the caprice, the daring – their bygone power, authority, and sovereignty. 'Amos,' 'vaqueros,' and 'mestizas,' for their part, personified the class and gender hierarchies of the hacienda and its social world.

But at the same time the spectacle staged something else, which might be called Indian *mestizaje*: an unruly exchange of positions, personae, and languages. In the performance, everyone, as the pig butcher said, could be *indio* – even pretentious, Greek-reciting gringos. Wealthy landowners impersonated vaqueros and mestizas; lowly mestizos, playing Indians, briefly ruled their betters. It must have seemed the greatest of put-ons – one that conjured Gonzalo Guerrero, if only to exorcise him in the end. It was a put-on that momentarily defied the social roles of hacienda society, even as it concealed their conditions of possibility: the land theft, hunger, forced labor, rapes. And in the end, the festivities restored the wealthy landowner to his station, the butcher to his filthy stall, and the Anglo explorer to his privileged road of travel and discovery.

By the latter half of the 19th century, however, the *representaciones pastoriles* seem to have disappeared from the rural *vaquerías*, or at least in recorded descriptions of them. In the wake of the construction of the first theatres in Mérida in the 1830s, most theatrical performances in the Yucatecan historical record are urban performances of European works by Spanish and Italian troupes: Spanish sainetes and zarzuelas, French romantic theater, Shakespeare and the like. In the last quarter of the 19th century, itinerant, popular Cuban troupes brought *teatro bufo*, often featuring actors in blackface (Cunin 2011; Lane 2005). Yucatecan dramaturges produced works of regional significance – dramas depicting events of the Caste War – but cast in the forms of European comedy and drama (Gamboa Garibaldi 1946). In such theatres, the performative practices of Yucatecan *mestizaje*, whether festive or dramatic, found little place.

Late in the century, however, inspired by the advent of '*costumbrismo*' in Spain, Yucatecan *costumbrismo* emerged as a didactic literary genre focused upon the representation of daily life and popular culture. A space therein opened for the representation of 'typical' mestizo characters and cultural practices. The mestiza was a particular focus – a rustic, simple, goodhearted woman, and an object of desire, offered up as a contrast to indigenous savagery or the duplicity of wealthy Hispanic elites (see Ancona [1861] 1950).[11] Most notable among these works was García Montero's (1901) play, *El rábano por las hojas*, with its dramatization of elite shenanigans in a pueblo fiesta. *El rábano* put not only mestizos but also *mestizaje*, on the theatrical stage: the actors mixed Spanish and Maya, and mestizo festivities were central to the performance. But the *mestizaje El rábano* featured was political, as well, presenting 'traditional' mestizo culture as a corrective to the corrosive effects of commercialism and elitism. Audiences, to judge by published reviews, took the play as demonstrating the way mestiza honor and mestizo culture underwrote moral honor, political order, and social peace.[12] Long before

Manuel Gamio proffered Yucatán's *mestizaje* as a model for nation making, *costumbristas* like García Montero put *mestizaje* on stage, to model a Yucatecan, if not a Mexican, patria.

Such *costumbrista* works set the stage for the most notable theatrical expression of *mestizaje* in Yucatán: the Yucatecan *teatro regional*, which came into its own as a popular commercial theatre in the wake of the Mexican Revolution. The *teatro's* incorporation of Maya phrases, scenes of country life, and *jarana* music and dance has led some to emphasize its indigenous roots (Cervera Andrade 1947; Muñoz 1987; Tuyub 2008). But placed in the context of the performance traditions surrounding Yucatecan *mestizaje*, it becomes clear that teatro regional is an 'in-between' genre – less indigenous than mestizo. It incorporates *vaquería* festivities and mestizo and mestiza *traje*; while Maya appears in word play, songs, and interjections, the language used in teatro regional is mostly Spanish, albeit strongly inflected by Yucatecan accent and regional usages. It echoes the *representaciones pastoriles* and *costumbrista* dramatic literature, but with a mix of other genres: from 19th-century Spanish *zarzuelas* and *sainetes* to 20th-century Mexican and Hollywood movies – and, more recently, televised soap operas (*telenovelas*), all of them irreverently spoofed and spun. While actors and authors typically are light-skinned urban dwellers, most with Hispanic surnames, teatro's audience crosses divides, joining constituencies both urban and rural, and of diverse ethnic, class, and political affiliations.

Teatro regional, while a commercial entertainment, often has had a critical edge, perhaps carrying the imprint of its emergence in times of revolution. It alternately levels radical social critiques, purveys official propaganda, and traffics in hackneyed stereotypes; it has met both censorship and cooptation by government officials. The 1930s brought ever more ambitious attempts to stage performances of regional mestizo and indigenous cultural identity, from large-scale theatrical performances of Yucatecan traditions and Maya sagas, to Maya-language theatre works used as vehicles for official propaganda (Pacheco Cruz 1940; Rosado Vega 1929). When the rise of cinema undercut the commercial basis of the urban theatre, the troupes survived as itinerant companies, supplementing occasional runs in Mérida with performances at festivals and carnivals pitched to popular audiences.

Issues of racial, class, and sexual identity figure centrally, and irreverently, in the *teatro*, which traffics in stereotypes of ethnicity, class, and gender. These take shape in stock characters (Cervera Andrade 1947); *teatro* regional features dim-witted or crafty Indians, and Lebanese (a.k.a. *Turco*) and Chinese immigrants as scoundrels and cheats, even as it mocks the pretensions of Spanish-descended elites, *hacendados* and mestizos, and the occasional gringo. Mestizo and mestiza characters alternately enact and deconstruct stereotypes of gender and sexuality through words and deeds: of salacious old men and naïve mestizas; villainous seducers and earnest suitors; cuckolded men and domineering women; sanctimonious priests and affable cross-dressers. While a kind of performative *mestizaje* is fundamental to the genre of *teatro* regional, occasionally teatro regional performers and dramatists engage in what might be called acts of meta-*mestizaje*: self-consciously reflecting upon, critiquing, and mocking, official discourses of *mestizaje*.

Debuting in Mérida in 1946 with the Herrera troupe, *Chayas contra cazón* was in some respects a conventional work. In the one-act comedy Casiano surreptitiously courts young Milaneza, is found unacceptable by her father Úrsulo Canché (a Maya surname), and must engage in a physical and verbal contest to gain acceptance. Here, though, the standard plot line is additionally freighted with the combination of both cultural proximity (i.e. a shared Maya heritage) and regional animus that characterizes relations between the natives of Yucatán and Campeche (hence 'chaya,' a Yucatecan leafy vegetable, versus *'cazón,'* or dogfish, a key item in the cuisine of Campeche). Úrsulo, patriarch of the '100 per cent campechano' Canché family, espouses a visceral hate toward Yucatecans like Casiano, who in his view 'believe themselves to be superior to everyone else (*Chayas* 1946, 3).' Casiano, in conversation with Milaneza, mocks that notion:

> Yes, of course! The Yucatecan race is practically like the Aryan race! All we need is our own Hitler, so we can dominate the world! You, the *campechanos*, are direct descendants of the noble Yucatecan families that bequeathed to you some of our glorious pedigree, and some of our blue blood. That is why we can accept you as blood relatives. But as for the rest of the Republic, we have to improve their race, so that all of Mexico might be inhabited by a superior race, like the Maya, the Yucatecan race and the race of Ah Kin Pech [preconquest Maya leader and founder of Campeche]. That is why you should tell your father that he should feel honored to accept into his family a descendant of the glorious heroes of the Caste War, Venancio Pec and Cecilio Chí, crossed with Ah Kin Pech. (*Chayas* 1946)

As Casiano holds forth, Úrsulo arrives unexpectedly, and declares, in a play on double meanings of Pec (dog) and chi (to be born) in Maya: 'Hey, Pec-chí, do you think that I would feel honored to include a Pec in my family? So that my grandchildren come out barking?' (*Chayas* 1946)

As a comedic commentary on *mestizaje, Chayas contra cazón* offered audiences an inversion of the ideology of *mestizaje*, presenting it – in Casiano's words – as a process by which superior peoples of Maya descent might find common cause in the racial 'improvement' of inferior Mexican others, through the infusion of their 'blue blood.' Yet, Casiano's embrace of an ideology of Maya racial superiority and *mestizaje* is proffered in jest, as Úrsulo's irreverent Maya wordplay makes clear, shifting back to a kind of impure *mestizaje* that produced not pseudo-Aryans, but dog-like mongrels. But the dueling *mestizajes* of both men meet their match in the words of Milaneza's mother, Doña Ciriaca, who offers a love-based *mestizaje* that dissolves all racial distinctions: 'when a woman falls in love,' she opines, 'she does not recognize lineage or race, and when she gives her heart to someone, it does not matter if the man she loves is American, Eurasian, Polynesian, or even a Visigoth!' (*Chayas* 1946, 2). Úrsulo eventually assents to Casiano's courtship of Milaneza, lending a kind of victory to Casiana. But audiences surely were entertained less by the outcome than by the contention between the *mestizajes* proffered by Casiano, Úrsulo, and Casiana, which left any sanctimonious official *mestizaje* in pieces.

Meta-*mestizaje* is also at work in another Herrera company play entitled *Un año con calendario* (1955). Throughout *Un año*, a character dressed in old sandals and shabby rags, simply called 'Indio,' is the target of racist jibes. Mocking Indio's linguistic confusions another character tells him: '¡Nunca vas a pasar de ser indio! … .Learn how to speak, you Indian' (5, 6). Yet more often than not, Indio made further jokes of his critics' words, using wordplay and puns to subvert their attempts to put him in his place. The greatest put down unfolds on a street in Mérida, where Joseíto Ek stands in fine mestizo attire, accompanied by Indio. Ek, musing distractedly, tells Indio that he is having a *'remembranza'* (remembrance) – and when Indio, not understanding that word, suggests that Ek see an herbalist, the mestizo holds forth: 'My dear aborigine, this can't be cured with herbs or medicines, because this is not an illness. It is a memory of the past, and of this month of October, when we remember the moment that laid the foundations for the formation of an entire race. When America was discovered.' Indio again misunderstands, thinking Ek is referring to the time when 'América Cauich was discovered ... with a married man!' (30).

All of Ek's explanations meet similar misconstruals until, frustrated, the mestizo calls Indio an 'animal' and addresses him haughtily: 'You, poor Indian, accept your sad destiny. The autochthonous races like yours must end, in order to open the way for Progress, for the new race like me – finer, more intelligent, and more refined. Of lighter skin color.' (*Un año con calendario* 1955, 31). After Indio responds angrily – 'Do you mean to suggest that we aren't equals?' – Ek explains: 'You are a pure-bred Indian, while my blood is mixed with Spanish. I have blue blood.' Indio explodes: 'You're descended neither from the Spanish, nor even from the Indians, do you hear me? If there is color in your blood, it is yellow, because you descend from the Chinese!' (32). After Indio proceeds to remind Ek of the Chinese street vendor who showed Ek and his mother affections when Ek was a child, giving him peanuts for free, Ek responds by spewing series of racist slurs. In his excitement he loses control, bending over, narrowing his eyes to slits and shuffling a few steps. Indio declares: '*¡Ahistá!*…You are Chinese, and moreover, of the peanut-selling kind!' Resigned, Joseíto Ek makes the best of the situation, in a Shylockian twist: 'Fine. Even supposing I am Chinese or have Chinese blood, is there any dishonor in that? Aren't the Chinese people too, just like us?' (*Un año con calendario* 1955)

Indio's rejoinders to Joseíto Ek were the most pointed of all his ripostes – not only besting his pompous mestizo friend but also giving the lie to the official Mexican ideology of race mixture in the process, unmasking it as a put-on. Against *that mestizaje*, he offered *this mestizaje* – Indian *mestizaje*, a confusion of peoples and tongues. Indio's version of *mestizaje* deployed stereotype against stereotype, subverting austere official sanctimony with salty mockery from below. While some in the audience might have laughed more heartily at Ek's racist put-downs, and others more loudly cheered Indio's rejoinders, most probably savored the whole spectacle, making the theatre neither a staging ground for racist stereotypes, nor a place for their dismantlement, but a space in between.

Theatre critic Lionel Abel famously called many theatrical genres, particularly popular traditions, 'metatheatrical:' they indulge in a variety of antirealistic devices, like audience-directed asides, that call attention to the fictitious nature of the theatre, encouraging a meta-level awareness of and its conventions (Abel 1963). By enacting public crossings of languages, ethnic categories, and class, gender and sexual roles, Yucatecan mestizo performance takes such awareness to a particular intensity. It is thus not only meta-theatrical but also meta-social, and therein its politics reside. It is a politics that is not only evident in Indio's rejoinders but also in the words and actions one century before of another mestizo playing Indian – the pig butcher, as cacique. In both cases, to play mestizo – which included taking on 'Indian' as well as 'mestizo' personae – was to engage in a meta-social performance: one where contrary social identities could be recombined, played against each other, exposed as artifice, dismissed.

This, then, was Indian *mestizaje*. It was not about the makings of a *raza cósmica*, but of a *raza cómica*. It played upon a long history in Yucatán – upon complicated and conflicted genealogies of looking, speaking, and playing mestizo. In some ways the kind of *mestizaje* that emerged in Yucatán from the mid-19th century forward might seem to converge with the ideology of *mestizaje* that became hegemonic in Mexico in the revolutionary and postrevolutionary periods. But at moments – as in Ticul's cacique skit, teatro plays like *Chayas contra cazón* and *Un año con calendario*, or the *vaquería*'s festive dances – a different kind of *mestizaje* was staged: neither 'from above' nor 'from below,' but in the spaces in-between.

To trace the complicated histories of *mestizaje* in Yucatán is, however, to concede one point to Joseíto Ek: namely, the aspect of remembering (cf. Roach 1996; Taylor 2003) that may be intrinsic to Yucatán's mestizo performances: whether in festivity, speech, or theatre. All of these mestizo acts may collectively constitute Yucatán's other *Monumento al mestizaje*, its lighter or darker side, a trace or reminder of 'mestizo' as something put-on – and a mocking rebuke to any bio-racial ideology or identity, whether from above or below. It was, and is, a *mestizaje* that is less about the making of a new race, nor even about the abolition of race, than it is about reveling in all kinds of impurity, at least as long the show lasts. It is almost as if Indio – or Casiano and Ciriaca, in their way – were echoing the words of the pig butcher, but this time with a twist: *We are all mestizos, together.*

Notes

1. For a Yucatecan author's earlier recognition of Guerrero, see Trujillo (1946).
2. Eiss, introduction to this volume.
3. On contemporary categories see Hervik (1999); and Loewe (2010).
4. On Maya use of instruments, see Heller (2007, 185, 197); Norman (1843, 104); also see José Bartolomé del Granado Baeza, cited in Rugeley (2001a, 29).
5. See also, Norman (1843, *Rambles in Yucatan*, 98–100); and Rugeley (2001b, *Of Wonders and Wise Men*, 92).
6. Similar views of the Caste War remained characteristic of Yucatecan commentary on *mestizaje* over the ensuing century. See Trujillo (1946, 325–326).
7. Ruz (1846); and Ruz (1847). See also Baeza cited in Rugeley (2001a, 23).
8. See verses in, García Montero (1901); and García (1856).
9. On elite children learning Maya from indigenous wet nurses, see Baeza cited in Rugeley (2001a, 21).
10. See also 'U kabetil le mayabthano,' in Pacheco Cruz (1914a, 85–91).
11. On Yucatecan costumbrismo see Esquivel Pren (1975).
12. These reviews are transcribed in García Montero (1901).

Acknowledgments

I am grateful to Joanne Rappaport and anonymous readers for their helpful feedback. Many thanks as well to Michal Friedman, Terry Rugeley, Rihan Yeh, and seminar participants at Carnegie Mellon University and Colby College for their comments on earlier versions of this article.

References

Unpublished sources

Alvarado, S. 1915. "Cartilla revolucionaria para los agentes de propaganda." Archivo General del Estado de Yucatán, Poder Ejecutivo, Gobernación, Box 473, September 3.
Chayas contra cazón. 1946. Private collection.
de Zayas Enríquez, R. 1891. "Fisiología del crímen." *El Siglo Diez y Nueve*, October 30.
La Libertad (México, D.F.). 1879. November 12.
Otro año con calendario. 1955. Private collection.
Registro Yucateco. 1845. Vol. 2, 218.

Published sources

Abel, L. 1963. *Metatheatre: A New View of Dramatic Form*. New York: Hill and Wang.
Adorno, R. 2007. *The Polemics of Possession in Spanish American Narrative*. New Haven: Yale University Press.
Alonso, A. M. 2004. "Conforming Disconformity: 'Mestizaje,' Hybridity and the Aesthetics of Mexican Nationalism." *Cultural Anthropology* 19 (4): 459–490. doi:10.1525/can.2004.19.issue-4.
Ancona, E. 1878–1880. *Historia de Yucatán, desde la època más remota hasta nuestros días*. Vol. 2. Mérida: Imprenta de M. Heredia Argüelles.
Ancona, E. 1889. *Historia de Yucatán, desde la època más remota hasta nuestros días*. Vol. 4. Barcelona: Imprenta de J. J. Roviralta.
Ancona, E. [1861] 1950. *La mestiza, novela yucateca*. Mérida: Editorial Yucatanense "Club del Libro".
Anzaldúa, G. 2012. *Borderlands/La Frontera: The New Mestiza*. 4th ed. San Francisco: Aunt Lute Books.
Aznar Barbachano, T., and J. Carbó. 1861. *Memoria sobre la conveniencia, utilidad y necesidad de erigir constitucionalmente en estado de la Confederación Mexicana el antiguo distrito de Campeche*. Mexico City: Imprenta de I. Cumplido.
Barbachano y Tarrazo, M. 1986. *Vida, usos y hábitos de Yucatán al mediar el siglo XIX*. Mérida: Maldonado Editores.
Barrera Vásquez, A., ed. 1980. *Diccionario Maya Cordemex*. Mérida: Ediciones Cordemex.
Basave Benítez, A. 1992. *México mestizo: A nálisis del nacionalismo mexicano en torno a la mestizofilia de Andrés Molina Enríquez*. México City: Fondo de Cultura Económica.
Beltrán de Santa Rosa, P. [1746] 1859. *Arte del idioma maya reducido a sucintas reglas y semilexicon yucateco*. Mérida: Imprenta de J.D. Espinosa.
Berkley, A. 1998. "Remembrance and Revitalization: The Archive of Pure Maya." Phd diss., University of Chicago.
Carrillo y Ancona, C. [1870] 1937. *Disertación sobre la historia de la lengua maya o yucateca*. Mérida: Imprenta del Editor.
Cervera Andrade, A. 1947. *El teatro regional de Yucatán*. Mérida: Imprenta Guerra.
Cunin, E. 2011. "Negritos y mestizos en Mérida en la primera mitad del siglo XX. Mestizaje, región y raza." *Revue Européenne des Migrations Internationales* 27 (1): 147–169. doi:10.4000/remi.
de Landa, D. 2011. *Relación de las cosas de Yucatán*. Newark, DE: Juan de la Cuesta.
de Zayas Enríquez, R. 1908. *El estado de Yucatán: Su pasado, su presente, su porvenir*. New York: J. J. Little & Ives.

Dumont, D. 1997. *The Machete and the Cross: Campesino Rebellion in Yucatan*. Lincoln: University of Nebraska.

Dutt, R. 2014. "Crossing Over: Caciques, Indigenous Politics, and the *Vecino* World in Caste War Yucatán." *Ethnohistory* 61 (4): 739–759. doi:10.1215/00141801-2717849.

Earle, R. 2007. *The Return of the Native; Indians and Myth-Making in Spanish America, 1810–1930*. Durham: Duke University Press.

Esquivel Pren, J. 1975. *Historia de la Literatura en Yucatán, t. 9: Los costumbristas y humoristas del siglo XIX*. Mexico City: Ediciones de la Universidad de Yucatán.

Fallaw, B. 2008. "Bartolomé García Correa and the Politics of Maya Identity in Postrevolutionary Yucatán, 1911–1933." *Ethnohistory* 55 (4): 553–578. doi:10.1215/00141801-2008-013.

Farriss, N. 1984. *Maya Society under Colonial Rule: The Collective Enterprise of Survival*. Princeton: Princeton University Press.

Gabbert, W. 2004. *Becoming Maya: Ethnicity and Social Inequality in Yucatán since 1500*. Tucson: University of Arizona Press.

Gamboa Garibaldi, A. 1946. "Historia del teatro y de la literatura dramática." In *Enciclopedia Yucatanense, Tomo 5, Historia de la Imprenta, del Periodismo, del Teatro, etc.*, edited by C. Echánove Trujillo, 109–315. Mexico City: Edición Oficial del Gobierno de Yucatán.

Gamio, M. 1916. *Forjando patria (pro nacionalismo)*. Mexico City: Porrúa.

García, M. 1856. *El toro de Sinkeuel; leyenda hípica, político-tauromaquica*. Mérida: Imprenta a cargo de Isac Manuel Avila.

García Montero, J. 1901. *El rábano por las hojas: Una fiesta en Hunucmá*. Mérida: Imprenta Nueva de Cecilio Leal.

Guss, D. 2000. *The Festive State: Race, Ethnicity, and Nationalism as Cultural Performance*. Berkeley: University of California Press.

Hale, C. 1989. "Political and Social Ideas." In *Latin America: Economy and Society, 1870–1930*, edited by L. Bethell, 357–442. Cambridge: Cambridge University Press.

Hanks, W. 2010. *Converting Words: Maya in the Age of the Cross*. Berkeley: University of California Press.

Heller, K. 2007. *Alone in Mexico: The Astonishing Travels of Karl Heller, 1845–1848*. Tuscaloosa: University of Alabama Press.

Hervik, P. 1999. *Mayan People Within and Beyond Boundaries: Social Categories and Lived Identity in Yucatán*. Amsterdam: Harwood Academic Publishers.

Joseph, G. 1988. *Revolution from Without: Yucatán, Mexico, and the United States, 1880–1924*. Durham: Duke University Press.

Knight, A. 1990. "Racism, Revolution, and *Indigenismo* in Mexico, 1910–1940." In *The Idea of Race in Latin America, 1870–1940*, edited by R. Graham, 71–113. Austin: University of Texas Press.

Lane, J. 2005. *Blackface Cuba: 1840–1895*. Philadelphia: University of Pennsylvania Press.

Loewe, R. 2010. *Maya or Mestizo?: Nationalism, Modernity, and its Discontents*. Toronto: University of Toronto Press.

Lomnitz, C. 2001. *Deep Mexico, Silent Mexico: An Anthropology of Nationalism*. Minneapolis: University of Minnesota Press.

Lund, J. 2012. *The Mestizo State: Reading Race in Modern Mexico*. Minneapolis: University of Minnesota Press.

Méndez, S. [1870] 1921. "The Maya Indians of Yucatan in 1861." In *Reports on the Maya Indians of Yucatan*, edited by M. H. Saville, 143–195. New York: Museum of the American Indian.

Mueller, R. 2001. "From Cult to Comics: The Representation of Gonzalo Guerrero as a Cultural Hero in Mexican Popular Culture." In *A Twice-Told Tale: Reinventing the Encounter in Iberian/Iberian American Literature and Film*, edited by S. Juan-Navarro and T. R. Young, 137–148. Wilmington: University of Delaware Press.

Muñoz, F. 1987. *El Teatro regional de Yucatán*. Mexico City: Grupo Editorial Gaceta.

Norman, B. 1843. *Rambles in Yucatan; or, Notes of Travel through the Peninsula, Including a Visit to the Remarkable Ruins of Chi-Chen, Kabah, Zayi, and Uxmal*. New York: J. & H. G. Langley.

Pacheco Cruz, S. 1912. *Compendio del 'idioma yucateco.' Dedicado a las escuelas rurales del estado: Obra propia para aprender la 'lengua maya' en muy poco tiempo*. Mérida: Librería de Espinosa.

Pacheco Cruz, S. 1914a. *Cuestiones de enseñanza y de educación social: Breves apuntes*. Hunucmá: Imprenta de R. Erosa P.

Pacheco Cruz, S. 1914b. *Traducción literal al idioma yucateco del decreto expedido a favor de los jornaleros de campo y de las circulares que se relacionan con estos*. Mérida: Imprenta "El Porvenir".

Pacheco Cruz, S. 1923. *Cartas desfanatizadoras: Escritas en Lengua Maya por un Indio convencido a otro que no lo está*. Mérida: Editora Mayab.

Pacheco Cruz, S. 1937. *Traducción al idioma maya del Artículo 123 constitucional: Con una crítica explicativa del artículo i de todos los incisos*. Mérida: Imprenta del Oriente.

Pacheco Cruz, S. 1940. *Teatro maya: Colección de obras escolares escritas en el idioma maya en pro de las campañas alfabetizantes, antialcohólicas, sanitarias, etc*. Mérida: Imprenta del Oriente.

Pacheco Cruz, S. 1953. *Recuerdos de la propaganda constitucionalista en Yucatán*. Mérida: Editorial Zamná.

Pacheco Cruz, S. 1969. *Hahil tzolbichunil tan mayab o verdadero diccionario de la lengua maya*. Mérida: Editora Pacheco Cruz.

Palma y Palma, E. 1901. *Los mayas: Disertaciones histórico-filológicas*. Motul: Imprenta Justo Sierra.

Patch, R. 1994. *Maya and Spaniard in Yucatan: 1648–1812*. Stanford: Stanford University Press.

Pérez Sabido, L. 1983. *Bailes y Danzas Tradicionales de Yucatán*. Mérida: Ediciones del Ayuntamiento de Mérida.

Pinkus Rendón, M. 2010. "Uso y costumbre de la jarana." In *Estampas etnográficas de Yucatán*, edited by F. F. Repetto, 153–182. Mérida: Ediciones de la Universidad Autónoma de Yucatán.

Pío Pérez, J. 1866–1877. *Diccionario de la Lengua Maya*. Mérida: Imprenta Literaria de Juan F. Molina Solis.

Ponce, A. 1873. *Relación breve y verdadera de algunas cosas de las muchas que sucedieron al padre fray Alonso Pone en las provincias de la Nueva España*. Madrid: Imprenta de la Viuda de Galero.

Rappaport, J. 2014. *The Disappearing Mestizo: Configuring Difference in the Colonial New Kingdom of Granada*. Durham: Duke University Press.

Redfield, R. 1941. *The Folk Culture of Yucatan*. Chicago: University of Chicago Press.

Redfield, R., and A. Villa Rojas. 1934. *Chan Kom, a Maya Village*. Washington, DC: Carnegie Institute of Washington.

Rejón García, M. 1905. *Los mayas primitivos: Algunos estudios sobre su origen, idioma y costumbres*. Mérida: Imprenta de la Lotería del Estado.

Restall, M. 1997. *The Maya World: Yucatec Culture and Society, 1550–1850*. Palo Alto: Stanford University Press.

Restall, M. 2009. *The Black Middle: Africans, Mayas and Spaniards in Colonial Yucatan*. Palo Alto: Stanford University Press.

Roach, J. 1996. *Cities of the Dead: Circum-Atlantic Performance*. New York: Columbia University Press.

Rosado Vega, L. 1929. *Payambe: Evocación de la tierra del mayab en cuatro escenarios*. Mexico City: Talleres gráficos de la nación.

Rugeley, T. 1996. *Yucatán's Maya Peasantry and the Origins of the Caste War*. Austin: University of Texas Press.

Rugeley, T., ed. 2001a. *Maya Wars: Ethnographic Accounts from Nineteenth-Century Yucatán*. Tuscaloosa: University of Oklahoma Press.

Rugeley, T. 2001b. *Of Wonders and Wise Men: Religion and Popular Cultures in Southeast Mexico, 1800–1876*. Austin: University of Texas Press.

Rugeley, T. 2009. *Rebellion Now and Forever: Mayas, Hispanics, and Caste War Violence in Yucatán, 1800–1880*. Stanford: Stanford University Press.

Ruz, J. 1846. *Colección de sermones para los domingos de todo el año y cuaremsa, tomados de varios autores y traducidos libremente al Idioma Yucateco por al padre Fray Joaquín Ruz*. Mérida: Imprenta de José D. Espinosa.

Ruz, J. 1847. *Catecismo y exposición breve de la doctrina cristiana*. Mérida: Imprenta de José D. Espinosa.

Sánchez de Aguilar, P. [1639] 1937. *Informe contra Idolorum Cultores*. Mérida: Imprenta Triay e Hijos.

Sierra O'Reilly, J. [1848–1851] 1994. *Los Indios de Yucatán*. Vol. 1. Mérida: Universidad Autónoma de Yucatán.

Stephens, J. 1848. *Incidentes del viaje en Yucatán*. Mérida: Imprenta de Castillo y Compañía.

Stephens, J. [1843] 1963. *Incidents of Travel in Yucatan*. Vols. 1 and 2. New York: Dover.

Taylor, D. 2003. *Archive and Repertoire: Performing Cultural Memory in the Americas*. Durham: Duke University Press.

Tenenbaum, B. 1994. "Streetwise History: The Paseo de la Reforma and the Porfirian State, 1878–1910." In *Rituals of Rule, Rituals of Resistance: Public Celebrations and Popular Culture in Mexico*, edited by W. H. Beezley, C. E. Martin, and W. E. French, 127–150. Wilmington: Scholarly Resources.

Trujillo, N. 1946. "Los 'Mestizos' de Yucatán." In *Enciclopedia Yucatanense*, edited by C. Echánove Trujillo, 321–340. Vol. 6. Mexico City: Edición Oficial del Gobierno de Yucatán.

Tuyub, G. 2008. *El teatro regional yucateco*. Mérida: Instituto de Cultura de Yucatán.

Vasconcelos, J. 1925. *La raza cósmica: misión de la raza iberoamericana*. Paris: Agencia Mundial de Librería.

Wells, A., and G. Joseph. 1996. *Summer of Discontent, Seasons of Upheaval: Elite Politics and Rural Insurgency in Yucatán, 1876–1915*. Stanford: Stanford University Press.

Zavala, M. 1896. *Gramática maya*. Mérida: Imprenta de la Ermita.

Foundational essays as 'mestizo-criollo acts': the Bolivian case

Javier Sanjinés C.

ABSTRACT

This paper engages Alcides Arguedas's 'Pueblo enfermo' and Franz Tamayo's 'Creación de la pedagogía nacional', two key foundational essays of early 20th-century Bolivia, as 'mestizo-criollo acts' rooted in the debates on the 'Indian problem' as a racial obstacle to nation-building and identity formation. The paper contends that both essays actually conceal the presence of European wild men, and construct a reality influenced by their interpretation of books and visual representations entrenched in the European imagination. They thus create an insurmountable ambiguity: a self-exotization brimming over with metaphors that actually deploy European wild imaginary sources to explain its Andean roots.

Complicated and elusive, *mestizaje* can elicit certain sociopolitical acts intended to solve national social 'disorders' that are considered to be of immediate and pressing importance. These 'mestizo-criollo acts' assert their apparent uniqueness by neglecting to engage in meaningful comparisons with similar situations in other countries and regions of the world. An example of such 'mestizo-criollo acts' springs from early 20th-century essays written by key Bolivian thinkers in the context of debates to solve the 'Indian problem', a fundamental obstacle encountered by national elites in their attempt to give a modern form to the nation-state.

At that time, the so-called 'Indian problem' was a central issue in mestizo-criollo consciousness. The Indian had been a source of constant anxiety for the criollo caste ever since the violent indigenous rebellions of the 18th century. Olivia Harris (1995) points to the late 19th century as a key historical moment when caste distinctions were being transformed into a complicated set of class relations. An emergent positivist discourse elaborated a negative image of the Indian, not only as uncultured and apparently alien to Western civilization, but also as situated outside the market economy. Liberal politics naturalized the idea of indigenous 'backwardness' to argue that the Indian was incapable of participating in the market initiatives that the mestizo-criollo sector practiced so assiduously. This allowed for the continued expansion of large agricultural estates, the appropriation of products that were once manufactured and marketed by indigenous communities, and the break-up of 19th-century pacts between Indians and criollos for the collection of indigenous tribute. The intellectuals of the early 20th century were essayists who belonged to the dominant mestizo-criollo class, yet were not necessarily tied to the oligarchy in power. Thus, they lacked the political influence enjoyed by an earlier generation of Latin American romantic fictions writers. This new breed of essayists, who generated what I call the 'mestizo-criollo acts', reinvented and updated the nation's racial and ethnic taxonomies and teleologies, adapting them to the political, economic, and ideological climate created by liberalism.

Following other well-known Latin American *Modernista* poets and essayists of the early 20th century, radicalized Bolivian liberals conceptualized their ideologies of race and nation by appropriating European theories, which they combined with their own understandings based on empirical observations of local cultures. Their *Modernista* discourse on the autochthonous, however, departed from the standard liberal discourse. Molded by positivism and social Darwinism, the liberal discourse turned on concepts of civilization and barbarism and predicated the stagnation of the autochthonous race. Alcides Arguedas (1879–1946) is the most important representative of this discursive tendency. Yet radicalized Bolivian reformists, such as Franz Tamayo (1878–1956) con-structed a more modern racial ideology in which the vital energy of the indigenous race was seen as infused with the telluric power of the environment. This discourse on the autochthonous generated ambivalent racial sentiments of pride, nostalgia, and fascina-tion with the Indian, while at the same time demonstrating repugnance for any breaking of racial boundaries that could not be rationalized and strictly controlled by mestizo-criollo consciousness. The idea that emerged was that the Indian race should be studied, disciplined, and exalted under the enlightened, paternalistic, and authoritarian political order. While this discourse on the autochthonous differed from the reigning positivist-liberal discourse that emphasized the innate racial inferiority of the Indian, both dis-courses hid the spectral presence of wild European ancestors, who haunted the nation's search for a healthy, civilized existence.

No research on Bolivian identity formation has considered racial issues as acts that actually conceal the presence of savages, or wild men entrenched in the European imagination. Coming from mythological mutations since the 16th cen-tury, the extravagant creatures that influenced the imagination of the local Bolivian elites at the turn of the 20th century might have remained in oblivion if they had not fitted into a complex series of historic circumstances. Such circumstances not only ensured the continuity of the myth but also came to constitute, as Mexican anthropologist Roger Bartra affirms, the most powerful symbol imagined by the West to represent the immense mass of *other* human beings, the inhabitants of the uncivilized regions of the globe (Bartra 1997, 78). At the core of this essay, I propose that in the heated racial debates of both Alcides Arguedas and Franz Tamayo, the two most prominent Bolivian essayists of the early 20th century, the 'Indian problem' may have been related to the figuration of the wild man that was generated within European imagination.

Since I am interested in recording both the historical course of this creature as it was exoticized by the European imagination and its presence in Bolivia's troubled modernity,

I will begin with an analysis of a few cases explored by Bartra regarding the mutations of the wild man in the heart of European society itself.

I

One of the most striking themes explored by Bartra is the fact that the myth of the European wild man has never been static but rather constantly reinvented over the centuries. Bartra shows how, in the long trajectory from Greek and Latin antiquity to the terrorism of today, the myth maintains a prodigious ability to change registers, constitute new syntheses, and modify its functions and messages as it leaps through time without following the linear outline of history,

Here, I will look briefly at four instances that marked the alterations of the European wild man from classical antiquity to the formation of European modernity in the 18th century. Doing so will help to reveal the often hidden or exoticized presence of the wild man figure in the representation of national constructions of Latin American societies in the 19th and 20th centuries. Bartra records the presence of the myth during the colonial times. My aim is to carry forward this transition from the European context to the particular reality of Latin America, at the moment when the myth falls in the hands of the key Bolivian foundational essayists.

From *Wild Men in the Looking Glass* (1994) through *The Artificial Savage* (1997) to his recent writing on terrorism at large, Bartra has studied the problematic construction of identities and differences in the changing sociohistorical reality of human beings. One of the sources of the wild man image is the European imagination itself; this image is, therefore, one of the keys to the Western culture. In effect, the wild man was the creation of the civilized people; it was their means of explaining their own identity, and at the same time it was their 'inner other', a stereotype rooted in the personal desires and fears that led them to explore the depths of their own being.

When the Greeks distinguished 'savages' from 'barbarians', – a topic of utmost interest for the study of 'mestizo-criollo acts', as we will see later on – they also created the first moment in the gestation of this 'inner other'. This distinction situated the barbarians 'outside' the civilized world, that is, at a distance from the polis. The barbarian or *agrios* was distinguished from the *hemeros*, the human or semi-human savage who lived, tamed and docile, inside the polis. The images of goodness and violence embodied in these figures formed the basis for its mythology. Thus, under the ambiguous sign of the positive and the pernicious, we have the full gamut of semi-human creatures: the nymphs, noble and dreadful; the centaurs, embodiments of the half-beastly; the fauns, satyrs, and sileni, as well as the Amazons, wild women with masculine traits.

The second phase of this mutation was the religious transformation of the Judeo-Christian ideology and vision of the savage. With the appearance of the Judeo-Christian tradition the savage was associated with the desert, where good and evil come together. A novel setting for the image of the savage, the desert expressed the need for culture to subjugate nature. And this need, which is the guiding principle of any national project, revealed that the desert, a metaphor for chaos, emptiness, and loneliness, was the wasteland that humankind should tame through sweat and tears.

The creation of *Homo sylvestris* is the third phase of the European savage's transformation. As Bartra points out, the Greek monster *agrios* and the troubling Judeo-Christian wasteland come together in this figure. With his body covered in wolf's hair, to differentiate him from a human, the male *Homo sylvestris* was a bearded, white-skinned, curly-haired being while the female's hair covered her entire body but left her breasts exposed. It might seem oxymoronic that *Homo sylvestris* came to be linked to Christian morality and that, at the same time, his social behavior patterns are considered wild, diametrically opposed to a man governed by morality. What then is the real nature of *Homo sylvestris*? This conceptual problem seems to haunt the Jesuit, José de Acosta, in the second half of the 16th century. The problem will reappear mutated, as we shall see later on, when discussing the 'Indian problem' at the beginning of the 20th century.

The fourth and final phase of transmutation of the savage is its full immersion in modern times. This could only happen when *Homo economicus* could defeat *Homo sylvestris* on its own playing field, and thus appeared one of the most important facets of modernity. Bartra shows how Daniel Defoe located his *Homo economicus*, represented by Robinson Crusoe, on a desert island as a symbol of the enterprising solitude of the modern man. Bartra reveals how this character is a composite of two allegorical figures: the European wild man and the American savage. The Mexican anthropologist adds that the former was part of a long-standing Western myth while the latter symbolized the peoples discovered and colonized by Europe. What is important, however, is that the wild man was the mythical subject of Western thought whereas the savage was the real object of colonial domination.

The dynamic between the mythical subject and the real object belongs to the complicated issue of how discourse becomes fetishized. This means that hidden behind the real object of colonization was the phantasmagorical way in which literature dealt with the conquest. Fetishizing refers to believing that both the European wild man and his transmutation over time explained what the natives were like in flesh and blood. Given that this was a complete lie, and that how the natives were depicted only obfuscated the condition of the real object of domination, to decolonize means to understand that the 'noble savage' of modernity was neither American nor particularly good. In other words, both the domesticated savage, which we will see in the liberal discourse of the early 20th century, and the 'noble savage', close to the discourse on the autochthonous proposed by radical liberal reformism – and theorized by Rousseau ([1781] 1990) as a way of man coming into contact with his natural condition – were European representations that had very little to do with the reality of the indigenous and Afro-American communities beset by colonization.

We should be aware that from the 19th century to the beginning of the 20th century the ways that liberal elites and Hispano-American *letrados* (lettered elite) represented reality were influenced by their interpretations of books and visual representations rooted in the Western culture. Therefore, it is impossible to fail to see that the representational practices in our foundational essays, whose aim was to supposedly uncover and lay bare the problems, actually created an insurmountable ambiguity: a self-exotization brimming over with metaphors that cover up and fetishize the true reality.

The following sections will return to Bolivia at the beginning of the 20th century. I will first look at both sides of a contentiously divided elite – the liberals and the reformist mestizo radicals. On the one hand, the ruling liberals, influenced by Alcides Arguedas's

Pueblo enfermo, a seminal essay on the necessary 'regeneration of the Indian', thought that domesticated savages could be assimilated to increase the voter populous, thus expanding their electoral base. On the other hand, the radical intellectuals, influenced by Franz Tamayo's *Creación de La pedagogía nacional* ([1910] 1975), developed the visual proposal of a savage that went beyond the model for liberal education, transforming the Bolivian liberal version of the *Homo sylvestris* into someone else – an Indian full of will and character, that, although seen as a source of creative energy for local culture, continued to be self-exoticized as a 'noble European savage'. In the final section, I will approach the debate concerning the 'Indian problem' not just from a local mestizo-criollo point of view, but in terms of its broader capacity to construct redeemable savages; I achieve the latter by examining the strange parallelisms linking the Bolivian case to an earlier European version from France, revealing the source of the 'mestizo-criollo act' as a message historically translated from one culture to another.

II

The first decades of the 20th century were a key moment in taking stock of the backwardness of the Bolivian nation. A moment of 'agonizing self-reflection', according to North American historian Brooke Larson (2001), it was during this period of liberal oligarchy that the rise of mestizo-criollos found contradictory expression in the social analyses undertaken by a select group of essayists from La Paz who were dedicated to reflecting on the nation's problems. These essayists, among whom Alcides Arguedas stood out, came from the dominant mestizo-criollo class. However, as pointed out earlier, they were marginalized from political decision-making and thus were not necessarily tied to the oligarchic sector in power.

Alcides Arguedas, a rural landowner born to criollo parents of Spanish ancestry, was the most important intellectual of the period. In 1905, he founded the *Palabras Libres* (Free Words) movement, which became an active center for studying the country's many problems. The youthful members of the movement, all imbued with positivist ideas, actively critiqued the contradictions of the liberal regime of President Ismael Montes (1904–1909 and 1913–1917) when the debates on the 'Indian problem' took place.

The *Palabra Libres* members grouped around Arguedas did not break with liberal ideology, but they did seek to correct the electoral excesses committed by Montes, who supported educating the indigenous masses exclusively for proselytizing ends. Their dissent led to the repression of the *Palabras Libres* movement and its disbandment as a studies center in 1906. For Arguedas, persecution meant exile in France, where he was welcomed by important Latin American intellectuals.

Armed sociologically with Positivism and literarily with modernism and realism, and saved from major economic distress by his family's position, Arguedas launched his career as a writer and thinker of Bolivian reality in Paris in 1906. There he began working on his sociological essay, *Pueblo enfermo*, which he would publish in Barcelona in 1909. It is important to bear in mind, however, that this essay underwent significant changes in the editions that Arguedas prepared in 1910 and 1937. All three versions have the same objective, however, to analyze Bolivian reality from a psychosociological and moralizing point of view.

Note that my focus here is not on the changes made by Arguedas in each version of the essay, but rather on the persistent view that Arguedas had of the races – their mechanistic relation between humans and the environment – that led him to propound a primarily fatalistic view of Bolivian reality. In Arguedas's thought, human groups are constituted by their geographical environment, and race determines their collective psychology. Together, geography and race formed the axes on which he then developed his analysis of national reality, not without some prejudice. Thus, the essential nature of the Indian, which could be changed through education, was paradoxically branded by fate, given that it was produced by the purely mechanical action that the highland plateau exercises on him. 'The Pampa and the Indian are but a single entity', Arguedas writes. 'The physical aspect of the plains … has molded the spirit of the Indian in a strange fashion. Note the hardness of character in the man of the high plateau, the dryness of sentiments, the total absence of aesthetic inclinations' (Arguedas [1937] 1986, 42–43). This deterministic relationship between man and environment, which Arguedas later extended to an explanation of the country's backwardness based on the land's rugged geography, was seemingly valid and objective. It overlooked other historical, economic, and social ingredients that could have been of equal or greater importance than the geographic factors that Arguedas presented. According to this version, which called into question the possibility of constructing a national culture, man had lost all capacity for transforming nature. This was also evidenced in the profound imbalance Arguedas saw between the landscape and the quality of its people. Therefore, the stability and harmony needed for progress was lacking. If Europe was a vast, uniform flatland, Bolivia was an uncouth and chaotic people. Thus, the geographic environment determined development.

Here, I will limit my analysis to the following four themes: first, I will observe the methodology Arguedas uses in his essay; second, I will focus especially on his concept of race; third, I will address the 'criollo act' itself; and finally I will refer, in a completely novel way, to the difference that Arguedas established between mestizo and Indian. It is in the psychological and moral nature of this difference that I find the identity of the European wild man unconsciously embedded. Medievalists are quite aware that the wild man is a stereotype that took root in European art and literature beginning in the 12th century. As Bartra shows us, however, the myth of *Homo sylvestris* spread far beyond the boundaries of the medieval world. Here, I argue that this theme reappears in Arguedas's essay. The difference that Arguedas lays out between Indian and mestizo reestablishes a mythic thread that runs through centuries, weaving the great problems of Western culture with the quandary posed by local Bolivian culture – the 'Indian problem'.

The title alone shows that *Pueblo enfermo* (*Sick Nation*) is governed by an organicist metaphor based on a value judgment that cannot be demonstrated objectively. If the nation is 'sick' because its character 'has the hardness and aridity of the wilderness' (Arguedas [1937] 1986, 43), or because it 'is assailed by profound and serious evils derived first and foremost from unfortunate atavisms' (32), we know little about how Arguedas constructed such observations or what he based them on. While *Pueblo enfermo* is governed by generalizations and subjective appraisals, nothing in the essay leads to a scientific proof that a nation can be sick in the first place. And even if we accept that such a thing is possible, the possibility that the nation might recover from its illness remains out of bounds. Indeed, how could a nation recover if its supposed 'sickness' is inscribed in its races, in the most intimate genes? Is not it paradoxical that Arguedas feels the need to redeem the people he has entrapped in racial determinism and biological fatalism? The Bolivian people thus remains steadfast, a prisoner of the same model that condemns it to being unable to mature. This may be why, in his critical take on the essay, José Enrique Rodó recommends that Arguedas be less drastic when he judges Bolivian reality, suggesting he call his people 'childish', rather than 'ill' (cited in Arguedas [1937] 1986, vii).

But Arguedas resorted to the illness metaphor because it fit well with rhetoric about the decadence of national identity. This transatlantic rhetorical style adopted the medical and psychological imagery that was being created simultaneously in Spain and Latin America in the early 20th century. Agustín Álvarez and Carlos Octavio Bunge were the two Argentine 'scientists' most directly associated with Arguedas's construction of illness as metaphor for the gloomy Bolivian reality, but we should not forget the transatlantic influences that directly affected Arguedas's thinking. A medley of European writers from that period – Bourget, Guyau, Le Bon, Lombroso, Taine, and others – led the Bolivian essayist to develop his own concept of geographical determinism, conceived within a frame of thought that was hardly democratic and that also asserted the existence of pathologies produced by racial hybridity and sexual degeneracy. Given the influence of these ideas on Arguedas, it is impossible to find an objective methodology for constructing reality in his essay. Quite the contrary, *Pueblo enfermo* offers the derogatory 'controlled' view of reality carried out by the subjectivity of a criollo thinker who observed the increasingly influential presence of mestizaje with tremendous suspicion. In Arguedas's view, this booming racial hybridity was a source of conflict because it ruled out any formation of the collective 'we' that is needed to lend meaning to nationality.

I will conclude these reflections on the organicist metaphor in Arguedas's essay by asserting that it makes little sense to study the essay only from the viewpoint of the empirical movement of identities, while treating the metaphor's purpose simply as background – the homogenization of a society debilitated by a racial hybridity that prevents it from discovering its national self. Rather than observe reality, Arguedas concealed it under the cloak of a metaphor that contains all the ills that hindered the social order. Granted, *Pueblo enfermo* hints at remedies for the ills of the social body – appropriate attention to education, including opening normal schools, centralizing the universities, educating the Indian, sending young men abroad for training – which would be important in creating the national character. However, in my opinion it is clear that his method of observation and the organicist metaphor that governs it make such prescriptions mere palliatives in the face of the profound illness which, according to Arguedas, afflicted Bolivia at the outset of the 20th century. In short, the 'illness' of mestizaje was the barometer of the human degeneracy by which Arguedas measured psychic and biological deterioration, damage that could scarcely be erased.

The organicist metaphor in the essay depends as much on the interaction between the races as on the relationship between races and the territory they inhabit. In this way, Arguedas treated the 'people' as an organism composed of two vital elements: the races and the environment in which they settle. But, as sociologist Salvador Romero Píttari has observed, despite the importance of Arguedas's essay, it never clearly defines the concept of race (Romero-Píttari 1993, 212). Indeed, Arguedas states in *Pueblo enfermo* that

The term *race*, used categorically to determine the slight variation that exists between the groups settled on Bolivian soil, appears out of place, and much more so if we bear in mind the restrictions and reservations that its use arouses today because science does consider it valuable or believe that its scope is concretely determined, for according to Novicow, 'no one has ever been able to state which traits establish the characteristics of race'. ([1937] 1986, 38)

He then adds:

In Bolivia, for example … it would be impossible to specify, or even outline, the differences that may exist between the so-called *white race* and *mestizo race*. The two are physically similar, or rather, are one. As soon as the *cholo* (mestizo race) rises in position he is a *señor* and thus belongs to the white race. No difference can even be detected in color, for the color appears to depend exclusively on the climate. ([1937] 1986, 38)

Observing the different races, Arguedas concludes:

The class which dominates the others is the mestizo, and the mestizos encounter little opposition as they invade the arbitrary and conventional circle created by a small group who consider themselves superior by blood, not because the latter differ in quality from the former grafted group but because of how they are denominated, the only distinguishing feature that seems to mark the difference attributed to the indigenous population of Bolivia. ([1937] 1986, 38–39)

Note that Arguedas did not have a neutral viewpoint on mestizaje. As mestizaje 'invades' the other races, it brings 'fateful consequences' ([1937] 1986, 39). His essay, which seems to lean towards a psychological conception of the races – the chapters in the book speak of the psychology of the indigenous race and of the mestizo race – sought to build a regional and national psychology that could explain the characters of the various ethnic groups: Aymaras, Quechuas, mestizos, and whites. And in order to achieve his aims, the author entered into murky explanations that sometimes emphasized the social and geographical context but at other times pointed toward the genetic mixing of mestizaje, while also, in a confused way, sometimes highlighted a combination of both factors.

Whatever the result of this combination of factors might be, it is clear that for Arguedas, race and the environment were the motors of history. As Romero Píttari points out, 'they determine the direction, the intensity, and the specific characteristics in the development of peoples' (1993, 212). Influenced by the Romanian historian X. D. Xenopol, Arguedas distanced himself from purely physical–biological explanations of the races so as to include moral and spiritual aspects, which as we will now see, gave rise to the contradictory 'criollo attitude' with which Arguedas approached Bolivian reality. Race and environment were the determinants of the nation's character. Thus Arguedas flexibly incorporated into *Pueblo enfermo* a pejorative, fatalistic, degenerate view of the biological inheritance, physical environment, and, finally, history of the social group being observed.

It was the influence of race on the historical composition of the nation and its collective psychology that outweighed other factors as explanations of Bolivian backwardness, particularly class interests, economic forces, and demographics. And in the explanation his essay provides of reality, Arguedas viewed mestizaje with repugnance:

> From the fertile arm of the white race, which dominates, and from the Indians, the dominated race, is born the mestizo race, bringing as their inheritance the characteristic traits of each...From the Iberian, his warlike spirit, his self-absorption, his pride and his vanity, his marked individualism, his rhetorical bombast, his invincible nepotism, his fanatical political favoritism; and from the Indian, his submission to the strong and powerful, his lack of initiative, his passivity in the face of wrongs, his abominable inclination for lying, cheating, and hypocrisy, his vanity, exasperated by motives of sheer appearance and without basis in any great ideal, his gregariousness, and finally, and to top it all off, his tremendous disloyalty. ([1937] 1986, 79–80)

And this 'cholo hybridity' gave birth to the nation's illness. The *cholo* is the representative type of mestizaje:

> The *cholo* – as politician, soldier, diplomat, legislator, lawyer, or priest – does not ever, at any time, cloud his conscience with wondering whether his actions are moral or not, taking 'morality' to mean 'the harmony of activities in view of the general welfare' (following the Positivist concept), for he thinks only of himself and only about satisfying his dreams of glory ... 'Think badly of others and you'll hit the mark'. This is the adage that, for the *cholo*, contains the best, most comprehensive, and most exact concept of human existence regarding man's relations with his fellow men. ([1937] 1986, 80–81)

Arguedas would say that the educated *cholo*, the *cholo letrado*, freed from ignorance, continued to feel conflicting emotions and to be credulous to the point of *naïveté* or skeptical to the point of viciousness. In broad terms, Bolivia had evolved in the wrong direction for human association due to its domination by the mestizo modality, which, by displacing the Iberian core, had made it lose its own qualities and inherit those of the subjugated race. In this way, the white man had also become *acholado*, 'cholo-ized'. In short, the possibilities for national development were visibly limited by the race and psychology of the various ethnic groups. And in this degenerative process, even education, one of the favorite remedies of the time, would prove insufficient to offset the weight of ethnicity.

The attentive reader cannot fail to have noticed how contradictory this 'criollo attitude' was. Contradictory, because Arguedas's sincere desire to turn history into a moral tale in action was weakened by the poverty of his organicist method of observing reality, which was completely inadequate for giving a scientific explanation of the reasons why Bolivia had enormous problems in entering modernity. As Romero Píttari points out, 'Arguedas, ranked by Bolivian commentators as a pioneer in sociological analysis in his country, was paradoxically one of the writers most indifferent to social dynamics' (1993, 214). Romero Píttari concludes that Arguedas was guilty of circular reasoning: 'he observed and thought he observed behaviors and attitudes derived from the psychology of peoples and even of races, and he was able to confirm this because people behave precisely in accordance to the way in which they are observed' (1993). The criollo attitude of denigrating the mestizo, calling him *cholo*, was thus a social–ethical criollo act that had nothing scientific about it; it arose instead from a caste prejudice that led the author of *Pueblo enfermo* to observe incorrectly the cultural dynamics among the various races, particularly those between Indians and mestizos.

Arguedas wanted to respond seriously to the social problems that ailed the Bolivian nation. But he sacrificed conceptual rigor and the rules of interpretation and documentary selection to his moralizing attitude, thus undermining the objective analysis of reality. This moralizing concept of history, which characterized the 'criollo act', adorned by the prestige of science, projected a vision of basically immutable ethnic groups, isolated from one another and alienated from relations of production. In Arguedas's view of historic events, barbarism did not come from the Indian, for it characterized the higher strata, particularly the mestizo ethnic group, and fell on the indigenous group like the yoke of fatality.

What and where were the origins of this Indian, basically Aymara, whom Arguedas described as belonging to the dominated ethnic group that 'has vegetated since time immemorial … savage and skittish as a wild forest animal, given to his pagan rites and to cultivating the sterile soil where, undoubtedly, his race will soon meet its end' ([1937] 1986, 42)? The presence of this savage being is not part of an objective analysis of reality but rather the product of a subjective relationship between race and environment, which is supported by the theory of fixed atavisms:

> The pampa and the Indian form but a single identity …. The physical aspect of the plains – the type of occupations, their monotony – has molded the spirit of the Indian in a strange fashion. Note the hardness of character in the man of the high plateau, the dryness of sentiments, the total absence of aesthetic inclinations …. Average in stature, perhaps taller rather than shorter, markedly coppery in color … his character has the hardness and aridity of the wilderness. [Note] the contrasts, too; for he is hard, spiteful, egotistical, cruel, vindictive, distrustful when he hates. Submissive and affectionate when he loves. He lacks will power, perseverance of spirit, and feels deep abhorrence for all that differs from him. ([1937] 1986, 42–45)

This is no scientific observation scrutinizing the Indian's nature; it is, rather, a historio-graphic invention that Arguedas gathers form his reading of the allegedly historical texts of Spanish chroniclers. It is the same 'narrow and tortuous conception of the Spanish invaders' (Rivera-Rodas 1993, 51) that we see repeated here in Arguedas's text, particu-larly his reading of the Jesuit José de Acosta, one of the most benevolent towards the indigenous people, who described them in his *Historia natural y moral de Las Indias* ([1590] 2002) as a transmutation of the European *Homo sylvestris*. Indeed, de Acosta mentions the wild men as the Indians' forebears:

> And the first men who entered [the West Indies] were savage hunters [*hombres salvajes y cazadores*, 'wild men and hunters'] rather than civilized folk … with no more laws than a bit of natural instinct (and even that somewhat clouded) and at most a few customs left over from their original country. Even though they came from civilized and well-governed countries, it is not difficult to believe that they forgot everything in the course of a long time and little use; for it is well known that even in Spain and Italy groups of men are sometimes found who except for their shape and faces, have no other resemblance to men. (de Acosta [1590] 2002, 71–72)

This 'first indigenous age' reappears, transformed, in *Pueblo enfermo* when Arguedas employs terms from the European wild man legend, calling the indigenous people 'idolaters', 'pagans' who 'lived like wild animals', 'without order or civility', in disorder and a state of utter savagery' ([1937] 1986, 22). This, then, is an Andean *Homo sylvestris* – or *Homo ferus*, as we will see they could also be termed – that Arguedas describes 'with more imagination than sociological reflection' (Rivera-Rodas 1993, 55), contradicting his own observations at the end of his essay when he conceptualizes all discourse based on the imaginary as something unreal, false, capable of disrupting our proper understanding of things.

This transmuted European savage, this ahistorical Indian defined by Arguedas as 'savage and skittish', also served to establish the differences between Indians and mestizos. This, ultimately, is the essay's purpose: demonstrating the *cholo*-ish nature of the mestizo, the illness that affects Bolivia because the *cholo* 'invaded' all other social groups. In this way, if the Indian is the savage, then the *cholo* must be the barbarian, the cultural element hindering the organization of the nation.

> The *cholo* … is unfailingly driven to the facile concept of a barbarous egalitarianism, as spread by every long-winded demagogue … [He] shows an innate tendency for lying …. His hallmark is to be barbarous because he cannot resign himself to seeing any member of the nation part ways with the barbarous customs and ancient habits of his tribe. (Arguedas [1937] 1986, 84, 131)

And as for mestizaje:

> The prevalence of mestizo blood is what has thus harmed the ethics of society, to the point that brazenness, cunning, and pretense are now the fashion, along with other evil practices that distance man, fatally, from the paths of his moral improvement, life's highest end …. And nothing can be done to remedy this anytime soon, because it is the mestizo blood that has in the end dislodged the Iberian blood and is now revealed in all its base and egotistical expressions, which are the patent sign of the sad state of Bolivian today, and of this sick people, more sick today than ever. (Arguedas [1937] 1986, 333, 337)

Finally, Arguedas denied with blind determinism that the dominated and subjugated Indian might possibly play a role in constructing the nation, but the prejudiced gaze of his moralizing view of history was also contradictory. Thus, he sometimes stated, surprisingly, that the indigenous race was not irremediably lost. These were the contradictions of a 'criollo act' that disqualified ethnic groups, denying them a social function. Arguedas sought to construct an odd national utopia that completely missed the fact that a viable social project needs to place the historic subjects that embody and form it. Therefore, Arguedas's 'criollo act' was roundly rejected by Tamayo's 'mestizo act', to which I now turn.

III

As a discourse of national construction, mestizaje arose during the first decades of the 20th century in the writings of a reformist upper class of *letrados* based in La Paz. Particularly influential to this sector was Franz Tamayo's 1910 essay *Creación de La pedagogía nacional*. After observing the constitution of Tamayo's subjectivity, I will focus on the bodily metaphor as one of the central topics through which the mestizo elite would imagine Bolivian modernity in this period. The visuality of this metaphor – constructed with the vitality of the Indian body and the intelligence of the mestizo mind – which marked the racial inclusions and exclusions of the reformist mestizo project, was what made Tamayo's discourse on the autochthonous so useful.

Yet despite the difference that the discourse on the autochthonous introduced in the observation of Bolivian society, it would be dangerous to idealize it and, hence, leave it untouched by the criticism it deserves. The image of the autochthonous was promoted by an incipient nationalist discourse that helped relocate the indigenous race within the mestizo-criollo view of the nation. The role of the mestizo intellectual, then, would be to discipline the ambiguous nature of his own reformist discourse by constructing an ideal image – an exalted spiritual image – that would solve leaders' problems in societies like Bolivia's, still marked by unsurmounted colonial relations. Franz Tamayo, the great modernist poet and essayist, played this exemplary role like no other mestizo upper-class intellectual.

Tamayo was an intellectually restless young man who had accompanied his father, Isaac Tamayo, on a long trip around Europe following the Federal Revolution of 1899, which changed the seat of government, moving it from the conservative city of Sucre to the liberal La Paz. The young Tamayo was profoundly marked by his father's solitary criticism of the 19th-century Bolivian elite, to which he himself belonged. Averse to the Francophile tastes of the elite, and mainly to the sociological ideas that would influence Alcides Arguedas's thought, the elder Tamayo instilled in his son the need to see Bolivia with his own eyes. According to Roberto Prudencio, another highly original Bolivian essayist, Isaac Tamayo was the first Bolivian intellectual to understand the value of the autochthonous, as well as the first to realize that the Indian and the *cholo* are Bolivia's deepest reality, 'the flesh of our reality' (1977, 31). The younger Tamayo's 1910 book was deeply influenced by his father's essay 'Habla Melgarejo' ('Melgarejo Speaks'), written in response to the policies of Mariano Melgarejo, one of the more barbarous *caudillos* of the 19th century, whose government officially dissolved indigenous communities as legal entities. Writing about Melgarejo gave Isaac Tamayo a chance to explore the natural results of republican life, in order to 'reassess our autochthonous values and build upon them a life of our own' (Prudencio 1977, 39). Isaac Tamayo eschewed Francophilia and put ideas in Melgarejo's mouth that would reappear in Franz Tamayo's book, above all the idea that Western progress could be studied and exploited, as Meiji Japan had done, so long as it did not run counter to the true strengths of Bolivian reality, that is, counter to its autochthonous culture.

Isaac Tamayo made an abiding impression on his son's intellectual work. The influence of Tamayo's mother Felicidad Solares was of a quite different nature. Little is known of Solares except that she was descended from a line of *caciques* (Indian nobles and community leaders). The only information we have is the short filial homage that Tamayo rendered to her in a scathing rebuttal to criollo essayist Fernando Diez de Medina, who had wounded Tamayo's sensitivities by referring to his alleged *cholo* origins in *Franz Tamayo, hechicero del Ande* ([1942] 1944). Rejecting the notion that he was of *cholo* blood, Tamayo wrote, 'On my mother's side, there is no *birlochaje* [the process of forming *cholos*] in my race or in my blood. Every virtue of the ancient American woman, further embellished by the light of Christianity, shone brightly in the proud Indian woman who was my mother' (cited in Diez de Medina [1942] 1944). Indeed, this was an interesting way to define himself: exalting the indigenous while suspiciously regarding the mestizo, who could so easily become degraded and *cholo*-ized. This aspect of Tamayo's subjectivity needs to be explored in more detail.

Tamayo was a thinker who, at the beginning of a century that stood out for its exaltation of positivist thought, chose to restore the mystical sentiments of introspection, of the journey within. Just as Jean-Jacques Rousseau ([1781] 1990) had already done with the ancient imagery of the wild man to reestablish it at the highest level in European culture, the same fascinating paradox seems to apply to Tamayo who, in his eagerness for subjectification, needed to lift his Indian tradition and place it on the central altar of his own ego. As we can see, for Tamayo the Indian was not the other: it was himself. In this sense, he could not be considered a social scientist but, rather, the reconstructor of an Aymara myth as a way of performing a great 'mestizo act' of self-identification. Consequently, Tamayo needed to lift the Indian out of his marginal existence by reconstructing him and admitting, as indeed Rousseau had already done, that the savage was nothing else but himself. This voyage into the empty pit of the ego forced Tamayo to explore the qualities of both the Indian and the mestizo.

Just as Tamayo interpreted the constitution of his own subjectivity, in his *Creación de La pedagogía nacional* he examined the Indian's devolution into *cholo* to discipline social facts with a bodily metaphor, which we will explore below. This metaphor was an ideologically ambiguous proposal. Tamayo appears not to have noticed the conflict it created between the internal and the external, between life and reason, a conflict that came to characterize the discourse on the autochthonous. Let us look at it more closely before returning to the subjectivist construction of his ideal mestizaje, what he called the *mestizaje ideal*.

One the most interesting aspects of *Creación de La pedagogía nacional* was the anticolonial tone that Tamayo gave to his discourse. Refusing to imitate the rationalist methods of European positivism, Tamayo aimed to reclaim the vital indigenous energy of Bolivia. Tamayo's anticolonialism, a precursor to the nationalist rhetoric of later decades, assumed the necessity of reconstructing an original identity. This assumption fused the notion of the autochthonous with the idea that Bolivia's indigenous roots were the source of its energy and vitality. In searching for the will of the 'noble savage', of the recuperated Aymara, his discourse on the autochthonous repudiated the degeneration – the *encholamiento* [choloization] – into which the criollo had fallen.

But this discourse, which sought to constitute a 'noble savage' by redeeming the Aymara, at the same time recreated the social fractures of the colonial order, for it could not resolve the contradictions between the indigenous 'interior' with its particular communitarian vision, and the mestizo-criollo 'exterior', ruled by European models of observation. Tamayo's discourse on the autochthonous reflected these contradictory impulses. By referring to the Indian's vital energy, Tamayo showcased his differences with Eurocentric forms, which, though deriving from the European romanticism and irrationalism that were both at odds with positivism, nonetheless added up to yet another foreign gaze on the local culture to which Tamayo hoped to return in strength and originality. In this sense, the search for a discourse on the autochthonous did not express the point of view of indigenous subalternity, but rather reproduced that of mestizo-criollo reason, which manipulated the people's energy and was capable of dominating society. This discourse proposed a different path than that of the 19th-century criollo oligarchy, which had divided reality into European civilization and American barbarism. Instead, the discourse on the autochthonous exalted indigenous culture, creating a local version of the 'noble savage', and the telluric strength of the environment, both of which, finally guided by mestizo intelligence, would overcome mechanic determinism and social Darwinism.

In his introspective search for the 'nation's soul', Tamayo, no different from Arguedas, attacked *cholaje*, the process of forming *cholos*. Indeed, Arguedas had argued for liberating the Indian, the local *Homo sylvestris*, from the social scourge of the *cholo*.

Tamayo, too, looked down on the *cholo* with profound disdain, but was much more cautious in promoting the liberal civilizing project. In *Creación de La pedagogía nacional* he criticized French-style positivism, which he termed 'Bovarysm', as well as the rationalist premises that supported evolutionary determinism. The concept of material progress that both ideologies shared, and which was promoted by the will of a European spirit imposed upon the barbarian body of Indo-American reality, was precisely what Tamayo rejected and countered with his utopian, irrationalist vision of mestizaje.

Creación de La pedagogía nacional cannot be judged through the lens of the positivist ideas that guided progress and modernity. In his search for the authentic, for the autochthonous, Tamayo aspired to present the indigenous potential of his Andean 'noble savage' as a source of vitality and energy that would overcome the opposition between civilization and barbarism. According to this reformist vision, the nation would only transcend the limitations of the present when the elite changed morally and culturally and put all of their efforts into redeeming and giving him a new form to the Indian.

Moving from Rousseauian subjectification into German irrationalist thought, and influenced by Schopenhauer, Tamayo argued that Bolivian backwardness could be overcome through self-perception and the development of the ability to intuitively recognize the national will. This complicated and rather unclear procedure reinforced subjectification, complementing it with the idea that the world could only be known through the self-reflexive gaze of the observer. This was a form of knowing that Tamayo applied to his conceptualization of mestizaje. Tamayo thus reflected on his own physique before constructing the bodily image of the nation. This form of perceiving reality was an optical, visual process that followed Schopenhauer's ([1818] 1966) revolutionary principal that the understanding of the objective nature of the exterior world had to first pass through the construction of subjectivity. In other words, it is through one's own self, one's own microcosm, that one apprehends the social world, the external macrocosm. The key is in self-reflection, in coming to understand one's own will.

Before delving into the hidden bodily metaphor of *Creación de La pedagogía nacional*, let me make some observations on Tamayo, the observer. Let us first remember that in his *Discours sur l'inégalité*, Rousseau ([1781] 1990) affirms that in order to discover the principles that preceded reason, it is necessary to abandon all the scientific books and 'meditate'. Rousseau's image of the wild man was the product of meditation, not of historical or ethnological research. In a strikingly similar fashion, Tamayo asked his hypothetical readers not to be guided exclusively by books and other structured forms of looking, but to direct their attention to the centrality of visual experience in everyday life. He noted that we should 'deal with life not with the dead letter' (Tamayo [1910] 1975, 26), and argued that we 'should close our books and open our eyes' (27). *Creación de La pedagogía nacional constantly* reminds us that 'Bovarysm' meant losing a vigilant spirit able to 'see' life directly. Following Goethe's maxim, *Glaube dem Leben*, Tamayo's belief in life invites us to reject the mechanical appropriation of artificial models of progress (47). As he noted, 'Our Bovarysts are convinced that European models can do everything …. This illusion robs us of energy and time' (35). Moreover, Tamayo, the observer of national reality, understood that national consciousness is 'a moment of reflection on ourselves, an opening of our eyes to our own nature, and then to the external world' (183). This self-reflexive movement from the internal to the external is precisely what led Tamayo, now under Schopenhauer's influence, to construct his bodily metaphor.

The movement of self-reflection allows us to ask the following: What happens when the anatomical parts of the observer – the musculature, the fat content, and so on – are the necessary conditions for making observations? And, particularly important for the purpose of this essay, how does self-reflection turn the Aymara *Homo sylvestris* into the 'noble savage'? Tamayo's own corporeality, as reflected in his essay's metaphor, became the privileged place for observing the entire project of national culture. His project, tied to the 20th-century visual science that investigated the physical composition of the human, was particularly influenced by the narcissistic visions of Goethe, Schopenhauer, and Nietzsche, who, as well as Jean-Jacques Rousseau, were fundamental to his Western-oriented subjective vision. Opposed to Alcides Arguedas's 'criollo act', Tamayo located Bolivian morality and vitality in its indigenous people's physical constitution: indigenous muscle contained 'ninety per cent of our national energy' ([1910] 1975, 72). Tamayo affirms, 'The builder of our house, the worker of his own land, the weaver of his own clothing, the maker of his own work tools …. The Indian is the storehouse of national energy (71).

But this great moral and physical 'will' was not accompanied by intellect: 'Intelligence is what the mestizos have inherited from their white forebears' ([1910] 1975, 113). Tamayo even stated that, before entering into contact with Western thought, mestizos were already endowed with 'natural intelligence'. Mestizo intelligence nevertheless lacked will. This was why the mestizo head, bereft of character, had to join the indigenous musculature. Only that physical vigor could infuse mestizo intelligence with passion and determination. For Tamayo, then, the *mestizo ideal* – the mutated Andean 'noble savage' of modernity – was the synthesis of indigenous will and mestizo intelligence. This ideal wild man would require rigorous guiding and control, for just as bodies accumulate excessive fat when they are sedentary, so mestizos tend to over-imagine rather than reason. The function of pedagogy was to control these excesses, so that they would not endanger the project of national construction. Thus subaltern *cholaje*, the excess fat of the social body, had to be eliminated. The *mestizo ideal*, then, was not the *cholo*, who was erased from the social imaginary. Tamayo thus constructed, via Western visuality, the fascinating bodily image of the ideal Bolivian, capable of introducing to society the changes needed for constructing the nation. This ideal being would have the Indian's wild but vital physique, combined with the educated mind of the mestizo, on whom the function of directing the nation-building project would fall.

The model for Tamayo's visual reflections on will and intelligence was foreign to Aymara culture, whose 'interior' dynamics Tamayo never bothered to study. On the contrary, Tamayo depicted a surprisingly similar relation between intellect and will as the optic regime of Schopenhauer's ([1818] 1966) *The World as Will and Representation*, which the German philosopher wrote when the European science of optics was moving from Cartesian perspectivism to an observational model that emphasized anatomy and the perceptual separation of the senses (Jay 1988). Where Schopenhauer summed up this relation as that of 'a robust blind man who carries a seeing cripple on his shoulders' ([1818] 1966, 421), we could say that Tamayo's *mestizo ideal* was a muscular wild Indian carrying an intelligent mestizo inside his head. The will, like the muscular but blind indigenous body, carries the intelligence, which, like a crippled mestizo, can only see and serve as a guide from the shoulders of the indigenous body. Schopenhauer's truly revolutionary visual theory anticipated modernist aesthetics; Tamayo made it possible to observe the man of the Andes in an inward, subjective way, without relying on the outward, distant, coldly objective Cartesian mind's eye.

As we have seen, Tamayo's subjectification connected with Rousseau, particularly with the famous phrase in the *Essay on the Origin of Languages*, 'When one wishes to study men it is necessary to look close to oneself; but, in order to study man, it is necessary to direct one's gaze afar; it is necessary first to observe the differences so as then to become aware of one's own qualities' ([1781] 1990, 89–90). Rousseau looks at what 'is distant' but not 'outward' – in order to observe what is faraway, he directs his gaze inward, very far into the interior of himself. And Tamayo, influenced by Rousseau, also saw a surprisingly similar movement in Schopenhauer, from whom he borrowed the concept of the inner will of modern man. This allowed Tamayo to construct the bodily metaphor of his *mestizaje ideal*. However, the vitalism he observed in the Indian body was not based on Schopenhauer, but on Nietzsche's more dynamic and positive philosophy. Schopenhauer had insisted, with pessimism that Tamayo never shared, that the will had no social aim. The Bolivian poet and essayist abandoned this view of the will, and instead followed the social goals proposed by Nietzsche.

Just as Nietzsche drew on Darwinian thought to depict human evolution in positive terms (see Simmel [1907] 1991), Tamayo found in the evolution of Bolivia the possibility of fully saying, with Nietzsche and Goethe, 'yes' to life. Consequently, Tamayo took up Nietzsche's energy to argue for the triumph of his *mestizaje ideal*. Furthermore, he believed that life's inner worth depended on neither pleasure nor pain, but on governing energy that is born, like an 'anonymous and powerful will' (Tamayo [1910] 1975, 51) in nature. Based on this theory of energy, which resembles Nietzsche's notion of will, Tamayo recognized the land itself as holding the world's vitality. Will is the vital nexus that ties man with the land, and man must try to capture all the virtues and determination of the land's will. Tamayo saw this vital energy not as a hostile force but as a positive impulse that was responsible for the existence of the man of the Andes. This would become, in the next decades, the source of the telluric mysticism of Tamayo's followers.

The motto *Glaube dem Leben* (Faith in Life), which Tamayo took from Goethe, was a way of overcoming the imperfections of the present. In other words, whereas Schopenhauer had no faith in the possibility of human redemption, Tamayo escaped such pessimism, which takes away the meaning of life, and affirmed the possibility of an ideal mestizaje that would make national construction possible. His *mestizo ideal*, a mutated version of the European 'noble savage', was thus the bridge that let Tamayo cross over from the chaos of the past into the order of the future. Yet his thought never broke with the notion of progress that is at the base of Western historiography. By combining his round rejection of early 20th-century Bolivia with an equally forceful affirmation of its future promise, Tamayo hoped to cast light on the path to social perfectibility. Despite his arguments against *cholaje*, Tamayo's book projected a much more positive view of the nation than Arguedas' *Pueblo enfermo*.

Tamayo had a vital and mysterious relationship with the land of Bolivia. This sense of mystery, which can be found in both his pedagogical ideas and in his modernist poetry, separated him from the existent-denying emotional abyss of Schopenhauer. Given that Tamayo's thought was motivated by moral themes rather than metaphysical problems, his bodily metaphor in *Creación de La pedagogía nacional* makes us look at Bolivia through a vitalism that does not derive from a rational explanation of society, but rather from a Schopenhauerian 'all-in-one' optic that harmonizes the races. With his metaphor of *mestizaje ideal*, Tamayo thus transformed empirical reality into an imaginary representation of life. As sociologist Juan Albarracín has noted, 'Tamayo believed in a national awakening based on the natural supports of land and blood, mythified by a prodigious vital energy that nurtured everything existing on Andean soil, giving it strength and power'(1981,10).

Finally, what interests me is to emphasize the importance of preconceived European schemas in Tamayo's 'mestizo act' that are interwoven into the apparently local theme of the 'Indian problem', which, as we have seen, refers to Europe. Indeed, Tamayo, a moderate metropolitan thinker, can only be understood if we link his thoughts to the European thinkers I have mentioned above. Foreign models of observing were never questioned at any point in the 20th century. Tamayo insisted that he had nothing to do with aping European thought, that he was entirely motivated by his enthusiasm for autochthonous originality. But his 'mestizo act' concealed his European intellectual sources to explain its Andean roots. Thus, Tamayo was able to pass off European romanticism and irrationalism as his own 'national pedagogy'.

IV

As the last topic of what I understand to be 'mestizo-criollo acts', I would like to reinforce the idea that these social 'acts' are not truly local by returning to the notion that they are neither unique nor exceptional. Rather, these acts represent a Eurocentric gaze constructed not only with the philosophical and sociological theories we have seen so far, but also with imaginaries populated by the troublesome images of the wild creatures I mention throughout this paper. These troublesome images may also be considered re-appropriations of a vision that, coming from the European past, defines the 'other' and at the same time determines the possibilities for how this 'other' might be either redeemed, as in Tamayo's take on the Indian, or forever socially chastised, as in Arguedas's pessimistic conceptualization of mestizos and Indians.

Let us consider some of these re-appropriations of the past. The European myths of the redeemed savage belong to a storytelling that has not been sufficiently explored in Latin America. In their transatlantic voyages to Latin American territories, the myths turn into 'mestizo' and 'criollo acts' rooted in 19th and early 20th-century discussions that present the Indian as a social prototype. In this sense, the Bolivian dispute on how to manage the 'Indian problem' may not have been just a local attempt to formulate the social viability of the nation-state, but also the re-enactment of a much wider cultural sensibility fixated on 'savages', or wild men that represent the real dangers besieging the well-being of Western societies.

Here, I find it important to make a parenthetical remark on the peculiar mutations that Roger Bartra has found throughout the history of the myth of the wild man. In his book *The Artificial Savage* (1997), Bartra proposes to seek out the mutations that will allow him to understand the continuing presence of the myth of the wild man throughout the centuries. After examining the ways in which pagan folklore influenced mythical thought, whether in the popular lyrics of the poets of the Reformation or in Spanish Renaissance humanism, Bartra introduces us to a chain of mutations that connects eaters of human flesh with the horrific cannibals painted by Goya and Frankenstein's monster of Mary Shelley. Through studying these mutations, Bartra contests what Ferdinand Braudel called *histoire événementielle*, an evolutionary history of ideas that emphasizes the narration of intellectual achievements as major events produced in the course of human history. According to Bartra, this view, impregnated exclusively with the evolution of grandiose events, ignores the malign, aggressive and dangerous facets of the myth of the wild man, without which, Bartra asserts, one cannot comprehend both the extraordinary complexity of myth and its enormous plasticity. Consequently, Bartra proposes a 'neo-evolutionist' approach to the history of myths that goes beyond the sequential narration of major events and focuses his attention on certain transitional moments that are symptomatic, both in relation to the composition of the myth and its functions within the surrounding cultural texture (15–18).

Transported to Bolivia, this discussion could be applied to 'mestizo acts' in ways that local historians and social scientists have not taken into consideration. For this reason the example of Franz Tamayo and the metaphysical construction of his *mestizo ideal* seems revealing to me. What determines the peculiar composition of Tamayo's culturally divided noble creature, half mestizo and half Indian?

From an anthropological perspective concerned with the history of constructing myths, we could claim that a mythical structure deeply anchored in the human spirit sends messages that are translated into concrete forms by each culture – in this case by the Bolivian early 20th-century debate on the 'Indian problem'. However, Tamayo's metaphysical construction of his bodily metaphor does not reflect the codified reception of certain 'instructions' that originate, as Bartra observes critically, 'in a deep structure (a kind of generative grammar) in which the nature-culture has crystallized' (1997, 15). Instead, Tamayo's metaphor may very well be a mutation of the *Homo sylvestris*. Such a mutation shows the persistence of a myth that evolves throughout the centuries. Connected to the 'Indian problem', the myth of the wild man is readopted in the early 20th century. Science, sanctioned and stimulated by myth, may have given an impulse to its continuity. Tamayo's ideal mestizo is also a peculiar metamorphosis of the myth of the wild man: the disturbing hairiness of the traditional wild man is exchanged for a muscular bodily metaphor, a deviation that indicates the myth's plasticity of structure and its capacity to take on many forms and to adapt to very different cultural contexts.

Obsessed with the 'other' as a way to reinforce the construction of the 'self', Tamayo's creation of a 'national pedagogy' may also be the local reenactment of a Western legend that – historically connected to the transatlantic voyage of the savage as a mythical figure capable of redemption – mutated a century later into a different culture. I am referring here to what Bartra found as a spectacular case, much discussed at the beginning of the 19th century, which generated the legend that is still circulating today: the true story of Victor, the child from Aveyron, who was found in 1797 in the woods near Saint Sernin-sur-Rance and who, lacking language, was studied by the Parisian scientist Jean-Marc-Gaspard Itard (see Itard [1801] 2003).

Those children who have grown up in harsh situations of depravation with minimal human contact are seen as feral or wild. Since language acquisition, especially with feral children and the consequences of late development, are not well documented, opportunities for this research are rare to nonexistent. The best case study with enough documentation for serious consideration is Victor, the wild boy of Aveyron. Could a language-less human being hold the clues to learn what is characteristic of being human? Feral children, as well as savages, represent our unknown past, a clue to what our lives were like before we settled into our modern routines. Savages and wild men, that is, human beings perceived by 'civilized' people to be uncivilized, primitive, brutish, were once considered subhuman, a separate species called *Homo ferus* (Cayea 2006). While the *Homo sylvestris* and the *Homo ferus* were not considered inhuman, they were still regarded as a possible source of information about humanity's nature. Such is the case of Victor, documented thanks to the meticulous note-taking of Jean-Marc-Gaspard Itard, the scientist who later wrote *de l'education d'un homme sauvage* ([1801] 2003). Victor appeared little more than an animal, and was both reviled and pitied by his finders. He was not even a savage, but a poor soul who had been abandoned in the woods. When found at the age of seven, he was a *tabula rasa*, a clean slate waiting to receive input. In some ways, Victor was fortunate because he appeared when the philosophical ponderings of the Enlightenment were beginning to show practical results with the birth of 'philanthropy'. And so the wild boy was scientifically useful as an experiment that would tell something about what was innate in being human and what was acquired through civilization and culture.

The debate on whether the wild boy was an idiot, or just so deprived of the period of language acquisition that he was unable to acquire language, also centered on the question of whether Victor was an idiot because he was left in the woods, or whether he was left in the woods because he was an idiot. Siding with the probability that Victor would evolve with training, Itard took up the challenge and sought to awaken Victor's senses to further education through a series of sense-stimulating exercises. Itard believed that seven or so years of isolation from all human society was enough of a reason to explain Victor's condition. Studying the wild boy of Aveyron provided the potential to scientifically answer the question that obsessed philosophers: What is the nature of man? When Itard began to examine the boy from Aveyron, however, he already had an answer to the question; his first report on the boy in 1801 began with these words:

> Thrown upon the world without physical strength and without innate ideas, without the capacity to obey by himself the constitutive laws of his organization, which call him to occupy the first rank in the system of beings, man can only find within society the eminent place in nature that was designated for him; and without civilization he would be one of the weakest and least intelligent of animals; this is a much repeated truth which has, however, not been in any way rigorously proved. ([1801] 2003, 185)

A century later, Tamayo, like Itard, seemed to be stimulated and guided by the same desire to prove that local 'savages' could be civilized, thus reenacting Itard's early research in Bolivia. And the parallelisms are striking because Victor was the first potentially redeemable savage to be created by the French Revolution. Likewise, Tamayo's Indian-turned-mestizo became crucial to the creation of the aesthetic politics that led to the Bolivian nationalist Revolution of 1952. The imaginary voyage of the Aveyron savage to Bolivian soil initiates two different historical moments united by the same guiding principle: the capacity to answer, both scientifically and aesthetically, the question about the nature of humankind, which had haunted moral and social philosophy ever since its search for man in a pure state of nature. And Itard's redeemable savage, just like Tamayo's Indian-turned-*mestizo ideal*, became the living proof of Rousseauian arguments concerning human nature's evolution since its purest state.

However, this discussion of the capacity to construct redeemable savages does not end with Itard. Refuting Itard's diagnosis of the savage boy, Phillipe Pinel, the eminent French scholar of mental illnesses, known to be the 'father of psychiatry', concluded that Victor was an incurable idiot and would not train him (see Lane 1976). Pinel's report, however, was most curious in the fact that it did not investigate nor explain scientifically what would have been wrong with the wild boy. For Pinel, education and training would do little to bring Victor into the sphere of humanity. He repeatedly talks about the boy's 'animal instincts', about his 'absence of reason', his lack of 'inborn intelligence' (57–69).

In a strange parallelism, the discussion between Itard and Pinel could be considered an early European version of the discussion that took place, like a message translated from one culture to another, between Tamayo and Arguedas at the beginning of the 20th century. Let us remember that, for Arguedas, while mestizaje was the illness that corroded the 'nation's soul', the Indian – 'solitary, unsociable' and 'clinging to bestial atavisms' – was still as subhuman as Victor, the wild boy of Aveyron, if we follow Pinel's report. Arguedas would also agree that solitary life, at the margins of civilization, corresponds to that of an *Homo ferus*, whose cretinism cannot be reversed with education and training, least of all by a pedagogical effort that would attempt to incorporate the Indian race into society by making it the source of energy and vitality needed to create the 'nation's soul'.

In the Arguedas-Tamayo debate around the 'Indian problem', however, what remains truly interesting about the savage-turned-*mestizo ideal* is the possibility to retrieve European imaginaries that are connected to racist and colonialist purposes. Gone largely undetected by the social sciences, the presence of the *Homo sylvestris* inside the foundational essays of our lettered culture is another proof of how European imaginaries weighed heavily on the Latin American construction of the 'self/other' identity formation.

Of course, this self/other aspect of nation building cannot be limited to the early 20th-century debate on the 'Indian problem'. The question of *cholaje*, vilified by both Arguedas and Tamayo, comes immediately to my mind as another 'mestizo act' of particular relevance. It could be considered to be a deeper 'Mestizo problem' that I simply mention here as I end this paper. There remains the need to continue tracing the still understudied map of the myth of the wild man within the evolution of *cholaje*. Its landmarks, its meanderings, its boundaries, and its connections must be uncovered. Bartra has already opened up the path to new discoveries from an anthropological point of view. In dialogue with his research, I have established in this essay a kind of cultural selection on the controversial nature of 'mestizo-criollo acts' that designate the 'Indian problem' as a key moment of Bolivia's 'being' as a nation-state. Since I concentrated my attention on Arguedas and Tamayo as a way to configure Bolivia's vision of reality at the turn of the 20th century, it would be appropriate to register in more detail the high-cultured predisposition to think Bolivia in terms of 'being', in contrast to the idea of 'becoming', which seems to be in tune with the popular and mass-cultured *cholaje*. I hope to have initiated this discussion by selecting the 'mestizo-criollo act' that initially started a historical debate by both separating and uniting civilization with wild life. It remains to be seen how *cholaje* deploys the image of the wild man when constructing its representation and figuration within movement and change.

References

Albarracín-Millán, J. 1981. *El pensamiento filosófico de Tamayo y el irracionalismo alemán*. Vol. 1. La Paz, Bolivia: Akapana.

Arguedas, A. [1937] 1986. *Pueblo enfermo*. 3rd ed. La Paz, Bolivia: Librería-Editorial "Popular.".

Bartra, R. 1994. *Wild Men in the Looking Glass: The Mythic Origins of European Otherness*. Ann Arbor: The University of Michigan Press.

Bartra, R. 1997. *The Artificial Savage: Modern Myths of the Wild Man*. Translated by C. Follett. Ann Arbor: The University of Michigan Press.

Cayea, W. 2006. "Feral Child: The Legacy of the Wild Boy of Aveyron in the Domains of Language Acquisition and Deaf Education." PhD diss., Rochester Institute of Technology. Accessed August 3, 2016. http://scholarworks.rit.edu/cgi/viewcontent.cgi? article=5163&context=theses.

de Acosta, J. [1590] 2002. *Natural and Moral History of the Indies*. Translated by F. López-Morillas and edited by J. Mangan. Durham, NC: Duke University Press.

Diez de Medina, F. [1942] 1944. *Franz Tamayo. Hechicero del Ande*. La Paz, Bolivia: Editorial Puerta del Sol.

Harris, O. 1995. "Ethnic Identity and Market Relations: Indians and Mestizos in the Andes." In *Ethnicity, Markets, and Migrations in the Andes: At the Crossroads of History and Anthropology*, edited by B. Larson, O. Harris, and E. Tandeter, 351–390. Durham: Duke University Press.

Itard, J.-M.-G. [1801] 2003. *De l'éducation d'un homme sauvage*. Reproduced in Lucien Malson, *Les enfants sauvages. Mythe et réalité*. Paris: Bibliothéque 10/18, nº 157.

Jay, M. 1988. "Scopic Regimes of Modernity." In *Vision and Visuality: Discussions in Contemporary Culture*, edited by H. Foster, 3–23. Seattle: Bay Press.

Lane, H. 1976. *Wild Boy of Aveyron*. Cambridge, MA: Harvard University Press. (Includes Philippe Pinel's diagnosis in his report to the Société des Observateurs de l'Homme [29 November 1800]).

Larson, B. 2001. "Indios redimidos, cholos barbarizados: Imaginando la modernidad neocolonial boliviana (c. 1900-1910)." In *Visiones de fin de siglo. Bolivia y América Latina en el Siglo XX*, edited by D. Cajías, M. Cajías, C. Johnson, and I. Villegas, 27–48. La Paz, Bolivia: IFEA/Coordinadora de Historia.

Prudencio, R. 1977. "Isaac Tamayo y su obra." In *Ensayos literarios*, 279–299. La Paz, Bolivia: Fundación Manuel Vicente Ballivián.

Rivera-Rodas, Ó. 1993. "Pueblo enfermo: Los fracasos de la utopía y la historia." *Signo. Cuadernos bolivianos de cultura* 39–40 (May–Dec): 41–68.

Romero-Píttari, S. 1993. "Alcides Arguedas: Entre el pesimismo y la esperanza." *Signo. Cuadernos bolivianos de cultura* 39–40 (May–Dec): 211–216.

Rousseau, J.-J. [1781] 1990. *Essai sur l'origine des langues ou il est parlé de la mélodie et de l'imitation musicale*. Edited by Jean Starobinski. Paris: Gallimard.

Schopenhauer, A. [1818] 1966. *The World as Will and Representation*. 2 Vols. Translated by E. F. Payne. New York: Dover Publications.

Simmel, G. [1907] 1991. *Schopenhauer and Nietzsche*. Translated by H. Loiskandl, D. Weinstein, and M. Weinstein. Urbana: University of Illinois Press.

Tamayo, F. [1910] 1975. *Creación de la pedagogía nacional*. 3rd ed. La Paz, Bolivia: Biblioteca del Sesquicentenario de la República.

Mestizaje as ethical disposition: indigenous rights in the neoliberal state

Deborah Poole

ABSTRACT

This article explores the modes of aspiration, skepticism, and suspicion that constitute the inheritance of mestizaje in neoliberal Peru. Drawing on recent controversies regarding the metrics deployed to determine access to indigenous rights, it argues for the need to move away from liberal understandings of mestizaje as a bounded 'identity' claim, to consider instead how the politics and discourse of mestizaje shape a more generalized affective politics of skepticism regarding all identity claims. More specifically, I argue that mestizaje acquires particular affective and ethical force in relation to the fiscal and technical norms that underwrite postregulatory government in Peru. What interests me in pursuing this argument is to understand how, in its move away from the forms of citizenship, constitutive rights, and recognition that fueled the liberal state, neoliberalism has simultaneously gained force from the ethos of suspicion that surrounds any claim to an antecedent or foundational (cultural, racial, or ethnic) identity, and forwarded new technologies of governance that render illegible emergent claims to national, territorial, or cultural 'rights' or 'identities'. In this article, I track this intersection of historical idioms of mestizaje and new technologies of government by looking at the technical instruments through which the Peruvian state sets out to reshape the territorial underpinnings of community and indigenous identity, and the implications of such technologies for the implementation of indigenous rights to prior consultation.

As Latin America's signature racial and cultural ideal, *mestizaje* can be glossed as an ideology of mixture that extends the illusion of defined 'racial' identities as it simultaneously portends the erosion of ethnic hierarchies. Thus while 'the mestizo' is frequently imagined as a more or less stable 'identity' or type that can be either assigned to, or claimed by, individuals and groups, in both daily practice and historical patterning the actual category or 'label' of mestizo turns out to be remarkably pliable, if not illusive (Cope 1994; de la Cadena 2000; Rappaport 2014; Wade 2005). At the same time, however – and as the various articles collected in this issue explore in some detail – mestizaje has also worked to deepen the racial distinctions and exclusions that characterize postcolonial society. In this respect, we might take mestizaje – as I do in this article – not as a category that allows us to access either the reality or meaning of difference and identity in Latin America, but rather as a diffuse cultural ethos or ethical disposition that frames 'racial' differences as at once empirically verifiable *and* politically suspect. Though grounded in colonial anxieties concerning status and caste, this ethos was shaped in distinctive ways by liberal political ideals that drew on disciplinary languages of racial and cultural classification to project a utopian, nationalist horizon of equality and inclusion (Appelbaum, MacPherson, and Rosemblat 2003; Dawson 2004; Gould 1998; Hale 2006; Poole 2004, 2011; Wade 2007). As mestizaje moved from being a nationalist aspiration to a generative principle of demographic government, however, its unifying nationalist ethos has been substantively transformed into an empirical under-standing of 'populations' and identities as entities that can be mapped – and governed – through the statistical patterning of bounded racial identities (Loveman 2014).

The distance separating these governmentalist understandings of population from the normative *ideal* of a 'mestizo identity' that could, someday, be shared by diverse peoples and groups, is further deepened if we consider how mestizaje is differently configured through acts of naming and acts of claiming. In the Peruvian case considered here, for example, the state has historically deployed ascribed 'ethnic' identities to both limit and extend rights to citizenship and territory (Méndez 2005; Remy 2013a). Thus, for example, after centuries of erasure and denial, 'indigenous communities' were finally recognized in the 1930s as juridical entities whose members were afforded the same 'special' or 'protected' status as minors.[1] Some 40 years later, however, under the government of General Juan Velasco Alvarado, these same communities were reconfi-gured as 'peasant communities' whose special political and juridical status derived not from their identities as 'first nations' or indigenous peoples, but rather from their subordinate position within Peru's class and economic system. Such a re-assignment allowed 'peasants' to shed the moniker of 'Indian', with its negative racial connotations and decreased citizenship rights. At the same time, the peasants' increased visibility and ideological significance in Peru's reformist left-leaning government deepened elite perceptions of coastal and Andean peasants as racially inferior 'Indians' (Mayer 2009). In this respect, and as various scholars have argued, the class-based military reforms of the 1970s have worked over time to deepen the historically inscribed forms of racism through which indigenous peoples continue to be excluded from normative definitions of a national 'mestizo' or criollo society. This pattern was, if anything, further consoli-dated in the 1980s through a counterinsurgency war in which insurgents and counter-insurgents alike relegated Andean peasants to the racially suspect status of 'backwards' Indians (Poole and Renique 1992).

This historical narrative of shifting governmental priorities provides a sense of how such things as census categories, penal codes, and juridical definitions of community have constrained the emergence of *ethnically* defined political and social organizations in *some* parts of Peru (Degregori 1993; García and Lucero 2011; Pajuelo Teves 2006, 2010). It does not, however, adequately explain the very deep forms of suspicion that seem to surround *all* claims to ethnic or racial identity in Peru. It is here that we can usefully turn to mestizaje not as a normative or allegedly stable category of racial or social identity, but rather as an ethos of suspicion that colors all discussions of identity and belonging in Peru. In considering this ethos, we would do well to start with the fact that claims to mestizo status in Peru as elsewhere, have been tied historically to improved social status and – sometimes – rights. Like the ideology of inclusion or mixture they invoke, such claims are both issued and received as deeply *political*. At the same time, all claims to mestizo status are haunted by the 'mestizo's' empirically verifiable genealogical or historical relationship to the supposedly 'inferior' cultural and racial categories of the 'indian' and/or the 'black' (de la Cadena 2000). In this sense, in Peru as elsewhere in Latin America, to claim mestizo status is to claim an 'identity' that is not only emergent or incomplete, but also shadowed by doubt. This shadow, I argue, is cast by the fact that the very language of mestizaje necessarily links claims to racial and social mobility or 'improvement' to antecedent racial identities that are imagined as having clearly consolidated boundaries and attributes.

In this article, I explore how the ideals of inclusion, assimilation, and impurity associated with historical understandings of mestizaje acquire new force and meaning in relation to the specific tools of technical governance through which the Peruvian state assigns 'identities' to populations in a context of expanded international indigenous rights. I approach mestizaje as an ideology of racial and political becoming and as a process of continual differentiation (Deleuze 1995), which rests uneasily with liberal understandings of identity as a fixed, inherited, or embodied essence. Rather than tracking mestizaje as a defined ideology or identity formation, I explore this aporia within mestizaje as generative of what I call an 'ethics of suspicion' in which all claims to identity are both articulated and received as inherently 'political' and thus suspect. To understand how this ethics takes hold in contemporary Peru, I ask three questions as follows. First, I am concerned to understand how 'mestizaje'– as a largely aleatory, open ended, and ongoing process that is itself grounded in the continual production of difference – resonates with the distinctively open-ended temporality and distributed sovereignty of Peru's post-regulatory, decentralized state.[2] Second, I am interested in understanding to what extent the ideal of mestizaje, as a form of assimilation or inclusion, shadows neoliberal commitments to participatory and multicultural government in Peru.[3] Third, I am interested in understanding how the metrics that give both legal form and technical precision to ethnic identities in Peruvian administrative law are framed by the specter of mestizaje as a harbinger (if not sign) of racial and cultural 'passing'. Whereas the Peruvian state once viewed with suspicion all individual and group claims to a racially 'improved' or mestizo status, today mestizaje is taken as the normative or default identity for non-elite subjects, while other sorts of identity claims are viewed as interest driven and thus as shadowed by doubt. By rendering suspect the very racial and ethnic categories that mestizaje claims to undo, this politics of naming and claiming effectively reverses historical understandings of mestizaje as a 'natural' process that leads to categorical confusion and misrecognition (Rappaport 2014). Instead, mestizaje is taken *not* as an ideal to which society aspires, but rather as an achieved or normative status against which all claims to difference are articulated and judged.

As an example of this inversion in the political and ethical sensibilities surrounding mestizaje, in this article I look at discourses and practices surrounding the implementation of indigenous rights to free prior and informed consent (*Consentimiento previo, libre e informado*, or CPLI; in Peruvian law free prior and informed 'consultation'). The right to CPLI enters Peruvian constitutional law by virtue of the national government's signature on International Labour Organization (ILO) Convention 169. It thus provides a strong example of an international governance device whose implementation unfolds in relationship to specific racial and national formations. In the case of Peru, which signed the ILO 169 in 1994, indigeneity has historically been measured in terms of a group's proximity to (or descent from) pre-Columbian Andean and Amazonian 'cultures'. The ideals of cultural and racial purity that inform this genealogical calculus can be traced to the evolutionary perspectives forwarded by early Peruvian archaeology, criminology, and anthropology (Poole 1990). Their enduring hold on Peruvian political and social life, however, must also be explained in terms of the governmentalist frameworks (and modernist political ideologies – including those on the Left) through which 'indigenous' populations have been imagined as existing 'outside' the Peruvian polity and national culture. As we shall see, this same understanding of identity informs the design of the technical instruments through which the Peruvian Ministry of Culture defines which populations *might* someday access the ethnically circumscribed right to CPLI. Whereas the exclusions that result from such policies are clearly discriminatory and thus 'racist', my interest here is to understand how the concepts that enable racial thought gain political force through technical devices and metrics that are widely seen as objective or 'post-ideological'.

Indigenous indicators

On 23 June 2015, nearly four years after approval of the law ratifying Peru's signing of the ILO agreement, and more than three years after approval of the enabling legislation that stipulates how indigenous consultations are to be implemented in Peru, the Vice-minister of Interculturality (*Interculturalidad*) announced the publication of a database of indigenous peoples (*pueblos indígenas*).[4] The 2015 database, which lists 54 'indigenous peoples' organized around broad language families, was compiled in response to a legal mandate to provide a 'free public instrument for the purposes of identifying indigenous people' and as a 'reference tool' for the implementation of future 'indigenous consultations'.[5]

The 2015 database was a revised version of an earlier database that had been briefly posted on the Ministry of Culture's website in October 2013.[6] Coinciding, as it did, with some of Peru's most highly contested – and violent – mining conflicts, the 2013 database was greeted, even before its publication, with both public controversy and legal challenges. As a result, it was removed from the Ministry of Culture's website by executive order, less than 24 hours after its initial posting.

Controversy concerning the 2013 database centered on the implications of a technical device that held the potential to render the political promise of consultation actionable as a legal right. Both the Humala government and the mining companies, for example, objected that such a database – whose creation was mandated in the framework law on indigenous rights – would offer a misleading sense of juridical entitlement to those 'peoples' who were named as indigenous in the database. Indeed, government spokespersons, including President Humala, were quick to point out that the database should not be taken as constitutive of rights ('*no tiene carácter constitutiva de derechos*').[7] For these actors, the database was to provide a technical baseline for defining (or naming) those demographic groups that *might* someday have access to 'indigenous rights', including the right to prior consultation.[8] In addition, and as I describe in more detail below, even if the database had been described in law as a normative, rather than 'merely technical' instrument (i.e., an instrument that could be taken as constitutive of rights), the fact that it had been compiled by an administrative branch of the national government meant that it was legally non-binding. As a result of these two, mutually reinforcing limitations in the database's legal and administrative design, even those groups that were named in the database as 'indigenous peoples' were not therefore guaranteed rights to 'prior consultation' on any particular 'development' project.[9] Not only does such an indefinite formulation cohere with the open-ended temporality of a mode of planning in which the development projects that would be subject to 'consultation' are projected as a series of multiple *possible* scenarios (Abram and Weszkalnyu 2011; Amoore 2013; Faubion 2015; Poole 2015), it also places clear parameters on the agency of the many indigenous organizations that had actively lobbied for implementation of the 1994 Consultation Law.

Criticisms from indigenous organizations and the Peruvian Left, meanwhile, addressed: (a) the *timing* of the database's publication vis-à-vis existing extractive projects; (b) the specific criteria and metrics used to designate particular groups as 'indigenous' (or not); and (c) the impossibility of rendering the political concept (or category) of 'community' commensurate with the technical criteria used to decide who was (and was not) 'indigenous'. Indigenous concerns regarding the timing of the database centered on the government's repeated assertions that the right to consultation would not apply to either the exploration phase of petroleum and mining license, or to the exploitation phase of projects that had been previously approved or were already underway (see CEPPAW 2014; O'diana Rocca, Chuecas Cabrera, and Vega Díaz 2015).

In terms of the indicators used to define 'indigeneity', human rights activists and intellectuals objected most vociferously to the idea that language preference or mother tongue should be taken as a necessary marker of indigeneity. Peasant organizations, on the other hand, focused their critiques – and legal claims (*demandas*) – on the criteria of territoriality and the continuous possession of communal lands.[10] Such criteria, they argued, effectively excluded the large number of communities whose lands or territories had been coercively or violently taken from them. A final objection raised by indigenous and human rights organizations concerned the Vice-ministry's failure to meet legal requirements for public transparency, as well as their failure to consult indigenous peoples and organizations about the criteria it would use to decide who was – and was not – 'indigenous'. In this sense, a database, seen as a technical instrument for the identification of indigenous peoples, had violated the political rights that it was intended to facilitate – but not guarantee.

The distance separating the database's technical indicators of 'identity' from the political frameworks through which the state delegates citizenship rights, however, came through most clearly in criticisms leveled at the Ministerio's understanding of 'community'. The 2013 database, for example, divided its 52 'indigenous peoples' (*pueblos indígenas*) into 5571 communities. Of these, over 60 per cent were located in high Andean regions such as Cusco, Puno, Apurimac, and Huancavelica, where some of the country's largest mining and hydroelectric projects had already been approved, without the benefit of prior consultation (Amancio and Romano 2015; Ruiz Molledo 2012).[11] Not only did many of these 5571 – predominantly bilingual – peasant communities fail to meet the language and cultural criteria that the Vice-ministry considered necessary for classification as an 'indigenous people'.[12] They were also located in regions such as the Andean highlands which the Peruvian government and industry leaders had declared to be void of indigenous peoples, in large part *because* – as they argued – the 'communities' found in these regions already formed part of a modern Peruvian 'nation-state'. For some, such as Peru's Minister of Energy and Mining (MEM) it was simply 'absurd' to suggest that 'indigenous' consultations might need to be implemented for the 'peasant communities' that were affected by several (very) large gold mines located in the southern Andean region of Apurimac.[13] A year later, the general manager (*gerente general*) of one of Peru's largest mining consortiums (Buenaventura) similarly asserted that the consultation law could not possibly apply in the Peruvian highlands where, he claimed, 'there are no indigenous communities'.[14]

At stake in such arrogant assertions of 'fact' is an image of Peruvian territoriality in which 'indigeneity' is necessarily marginal to or 'outside' the bounds of the national polity. Conversely, the idea that 'peasants' who participate in political organizations or officially recognized 'communities' might also be considered indigenous was simply not allowed. Peruvian president Ollanta Humala, for example, repeatedly cited the 'agrarian' or 'peasant' nature of highland and coastal communities to suggest that many Andean and coastal communities could never meet the criteria necessary to qualify as 'indigenous'.[15] On other occasions, he cited as evidence of their non-indigenous character the fact that these communities also participate in Peruvian governmental programs.[16] For Humala, as for others, these historical patterns of integration or 'assimilation' into national administrative and political structures effectively negate the condition of marginality or exclusion, which government and industry spokespersons mistakenly interpret as ILO and UN prerequisites for recognition as an 'indigenous people'.[17]

In claiming that 'marginality' is equivalent to exclusion and that exclusion constitutes a necessary criterion for attaining status as an 'indigenous rights holder', Humala invoked long-standing traditions concerning both the irreversibility and the inevitability of mestizaje as a form of political or social inclusion, and long-standing European (and Catholic) understandings of *vecindad* as an identity and place claim that replaces (and is necessarily opposed to) indigenous understandings of political community.[18] Thus in denying indigeneity to peasant communities, Humala takes the additional step of forecasting the future 'integration' of the 'very few communities' that do not already have state-recognized political authorities, and the consequent likelihood that 'abuses such as those that occurred in previous centuries, are less likely to occur' (cited in Ilizarbe 2013).

To be 'indigenous' in Peru therefore requires that communities remain not only unassimilated or 'pure'. The abuses they endure as *unassimilated populations* must also be documented as permanent and unchanging.[19] Needless to say, these positions resonate strongly with inherited understandings of mestizaje as a condition that pertains to any group or individual who has *left behind* their indigenous identity to participate in 'modern' (or criollo) culture and society.[20] In such a context of *naming*, any attempts to *claim* indigenous status were received with suspicion as either inauthentic or 'political' in the sense that they were 'interest driven'. Indeed, the very fact of participating in – or demanding – a state-led 'consultation' was itself interpreted as an act that put into doubt the forms of separation, exclusion, or marginalization that the database deemed essential for the definition of an 'indigenous' people.

Commensuration and continual review

What unites these objections to the database from both the Left and the Right is the problem of how to accommodate the *political* and juridical question of who constitutes a collective rights-holding subject of law (in this case, an 'indigenous people'), with the *technical* (as well as governmentalist) question of who 'counts' as an indigenous population (cf. Galvez and Sosa 2013; Rousseau 2012). Faced with such a problematic, the Viceministry has attempted to defend their database by pointing out that technical criteria – much like politics itself – should be seen as both flexible and negotiable. Thus, in his response to the broadly political objections coming from both indigenous organizations and the mining sector, then vice-minister Ivan Lanegra noted simply that both the 2013 database and the criteria it deployed would, in the future, be 'subjected to continual revision' (La *República*, 25 October 2013). Here Lanegra offers 'continual review' as a solution to the question of how a database that purports to provide a neutral list of defined cultural 'identities' can be accommodated within the open-ended temporalities of neoliberal governance and planning (on planning, see Abram and Weszkalnyu 2011; Faubion 2015).

'Continual Review', however, also resonates with the skeptical disposition of mestizaje as a process and identity that cannot be fixed in time. Thus, for example, in a subsequent interview on the 2013 database, Lanegra defended the use of technical definitions of indigeneity on the grounds that they 'allow us to differentiate between cultural diversity and an indigenous people'.[21] If a community or group was to satisfy the criteria for inclusion in the database, it must do so by showing that it stands outside the historical currents of mixture, inclusion, and acculturation that have 'diversified' their communities and cultures – converting them, in the logic of 'mestizaje', into an 'imperfect' or less 'pure' form of indigeneity. At the same time, however, and as scholars have noted for other parts of the world, the forms of evidence required in law to prove the purity or 'authenticity' of an indigenous culture rely on the sorts of tangible or measurable attributes (or 'indicators') that cannot easily be accommodated with the idea of cultural 'continuity' in time (Povinelli 2002).[22] Seen from this perspective, a database might be said to be more useful for revealing the existence of a suspiciously mestizo diversity than it would be for certifying either 'authenticity' or 'indigeneity'.

The revised 2015 database offered technical adjustments as responses to the objections that were raised from both sides of the 2013 controversy. Specifically, in the new database the total number of recognized 'indigenous peoples' was increased by two (from 52 to 54). More significantly, the revised database addressed objections (and lawsuits) from highland peasant federations by including a rubric for 'Quechua (speaking) peoples'. Through such adjustments, the 2015 database reinforced ministerial claims that the database could be perfected through a 'continual review' of the specific indicators or criteria it deploys to define an 'indigenous people'. In this view of the database, all objections – including political objections to the idea that 'indigeneity' itself can be measured and defined – are necessarily received as suggestions for how to tweak or improve the instrument's technical parameters, rather than as broad political or epistemological critiques of the database's spirit and purpose.

At the same time, and as a commitment to the principle of 'continual review', the 2015 database also introduced a new strategy for how large, culturally 'diverse' language groups might be rendered commensurate with both the technical criteria required for the definition of an 'indigenous people', and government (as well as industry) concerns about the overrepresentation of majority indigenous groups. Thus, although the new database included a separate listing for 'the Quechua', which the database describes as 'the (country's) majority indigenous population', the attribution of a possible collective 'Quechua identity' is immediately qualified by the claim that members of this diverse group do not share a uniform 'identity' or 'denomination'. Instead, 'the Quechua peoples' are described as made up of 'a (varied) group of identities (*un conjunto* de *identidades*)' including the 'Chopccas, Huancas, Chankas, Huaylas, Q'eros, Cañaris, K'ana'.[23] At the same time, the Vice-ministry of Interculturality (VMI) has attempted to justify both this depiction of the Quechua as a 'diverse' group, and their reliance on language preference (mother tongue) as an indicator of indigeneity in the highlands, by alleging that 'little information is available on the history and culture of Peru's highland Andean communities' (Ivan Lanegra, cited in La *República*, 23 June 2015).[24] In this way, the database projects a category of 'Quechua peoples' that is both technically precise and open to continual review: In short, it provides a rubric that allows a large sector of Peru's peasant population (and 15 per cent of its own national population) to be included in the database as an 'identity' that is endlessly shadowed by doubt.

Contingent suspects

The database controversy speaks on several different registers to the forms of suspicion that I have argued constitute the legacy of mestizaje in 21st-century Peru. Not only are actual claims to indigenous status greeted with skepticism (if not outright refusal); even the technical criteria through which indigenous groups are to be legally identified are themselves framed either as contingent in the sense of being 'subject to continual review and improvement', or – as in the case of the sources cited in the Vice-ministry's 'History of the Quechua People' – judged to be insufficiently 'technical' and hence non-authoritative. In short, even the criteria that will be used to evaluate potential, future claims to indigenous status are framed by the database as epistemological uncertainties.

While the exclusions generated by the application of such criteria may well map quite neatly onto the racial, class, and regional categories through which certain populations have been historically rendered as either racially or culturally 'inferior', it is not, in my mind, sufficient to explain the workings of such devices as the ideological outcome of either racism, or an always and already racialized social formation (although both of these are very much present in the history of Peru; Drinot 2011; Sulmont and Callirgos 2015). Instead, it has been my argument here that the skeptical dispositions that shadow the database and consultations are not produced through ideational or representational inheritances alone (in this case the idea that human difference can be precisely cali-brated and described through a metric of 'race;' Poole 1997). Rather, these provocations to doubt gain both political force and social traction through governmental devices and administrative instruments that are widely understood as 'neutral' or technical devices. In making such a claim, I draw on a Foucauldian understanding that power is exercised through *both* the political rationalities (or ideologies) that inform and motivate the modern state as a constellation of political and economic interests, *and* the specific forms of intervention or procedures through which 'the state' makes its presence felt in the administration of everyday life (Foucault 2007; see also Elden 2007; Mitchell 2002). Seen from this perspective, ideas of both race and mestizaje acquire differentiated force as the object of government moves across the fixed certainties of territory to the uncertain dynamics and deterritorializing vitalities of biological populations and 'milieus' (Elden 2007; Foucault 2007).[25]

A particular – though not unique – convergence of territorial and biopolitical government has taken hold in Peru around the strong disciplinary languages that differentiate between the 'degenerate' or historical indigeneity of Peru's post-Inca Andean populations, and the more 'pristine' or 'ahistorical' indigenous formations of the eastern Andean and lowland Amazonian forests. As we have seen in the database example, these same dichotomies inform not only 'popular' or 'ideological' understandings of 'biopolitical populations' and 'race' in Peru (de la Cadena 2008; García and Lucero 2011; Greene 2006; Pajuelo Teves 2010); they also shape the material apparatus through which citizenship rights and 'identities' are defined and distributed in Peru's decentralized, administrative state.[26]

At the same time, however, neither reliance on disciplinary knowledge nor the calculative metrics of administrative or managerial government are necessarily 'new'. Indeed, it is the deep historical involvement of such disciplinary forms in state rule that accounts for their status in the shaping of entrenched 'common sense' understandings of both race and identity in Peru. Thus, since at least the early 20th century, Andean indigenous populations have been governed through ministries and technical directorates led by lawyers and anthropologists whose formation privileged positivist history, philology, and philosophy over the 'scientific' study of, for example, biology or 'race' (Poole 1997). Ironically, the histories of both prior civilizational achievement and subsequent degeneration that Peruvian intellectuals, politicians, and bureaucrats deployed in their arguments for the enduring nature of an indigenous 'Andean ethos', have worked to project the idea that these same rural Andean populations are *more* disposed than their supposedly uncivilized lowland counterparts to the forms of cultural, linguistic, and racial mixture that have been glossed, in Peru as elsewhere, as 'mestizaje'. At the same time, the emphasis placed in Peruvian indigenista and anthropological thought on the ideational and spiritual unity of highland Quechua and Aymara cultures led to a conceptual 'deterritorialization' of Andean indigeneity as an identity formation that exceeds any specific territorial or material home.[27] Indeed, the addendum on Quechua peoples that accompanies the 2015 database opens by noting that 'Quechua peoples' are dispersed across at least three national territories (Peru, Ecuador, and Bolivia).[28]

This deterritorialization of cultural and racial 'identities' in the Andes contrasts strongly with notions of Amazonian indigeneity as intimately *placed* (if not bounded) (Chirif and García Hierro 2007). More importantly for my argument here, however, it also resonates with a model of post-regulatory governance and state decentralization in which political responsibilities and technical competencies are themselves dispersed – or 'deterritorialized' – across multiple instances of local (municipal), regional, national, and international governance.[29] In such a state system, the forms of economic investment – or 'development' – that require prior 'consultation' from local stakeholders are regulated through international laws that exceed the sovereign territory of Peru. In Peru indigenous consultations, which are mandated by international treaties and agreements, represent a particular instantiation of this model of distributed sovereignty in that political and administrative responsibility for implementation of the consultations is dispersed across several different territorial and political layerings of Peru's newly decentralized state (Szablowski 2010).[30] Within this complex landscape of post-regulatory governance, it is significant that a state agency such as the VMI, which has no direct representation at the cabinet level, is assigned political responsibility for articulating the principle of consultation as a non-binding administrative policy or norm.

At the same time, responsibility for implementing such policies is assigned to Ministries (such as the Ministry of Mining and Energy and the Ministry of the Environment) with direct political representation on the cabinet level. Such an arrangement works not only to reinforce the strictly *technical* competencies and reach of the VMI's responsibilities; it also delegates responsibility for implementing consultations to ministers whose principal governmental responsibility is to forward the same investment and development projects that are, theoretically, subject to consultation. This segmentation of political authority, contrasts with other countries – such as Colombia – where competencies for both designing and implementing indigenous consultation are assigned to a single instance of the state (in Colombia, the Ministry of the Interior; Galvez and Sosa 2013, 11; see also; Padillo Rubiano 2013).[31]

This already complex regulatory landscape is further complicated by the Vice-ministry's status as a 'decentralized' agency whose technical and political competencies are distributed spatially and politically across 25 regional directorates that answer both to the Ministry of Culture and to their respective regional governments (DS 005–2013-MC). In addition, as one of two 'viceministries' within a ministry that was itself formed in 2010 as a replacement for the National Institute of Culture (INC), the VMI has unclear political status within Peru's national government. Thus, whereas the INC retained limited autonomy vis-à-vis the Executive Branch of Peru's national government, the Minister of Culture (who is appointed by the president) represents the VMI as one layering of a national ministry. It may also be worth noting that the VMI was itself created and designed with the mission of governing and regulating the same sorts of 'intercultural' relationships that both the government and the Vice-ministry's own mission statement evoke as signs of a 'mestizaje' (or diversity) that is understood to be contrary to the principal of 'indigeneity' as a pristine, or non-assimilated, identity.[32] In this way, claims to indigeneity (or indigenous consultation) acquire traction through the ILO 169 and other international instruments, only to be elided – or at best, rendered suspect – by the sorts of administrative and technical knowledges that make post-regulatory or 'neoliberal' government possible (Li 2015; Pinto 2009; Sabel and Zeitlin 2012). Political rights *and the groups that have access to those rights* are, in this way constituted through criteria that are forwarded as overtly 'technical', and thus 'non-negotiable'.

Conclusion

While few will question the need for both 'precision' and 'neutrality' in the administration of resources and rights, governmental reliance on technical devices such as databases presents novel challenges for the articulation of political responses to the use of such inherited concepts as mestizaje, race, and identity. Indeed, as the case of Peru makes clear, mestizaje – like other 'racial' and cultural discourses – has produced uneven and, at times, contradictory effects. One such effect is what I have called the ethos of suspicion within which all claims to racial, ethnic, and moral status are both enunciated and received. This disposition surfaces in state actors' responses to the idea that communities that speak Spanish, use cellphones, and participate in municipal budgeting or national elections do not qualify as 'indigenous peoples' who can access internationally mandated 'rights to consultation'.[33]

Mestizaje, in this view of the world, constitutes much more than a mode of differentiating racial and cultural categories. It colors the ethical postures and affective dispositions surrounding *all* individual and collective responses to the claims (and lives) of 'others'. My argument is that the forms of suspicion that run through the database controversy speak both to the idea of mestizaje as an inherited ethical disposition from which others' claims to identity and status are routinely questioned if not disbelieved, and to the *specific* ways in such skepticism is magnified by the forms of technical reasoning and administrative governance that characterize the post-regulatory neoliberal state. Thus, in the database example, we see how political *ideals* of diversification, mestizaje, and inclusion that were traditionally considered 'progressive' are reconfigured as empirical qualities – or 'indicators' – that not only disqualify certain claims to citizenship rights (the right to consultation), but also, in so doing, mark such claims as morally suspect, if not scandalous. In this respect, we might think of mestizaje as effecting a sort of permanent scandal in modern capitalist societies, insofar as the forms of suspicion that surround any and all claims to ethnic territories or rights disrupt liberal democracy's foundational discourse of equity, universal citizenship, and transparency.[34]

At the same time, as features of an allegedly 'neutral' database, the criteria deployed in the differentiation of indigenous and non-indigenous identities render such scandals technical rather than political in nature. Of course, critics and activists have been quick to denounce the exclusions that have resulted from the Vice-ministry's vacillation on indigeneity either as politically motivated or as overtly ideological or racist. In their engagements with the database controversy itself, however, these same critics have tended to accept the possibility that the database might in fact 'work', if we could only just improve – or refine – the criteria it uses to differentiate indigenous from non-indigenous communities. As a technical device, the database in this sense holds out the hope that such a project to craft a transparent, 'universal' metric for indigeneity might, some day, succeed.

I agree with these critics that the sorts of foot-dragging and denial that have characterized efforts to implement prior consultation in Peru speak quite eloquently to the Peruvian government's privileging of mining and macroeconomic indicators over the needs of its citizens and the environment. What interests me *here*, however, is to understand how racialized attitudes concerning who qualifies for 'indigenous' or 'special' rights are simultaneously masked and made possible by the *particular* sorts of technical and administrative reasoning that underwrite the formation of such a 'database'. As examples of such reasoning, we might think of the Vice-ministry's disclaimers regarding the lack of reliable (government generated) information on Quechua communities – and their consequent reliance on the 'soft data' they could cull from the inherently untrustworthy disciplines of anthropology and history. The Vice-minister's blanket dismissal of the substantial literatures on Andean history and culture will strike those of us who have spent our lives dedicated to the production of such knowledge as absurd. It may also resonate unpleasantly with the long history of both political disavowal and existential doubt that has surrounded the production of anthropological knowledge in the Andean region. What gives particular force to such a claim in 21st-century Peru, however, is the shared illusion that it is not only possible, but *desirable* to create a universal metric for gauging the purity of identities that are inherently fluid and political (García and Lucero 2011; Pajuelo Teves 2006, 2010; Paredes 2010; Rousseau 2012; Galvez and Sosa 2013).

Notes

1. Although Peru's 1930 constitution recognized indigenous communities as rights-bearing juridical subjects (Davies 1970), the national penal code defined indigenous subjects as 'minors' in need of protected status (Poole 1990). On ethnicity in early republican censuses, see Gootenberg (1991).
2. In the past decade, Peru's highly centralized state has been dramatically restructured through the delegation of administrative competencies to subnational layers of government (regional and municipal governments) that have very limited fiscal, juridical, or legislative autonomy vis-à-vis the national or 'central' state. In describing the new state form as 'neoliberal' I refer principally to the ideological principles of participation and subsidiarity that animate this model of administrative and political decentralization. In describing the state as 'post-regulatory', I refer to the governance mechanisms, including and especially international legal and regulatory agreements, through which sovereignty has been effectively redistributed across diverse layerings of national, international, and subnational government. On sovereignty in the post-regulatory state, see Black (2002), Broude and Shany (2008), Scott (2005), Szablowski (2007). On decentralization, see Ballon (2011), Eaton (2014), McNulty (2011), Remy (2013b). On neoliberal planning, see Abram and Weszkalnyu (2011), Beard, Miraftab, and Silver (2008), Poole (2015).
3. On neoliberal decentralization and ideologies of subsidiary, locality, and participation, see among others, Broude and Shany (2008), Obarrio (2014), Orta (2013), Pajuelo Teves (2006), Poole (2006), Remy (2011).
4. Ley 29,785 *Ley del Derecho a La Consulta Previa a Los Pueblos Indígenas u Originarios, reconocido en el Convenio 169* de La *Organización Internacional del Trabajo*, 7 set 2011 (Peru Ministerio de Cultura 2012). For critical analyses of the law and its implementation, see Coordinadora (CNDH) (2012), Galvez and Sosa (2013), Ramos et al. (2011), Ruiz Molledo (2012), Sosa Villagarcia et al. (2012). On the role of Peruvian indigenous organizations and demands in the crafting of the law, see, among others, Herrera Rodríguez (2014), Ramos et al. (2011), Ruiz Molledo (2012), Sifuentes (2013).
5. Directiva No.03-2012/MC: 'Directiva que regula el funcionamiento de la Base de Datos Oficial de Pueblos Indigenas u Originarios,' Lima, Ministerio de Cultura, May 2012.
6. See, http://bdpi.cultura.gob.pe, accessed 9 September 2015; http://redaccion.lamulaverde. pe/2015/06/23/ministerio-de-cultura-concluye-primera-etapa-de-difusion-de-la-historia-de -54-pueblos-indigenas/ecabral/, accessed 30 July 2015.
7. See, for example, President Humala's interview with David Rivera and Nicolás Lúcar, *TV Perú*, 28 April 2013.
8. Article 29, Decreto Supremo No. 001-2012-MC *Reglamento* de La *Ley No29785*. 'Funciones del Viceministerio de interculturalidad,' *El Peruano. 3.IV. 2012, 44,594.*
9. 'Base de datos sobre pueblos indígenas es referencial: Se incrementará poco a poco,' *Servindi*, 27 October 2013. Accessed 28 August 2015. http://servindi.org/actualidad/95452.

10. Territorial criteria figure in the database in reference to a group's location in both national and 'ancestral' territories: 'historical continuity', which is considered a leading 'objective indicator' of indigenous status, is defined in terms of *permanencia en el territorio nacional desde tiempos previos al establecimiento del Estado;*' and 'Conexión territorial', is then defined as 'La *ocupación* de *una zona del pais por parte* de *los ancestros* de La*s poblaciones referidas*' (Directiva 03-2012/MC, Art.7.1.3).

11. A short time after congressional approval of the law, the Constitutional Tribunal ruled that prior consultation could not be made retroactive for projects approved before June 2010 (Sentencia 06316-209-PA).

12. On bilingualism in Peruvian Andes, see Harvey (1991, 2008).

13. In response to a query about the Apurimac projects, the Minister replied simply: '*Indios en Apurimac. No jodas!*' (Jorge Merino [2012], cited in Sifuentes 2013).

14. 'In the highlands of Peru, there are no indigenous communities only peasant communities' (Roque Benavides, cited in Diez 2013).

15. '*En las tierras andinas hay principalmente comunidades agrarias...las comunidades indigenas estan en su mayoria en* La *selva*' (D. Rivera and N. Lúcar, Interview with Ollanta Humala, *TV Perú*, 28 April 2013; cited in Galvez and Sosa 2013, 10).

16. '*Hoy en día son pocas las comunidades que no tienen una autoridad como un alcalde o teniente alcalde y así en cadena llegar al gobierno regional o al presidente* de La *República. Más aún, con el avance* de *los medios* de *comunicación como para que suceda un abuso como los que había en el siglo diecinueve o veinte*' (*Servindi.org*, April, 29, 2013). Through such claims, government spokespersons advance a criteria of authenticity in which *any* participation in governmental structures will be taken as a form of an urbanity or political modernity that effectively rules out antecedent claims to indigeneity. For other examples, see Ruiz Molledo (2012) and Marapi Salas (2013).

17. The ILO 169 nowhere states, as Humala and other Peruvian government spokespersons have claimed, that 'marginality' is a *necessary* condition for attaining indigenous status or rights.

18. On *vecindad*, see Arguedas (1968). In a more immediate sense, of course, Humala's claims also refer to the state's own reclassification of 'indigenous communities' as 'peasant communities' during the 1970s agrarian reform led by General Velasco Alvarado.

19. Here, I note the intriguing fact that both the database and the government consider documented 'abuses' as necessary criteria for defining indigenous people, thus suggesting that any group that aspires to remain 'indigenous' must also be prepared to forever endure the 'abuses' that the government considers constitutive of indigenous bodies and lands.

20. Humala himself frequently insists that only 'uncontacted' groups can be made to 'count' as indigenous. Interestingly, as of 2015, the same Vice-ministry charged with compiling the data base has taken on the task of locating – and producing studies of – all of Peru's 'uncontacted' indigenous nations. The question remains whether the fact of having been contacted by a government agency will be taken as evidence that such groups are no longer to be considered as 'indigenous'.

21. '*que nos permitan diferenciar una diversidad cultural frente a un pueblo indígena*' (Ivan Lanegra in interview with Javier Torres in La *Mula TV*, March 2013. Accessed 27 July 2015. https://redaccion.lamula.pe/2013/03/22/viceministro-lanegra-explica-retraso-en-publicacion-de-base-de-datos-de-pueblos-indigenas/jorgepaucar/.

22. Historical criteria such as authenticity generally carry greater weight in the legal definition of indigeneity in common law countries than in the civil law systems of Peru and other Latin American countries (see Poole 2012). Government programs for the promotion of tangible and intangible 'culture', have furthered technical understandings of both culture and indigeneity through policies designed to produce indicators for measuring the contributions of Peru's 'cultural DNA' to national development and economic growth. Such programs move away from the notion of culture or identity as a dynamic, continually emergent process, to project an ideal of culture (and identity) as a temporally stable essence (see Peru Ministerio de Cultura and UNESCO-CDIS 2015).

23. *'los pueblos quechuas no tienen otras denominaciones, más sí un conjunto* de *identidades, entre las que se encuentran: Chopccas, Huancas, Chankas, Huaylas, q'eros, Cañaris, Kana'* (accessed 20 August 2015, from http://bdpi.cultura.gob.pe/). The 'identities' cited refer to regional Quechua-speaking ethnicities associated with bounded communities or historical territories in the regions of Cusco (Q'eros, Kana), Ayacucho (Chankas; Huancas), Junin (Huaylas), and San Martin (Cañaris).

24. This assertion is repeated in the introduction to the 'History and Culture of the Andean Peoples' that accompanies the 2015 database. In this document, the Vice-ministry's decision to retain mother-tongue as key (technical) indicator of indigenous status in the highlands is justified by referring to the scarcity of 'official' or state-produced knowledge about Andean peoples: *'Frente a* la *escasa información oficial que el Estado peruano ha producido con relación a los pueblos indígenas andinos,* la *lengua indígena como idioma materno es un elemento clave que ha contribuido a* la *identificación* de *estos pueblos. No obstante, es importante precisar que* la *lengua no constituye el único elemento a considerar para* la *identificación* de *pueblos indígenas y que tampoco es una condición imprescindible.'* (accessed 20 August 2015, from http://bdpi.cultura.gob.pe/pueblo/quechuas).

25. These modes of 'disciplinary' and 'biopolitical' government are neither historically sequential nor mutually exclusive. Rather, as theorized by Foucault and as exemplified in the database example discussed here, biopolitical populations and sovereign territoriality are best approached as contemporaneous emphases or overlapping fields within both post-regulatory governance and the Peruvian neoliberal state.

26. The question of how to define 'indigeneity', also figured prominently in the 2016 Peruvian national elections; see http://www.servindi.org/actualidad-noticias/15/03/2016/las-promesas-de-los-candidatos-para-los-pueblos-indigenas (accessed 5 July 2016).

27. This view of Andean culture has been forwarded as both a political claim for the utopian qualities of Andean political formations (Flores Galindo 1993), and as an argument for the progressive nature of cultural and racial mixtures (*cholaje*) in the Peruvian Andes (see, for example, Garcia [1930] 1973); on indigenista appeals to mixture, see also de la Cadena (2000), Mendoza (2008), Poole (1997).

28. See http://bdpi.cultura.gob.pe (accessed 20 August 2015).

29. On decentralization in Peru, see, among others, Ballon (2011), Eaton (2010, 2014), McNulty (2011), Remy (2013b).

30. On dispersion of administrative capacity in decentralized and post-regulatory state forms, see Scott (2005).

31. In comparing the Peruvian and Colombian models, I do not wish to imply that the Colombian 'model' is in any way preferable or ideal. Rather, I contrast them so as to underscore the importance of tracking the particularities of both state form and the specific administrative and disciplinary technologies deployed in evaluating (and contesting) the outcomes of internationally mandated 'consultations'.

32. On its webpage, the Vice-ministry defines its objective as a governmental agency as that of 'Formulating policies programs and projects, that promote intercultural relations (la interculturalidad) as a means to…construct a citizenry (*ciudadanía*) that recognizes, respects, and is enriched through interaction with cultural diversity.' The Vice-ministry is organized into two directorates, the 'Directorate of Indigenous Peoples' and the 'Directorate of an Intercultural Citizenry': whereas the former is assigned responsibility for 'indigenous consultations', the latter is assigned responsibility for 'Indigenous Policies' (*Políticas Indígenas*). See http://www.cultura.gob.pe/interculturalidad (accessed 15 August 2015).

33. In an August 2013 confrontation over a proposed gas drilling project, Peruvian First Lady Nadine Heredia questioned the Vice-ministry of Inerculturality's jurisdiction over the project because *'un indígena que tiene celular ya no es indígena'* (Los Andes, 19 August 2013; see http://www.losandes.com.pe/Opinion/20130819/74074.html [accessed 5 July 2016]).

34. I do not want to argue that this 'scandal' is in any way unique to 'racialized' expressions of state power. Instead, I argue that the affects of suspicion and doubt that surround mestizaje can more productively be seen as expressions of the modes of uncertainty,

illegibility, and fear that typify modern state power as a zone of exception; see Asad (2004), Poole (2004). On scandal, see Deleuze and Guattari (2007).

References

Abram, S., and G. Weszkalnyu. 2011. "Introduction: Anthropologies of Planning – Temporality, Imagination and Ethnography." *Focaal-Journal of Global and Historical Anthropology* 61: 3–18.

Amancio, N. L., and V. Roma. 2015. "Los Secretos Mineros detras de la lista de comunidades indígenas del Peru." *Ojo Publico*, July 22. Accessed 28 August 2015. http://ojo-publico.com/77/los-secretos-detras-de-la-lista-de-comunidades-indigenas-del-peru

Amoore, L. 2013. *The Politics of Possibility: Risk and Security Beyond Probability*. Durham, NC: Duke University Press.

Appelbaum, N., A. S. MacPherson, and K. Rosemblat, eds. 2003. *Race and Nation in Modern Latin America*. Chapel Hill: University of North Carolina Press.

Arguedas, J. M. 1968. *Las comunidades de España yel Perú*. Lima: Universidad Nacional Mayor de San Marcos.

Asad, T. 2004. "Where are the Margins of the State?" In *Anthropology in the Margins of the State*, edited by V. Das and D. Poole, 279–288. Santa Fe, NM: SAR Press.

Ballon, E. 2011. "Decentralization." In *Fractured Politics: Peruvian Democracy Past and Present*, edited by J. Crabtree, 187–216. London: University of London Press.

Beard, V. A., F. Miraftab, and C. Silver, eds. 2008. *Planning and Decentralization: Contested Spaces for Public Action in the Global South*. New York: Routledge.

Black, J. 2002. "Decentring Regulation: Understanding the Role of Regulation and Self- Regulation in a 'Post-Regulatory' World." In *Current Legal Problems 54*, edited by M. Freeman, 103–146. New York: Oxford University Press.

Broude, T., and Y. Shany. 2008. *The Shifting Allocation of Authority in International Law: On Sovereignty, Supremacy, and Subsidiarity*. Oxford: Hart Publishers.

CEPPAW (Comisión Especial Permanente de los Pueblos Awajún y Wampis). 2014. *Lote 116' Pueblos Awajun y Wampis sin derecho de consulta previa, respuesta reciente del Viceministerio de Inerculturalidad*. Lima: CEPPAW.

Chirif, A., and P. García Hierro. 2007. *Marcando territorio: Progresos y limitaciones de la titulación de territorios indígenas en la Amazonía*. Copenhagen: IIGIA.

CNDH (Coordinadora Nacional de Derechos Humanos). 2012. *Análisis del Reglamento de la Ley de Consulta Previa*, DS Num. 001-2012-MC. Lima: CNDH.

Cope, R. D. 1994. *The Limits of Racial Domination: Plebeian Society in Colonial Mexico City, 1660-1720*. Madison: University of Wisconsin Press.

Davies, T. M. 1970. *Indian Integration in Peru: A Half Century of Experience, 1900-1948*. Lincoln: University of Nebraska Press.

Dawson, A. 2004. *Indian and Nation in Revolutionary Mexico*. Tucson: University of Arizona Press.

de la Cadena, M. 2000. *Indigenous Mestizos: The Politics of Race and Culture in Cuzco, Peru, 1919-1991*. Durham, NC: Duke University Press.

de la Cadena, M. 2008. "Alternative Indigeneities: Conceptual Proposals." *Latin American and Caribbean Ethnic Studies* 3 (3): 341–349. doi:10.1080/17442220802462501.

Degregori, C. I. 1993. "Identidades etnicas, movimientos sociales y participacion politica en el Perú." In *Democracia, etnicidad y violencia política en los paises andinos*, 113–133. Lima: IEP.

Deleuze, G. 1995. *Difference and Repetition*. Translated and edited by P. Patton. New York: Columbia University Press.

Deleuze, G., and F. Guattari. 2007. "Capitalism: A Very Special Delirium." In *Chaosophy*. Translated and edited by S. Lothringer, 35–52. New York: Autonomedia/Semotexte.

Diez, J. 2013. "En la sierra del Peru no existen comunidades indigenas." *La Mula*, September 22. Accessed 2 September 2015. https://.pe/2013/09/22/en-la-sierra- del-peru-no-existen-comunidades-indigenas/jonathandiez/

Drinot, P. 2011. *The Allure of Labor: Workers, Race, and the Making of the Peruvian State*. Durham, NC: Duke University Press.

Eaton, K. 2010. "Subnational Economic Nationalism? The Contradictory Effects of Decentralization in Peru." *Third World Quarterly* 31 (7): 1205–1222. doi:10.1080/01436597.2010.532612.

Eaton, K. 2014. "Disciplining Regions: Subnational Contention in Neoliberal Peru." *Territory, Politics, Governance* 3 (1–2): 124–146. doi:10.1080/21622671.2015.1005126.

Elden, S. 2007. "Governmentality, Calculation, Territory." *Environment and Planning D: Society and Space* 25: 562–580. doi:10.1068/d428t.

Faubion, J. D. 2015. "Stories of Things to Come, or Not." *The Futures We Want*. Accessed 15 June 2016. http://futureswewant.net/james-faubion-scenarios

Flores Galindo, A. 1993. *Buscando un Inca: Identidad y utopia en los Andes*. Lima: SUR.

Foucault, M. 2007. *Security, Territory, Population: Lectures at the Collège de France, 1978-1978*. Translated by G. Burchell. New York: Palgrave.

Galvez, A., and P. Sosa. 2013. "'El Problema del Indio': Una Mirada a la implementacion de la Consulta Previa desde la lógica del Estado y sus funcionarios." *Revista Argumentos*. Accessed 27 August 2015. http://revistaargumentos.iep.org.pe/articulos/el-problema-del-indio-una-mirada-a-la- implementacion-de-la-consulta-previa-desde-la-logica-del-estado-y-sus- funcionarios/

García, M. E., and J. A. Lucero. 2011. "Authenticating Indians and Movements: Interrogating Indigenous Authenticity, Social Movements and Field Work in Peru." In *Histories of Race and Racism: The Andes and Mesoamerica from Colonial Times to the Present*, edited by L. Gotkowitz, 278–298. Durham, NC: Duke University Press.

Garcia, U. [1930] 1973. *El Nuevo Indio*. Lima: Coleccion Autores Peruanos.

Gootenberg, P. 1991. "Population and Ethnicity in Early Republican Peru: Some Revisions." *Latin American Research Review* 26 (3): 109–157.

Gould, J. 1998. *To Die in This Way: Nicaraguan Indians and the Myth of Mestizaje*. Durham, NC: Duke University Press.

Greene, S. 2006. "Getting over the Andes: The Geo-Eco-Politics of Indigenous Movements in Peru's Twenty-First Century Inca Empire." *Journal of Latin American Studies* 38: 327–254. doi:10.1017/S0022216X06000733.

Hale, C. 2006. *Mas que un Indio (More than an Indian): Racial Ambivalence and Neoliberal Multiculturalism in Guatemala*. Santa Fe: SAR Press.

Harvey, P. 1991. "Drunken Speech and the Construction of Meaning: Bilingual Competence in the Southern Peruvian Andes." *Language in Society* 20 (1): 1–36. doi:10.1017/S0047404500016055.

Harvey, P. 2008. "Language States." In *A Companion to Latin American Anthropology*, edited by D. Poole, 193–213. Malden, MA: Blackwell.

Herrera Rodríguez, N. M. 2014. *La Ley de Consulta Previa en el Perú: La Problemática de las Comunidades Campesinas y Nativas*. Buenos Aires: Centro Internacional de Estudios Políticas, Universidad de San Martín. Accessed 19 July 2016. http://www.unsam.edu.ar/ciep/wp-content/uploads/2014/11/Nataly-Herrera-Rodriguez2.pdf

Ilizarbe, C. 2013. "El gobierno de Ollanta Humala y el discurso sobre los Pueblos Indígenas." *Servindi*, May 20. Accessed 19 July 2016. http://www.servindi.org/actualidad/87719

Li, F. 2015. *Unearthing Conflict: Corporate Mining, Activism and Expertise in Peru*. Durham, NC: Duke University Press.

Loveman, M. 2014. *National Colors: Racial Classification and the State in Latin America*. Oxford: Oxford University Press.

Marapi Salas, R. 2013. "Mantra politico. Donde están los pueblos indígenas en el discurso pre-sidencial de Ollanta Humala?" *Spaciolibre*. Accessed 31 July 2013. http://www.spaciolibre.pe/mantra-politico-donde-estan-los-pueblos-indigenas-en-el-discurso-presidencial-de-ollanta-humala/

Mayer, E. 2009. *Ugly Stories of the Peruvian Agrarian Reform*. Durham, NC: Duke University Press.

McNulty, S. L. 2011. *Voice and Vote: Decentralization and Participation in Post- Fujimori Peru*. Stanford: Stanford University Press.

Méndez, C. 2005. *The Plebian Republic: The Huanta Rebellion and the Making of the Peruvian State, 1820-1850*. Durham, NC: Duke University Press.

Mendoza, Z. 2008. *Creating Our Own: Folklore, Performance, and Identity in Cusco, Peru*. Durham, NC: Duke University Press.

Mitchell, T. 2002. *Rule of Experts: Egypt, Techno-politics, Modernity*. Berkeley: University of California Press.

O'diana Rocca, R., A. Chuecas Cabrera, and I. Vega Díaz. 2015. *Análisis de la aplicación de la consulta previa*. Magdalena del Mar, Peru: CAAAP. Accessed 5 July 2016. http://www.caaap.org.pe/website/wp-content/uploads/2015/08/consulta-previa18-marzo.pdf

Obarrio, J. 2014. *The Spirit of the Laws in Mozambique*. Chicago: University of Chicago Press.

Orta, A. 2013. "Forged Communities and Vulgar Citizens: Autonomy and its Limits in Semi-neoliberal Bolivia." *Journal of Latin American and Caribbean Anthropology* 18 (1): 108–133. doi:10.1111/j.1935-4940.2012.01249.x.

Padillo Rubiano, G. 2013. "Consulta previa en Colombia y sus desarrollos jurisprudenciales. Una lectura desde los pueblos indienas, los empresas y el Estado." In *Anuario de Derecho Constitucional Latinoamericano AÑO XIX*, 353–379. Bogotá: UNAM (Universidad Nacional Autonoma de Mexico).

Pajuelo Teves, R. 2006. *Participación política indígena en la sierra peruana. Una aproximación desde las dinámicas nacionales y locales*. Lima: Instituto de Estudios Peruanos.

Pajuelo Teves, R. 2010. "Movimientos indigenas y política nacional en los Andes: Ideas para un balance." *Peru Hoy*, July: 299–320.

Paredes, M. 2010. "En una arena hostíl: La politización de lo indígena en el Perú." In *La Iniciación de la politica: El Perú política en perspectiva comparada*, edited by C. Meléndez and A. Vergara, 213–244. Lima: Fondo Editorial PUCP.

Peru Ministerio de Cultura. 2012. *Derecho a la consulta Previa*. Lima: Ministerio de Cultura.

Peru Ministerio de Cultura and UNESCO-CDIS. 2015. *Culture for Development Indicators: Peru's Analytical Brief*. Lima: Ministerio de Cultura and UNESCO- CDIS. Accessed 15 June 2016. http://en.unesco.org/creativity/sites/creativity/files/digital-library/cdis/cdis_peru_analytical_brief_web_0.pdf

Pinto, V. 2009. "Reestructuración neoliberal del Estado peruano, industrias extractivas y derechos sobre el territorio." In *Minería y territorio en el Perú: Conflicos, Resistencias y propuestas en tiempos de Globalizacion*, edited by J. de Echave, R. Hoetmer, and M. Palacio Panéz, 87–106. Lima: Programa Democracia y Transformación Global; CONACAMI; CooperAccion; and Universidad Nacional Mayor de San Marcos.

Poole, D. 1990. "Ciencia, peligrosidad y represion en la criminología indigenista peruana." In *Bandoleros, abigeos y montoneros: Criminalidad y violencia en el Peru, siglos XVIII-XX*, edited by C. Aguirre and C. Walker, 335–364. Lima: Instituto de Apoyo Agrario.

Poole, D. 1997. *Vision, Race, and Modernity: A Visual Economy of the Andean Image World*. Princeton: Princeton University Press.

Poole, D. 2004. "An Image of Our Indian: Photography and Racial Sentiments in Oaxaca, 1920-1940." *Hispanic American Historical Review* 84 (1): 37–82. doi:10.1215/00182168-84-1-37.

Poole, D. 2006. "Los usos de la costumbre: Hacia una antropologia juridical del Estado Neoliberal." *Alteridades México* 16 (31): 9–31.

Poole, D. 2011. "Mestizaje, Distinction, and Cultural Recognition: The View from Oaxaca." In *Histories of Race and Racism: The Andes and Mesoamerica from Colonial Times to the Present*, edited by L. Gotkowitz, 170–203. Durham, NC: Duke University Press.

Poole, D. 2012. "La ley y la posibilidad de la diferencia: La antropología jurídica peruana entre la justicia y la ley." In *No Hay Pais Mas Diversa: Compendio de antropología peruana*, edited by C. I. Degregori, P. Sendon, and P. Sandoval, 200–246. Lima: Instituto de Estudios Peruanos.

Poole, D. 2015 "Conditional Devices: Territorial Scenarios in a Decentralized State." Unpublished manuscript.

Poole, D., and G. Renique. 1992. *Peru: Time of Fear*. London: Latin America Bureau.

Povinelli, E. 2002. *The Cunning of Recognition: Indigenous Alterities and the Making of Australian Multiculturalism*. Durham, NC: Duke University Press.

Ramos, P., A. Chirif, A. D. Alejandro, B. Clavero, H. Coronado, and C. Gamboa. 2011. *Consulta previa: Derecho fundamental de los Pueblos Indígenas e instrumento de la gestion estatal para el fortalecimiento de la democracia*. Lima: Congreso de la República.

Rappaport, J. 2014. *The Disappearing Mestizo: Configuring Difference in the Colonial new Kingdom of Granada*. Durham, NC: Duke University Press.

Remy, M. I. 2011. *Participación ciudadana y gobiernos descentralizados*. Cuadernos Descentralistas 28. Lima: Grupo Propuesta Ciudadana.

Remy, M. I. 2013a. *Historia de las comunidades indígenas y campesinas en el Perú*. Documento de Trabajo no. 202. Lima: Instituto de Estudios Peruanos.

Remy, M. I. 2013b. "Descentralización y gestión territorial en el Perú." In *Miradas cruzadas: Políticas públicas y desarrollo regional en el Perú*, edited by B. Revz, 133–148. Lima: Instituto de Estudios Peruanos.

Rousseau, S. 2012. "La ley de Consulta Previa y las paradojas de la indigeneidad en la sierra del Perú." *Argumentos* 6 (5). Accessed 12 July 2015. http://revistaargumentos.iep.org.pe/articulos/la-ley-de-consulta-previa-y-las-paradojas- de-la- indigeneidad

Ruiz Molledo, J. C. 2012. *La consulta previa de los Pueblos Indígenas del Peru: Un compendio de legislación y jurisprudencia*. Lima: Instituto de Defensa Legal.

Sabel, C., and J. Zeitlin. 2012. "Experimentalist Governance." In *The Oxford Handbook of Governance*, edited by D. Levi-Faur. New York: OUP.

Scott, C. 2005. "Regulation in the Age of Governance: The Rise of the Post-Regulator State." In *The Politics of Regulation*, edited by J. Jordana and D. Levi-Faur, 145–174. Chelgenham, UK: Edward Elgar.

Sifuentes, M. 2013. "La Consulta previa: Una fuente de conflictos dentro y fuera del gobierno." *La Republica* February 5. Accessed 5 July 2016. http://larepublica.pe/05-02-2013/la-consulta-previa-una-fuente-de-conflictos-dentro-y-fuera-del- gobierno

Sosa Villagarcia, P., J. Pérez Pinillos, M. F. Burga, and D. Uchuypoma Soria. 2012. "Los efectos de la fragmentación en las organizaciones indígenas y la dinámica política e institucional de la consulta previa en el Perú." *Politai: Revista de Ciencia Política* 3 (5): 157–177.

Sulmont, D., and J. C. Callirgos. 2015. "El país de todas las sangres? Race and Ethnicity in Contemporary Peru." In *Pigmentocracies: Ethnicity, Race, and Color in Latin America*, edited by E. Telles and the Project on Ethnicity and Race in Latin America, 126–171. Chapel Hill: The University of North Carolina Press

Szablowski, D. 2007. *Transnational Law and Local Struggles: Mining, Communities, and the World Bank*. Oxford, UK: Hart Publishing.

Szablowski, D. 2010. "Re-empaquetando el CPLI: Las conexiones globales y el debate sobre el consentimiento indígena para la extracción industrial de recursos." *Antropológica* 28 (1): 217–238.

Wade, P. 2005. "Rethinking Mestizaje: Ideology and Lived Experience." *Journal of Latin American Studies* 37: 239–257. doi:10.1017/S0022216X05008990.

Wade, P. 2007. "Identidad racial y nacionalism: Una visión teórica de Latinoamerica." In *Formaciones de Indianidad: Articulaciones raciales, mestizaje y nacion en America Latina*, edited by M. de la Cadena, 379–402. Popayan: Envión.

Racing to the top: descent ideologies and why Ladinos never meant to be mestizos in colonial Guatemala

John M. Watanabe

ABSTRACT

This paper asks what *mestizaje* as presently conceived could have meant in colonial Latin America before modern notions of race, nation, state, or culture. It explores the term *ladino* in contemporary Chiapas and Guatemala that refers to people of mixed descent who identify as 'not Indian.' More than a substitute for mestizo, *ladino* represents a descent ideology that stresses parentage over race in pursuit of relative advantage within a stratified, postconquest society. This descent ideology in turn derives from the 'republics' of Spaniards and Indians – and African slaves – in colonial Guatemala, and post-Reconquest Iberian ideals of 'purity of blood' based on, not race, but legitimate birth to a Christian family going back to before the Muslim conquest of Spain. The vagaries of genealogical reckoning inherent in descent ideologies help to rationalize why from the bottom up 'mestizo' identities came to depend as much on behavior as appearance, and from the top down, they provoked blanket phenotypic exclusions that eventually, but not primordially, found validation in biologized conceptions of race.

In typical anthropological fashion, this essay seeks to relativize *mestizaje* as an analytical concept by trying not to assume we already know what is being 'mixed' or 'crossed' when we invoke it. This may appear needlessly obtuse, given the undeniable admixture in Latin America between populations of Amerindian, European, African, and Asian descent – but that is precisely the point. In a post-eugenics, postcolonial, but still nationalist, ethnically stratified Latin America, it becomes nearly impossible to think of *mestizaje* as anything other than biological race mixture inflected with segregationist or assimilationist state policies and multiracial identity politics, however imagined or imposed, invented or institutionalized. Indeed, associating modern nation-state formation with European colonial domination of others elsewhere imbues modernity itself with notions like Hannah Arendt's 'race thinking' (Silverblatt 2004), Foucauldian 'race–class–gender ideologies' (Smith 1995), or arguments about 'racism without races' (De La Cadena 1998) that make *mestizaje* even harder to imagine otherwise. Compelling in retrospect, these presumptions beg the question of exactly how people envisioned and enacted *mestizaje* before present ideas of race, nation, state, or even culture, as a language of difference, developed (cf. Rappaport 2014, 224–226).

Methodologically, the more 'naturally' we imagine *mestizaje*, the more self-consciously we need to justify how far to generalize it analytically as the postcolonial process we imagine today. This pertains not to the empirical fact of admixture itself but to how participants in the process have variously understood and acted upon it, assuming with Weber ([1968] 1978, 4–22) that social actors' own subjective meanings and motivations serve to rationalize (for both actors and analysts) individual behavior, social arrangements, and historical developments. Such subjective orientations, however, emerge from received practices, idioms, and institutions that constitute (for analysts but not necessarily for actors) a historical, subjectless Foucauldian genealogy manifest in the partial, localized knowledges on which actors act (Foucault 1980, 85, 117).

For *mestizaje*, the slippage between actors' orientations and historical genealogy nowhere finds more ironic expression than in Mexico, home of the postrevolutionary, nationally mestisized 'cosmic race' but where people seldom refer to themselves as *mestizos*. Instead, they more commonly self-identify as *gente de razón* (people of reason), *gente decente* (decent people), *correctos* (polite company), *catrines* (fancy dressers), *vecinos* (resident citizens), or simply *mexicanos* (Mexicans) (Aguirre Beltrán, cited in Chance 1979, 154) – all terms that finesse race mixture in favor of behavior, culture, or political standing. Yucatán represents the limiting case where *mestizo* has come to include rural, Maya-speaking farmers who elsewhere would be identified by themselves and others as native or indigenous (Eiss 2010; this volume; Pitt-Rivers 1969, 463–464; Sullivan 2000, 214–216).

Similarly, in what was once the old colonial Kingdom of Guatemala extending from Chiapas to Honduras, El Salvador, and Nicaragua, the curious term *ladino* has supplanted *mestizo* and *mulato* regarding Spanish-speaking non-Indian part-Europeans (Colby 1966; Euraque 2004; Gould 1993, 397; Lauria-Santiago 1999, 498–499; cf.; Euraque, Gould, and Hale 2004). When not simply treating it as an awkward equivalent of mestizo, anthropologists and historians most often assume that the term emerged as a default catch-all for the colonial admixture and remixture of Spaniards, Indians, and Africans that eventually overwhelmed imperial efforts to order the ever-burgeoning permutations (Luján Muñoz 1976a, 53; Lutz 1994, 95, 1995, 120–121; Taracena Arriola 1982, 95–97; Tax 1941, 27; cf.; Gould 1998, 136; Mörner 1967, 68–70). Closer inspection, however, suggests *ladino* reflects less indeterminate race mixture than what I will call a 'descent ideology' that, paralleling the euphemisms of self-identification in Mexico, emerged to elide any reference to *mestizaje* – much less race – at all.

To construct the necessarily illusory Weberian ideal type to defend this assertion, I look first to ethnographic meanings of *ladino* in 20th-century Guatemala and Chiapas, then to historical, institutional, and ideological considerations that contributed to this formulation. This will reveal the importance of descent over race, familial and religious legitimacy over biological purity, and pursuit of relative advantage within a stratified postconquest society – what with due irony I will call 'racing to the top' – over preemptive racial prejudice or discrimination. My argument parallels Joanne Rappaport's (2014) about 'the disappearing mestizo' in early modern Colombia, and, given the contrasting colonial and demographic histories of Guatemala and Colombia, their mutual contrast with central Mexican representations of *casta* suggests the need to reconsider what we today so naturally generalize – and racialize – as *mestizaje*.

Being *ladino*

Ethnographically, anthropologist Julian Pitt-Rivers captured well the ambiguities of *ladino* in mid-20th-century Chiapas.

> A ladino is one who speaks Spanish correctly (or what is thought to be correctly); he is civilized …. The ladinos vary in physical type from European to Indian while the Indian population includes individuals who show traces of European descent. Negroid features are found among both. However, the upper classes are markedly more European in type and commonly believe themselves to be of purely European descent. Physical features are therefore a rough correlate of status, not a criterion of it, and are in no sense a determinant of ethnic affiliation. Anyone who claims to be a ladino and knows enough Spanish to play the part is accepted as such in face to face situations. Behind his back it may be explained that he is 'really an Indian' but this assertion relates to known descent and cultural accomplishments, not to phenotype. Moreover, of course, it is only said of those who do not occupy Indian status [by speaking a Maya language, wearing distinctive dress, farming maize, living in a rural village, practicing a localized 'folk' Catholicism]. The higher the social status of the speaker the more people he regards as 'really Indian.' (1967, 74–75)

Pitt-Rivers makes three key observations. First, and most often noted, being *ladino* is performative, not phenotypic – it means acting 'civilized' and 'playing the part,' especially speaking Spanish 'correctly.' Nonetheless, the term also imputes 'European,' or at the very least not Indian, identity and descent. Put the other way around, anthropologist Douglas Brintnall found in Guatemala that

> an Indian is defined as a person with Indian parents, and a Ladino a person with Ladino parents. And, no matter how much Spanish, education, or wealth an Indian might acquire in his community, everyone knows he is really an Indian, and 'real' Ladinos look down upon him and tend to exclude him because of it. (1979, 644)

Ladino thus indicates behavior associated with the ancestry – if not always appearance – of 'European descent.'

Second, and more insidiously, playing the civilized Ladino may suffice for outward acceptance from other Ladinos but not always for their private approval. Regardless of behavior, being *ladino* also depends on acceptance from others, especially other Ladinos. Indians wanting to pass as Ladinos can adopt *ladino* dress, speech, and ways, but as Brintnall implies, they have to leave their home communities (Colby and van den Berghe 1969, 91; Stavenhagen 1968, 53). When they do, however, Ladinos elsewhere have little reason to accept them (Adams 1988, 283). Indeed, the very possibility of passing as *ladino* only heightens other Ladinos' suspicions of any newcomer as 'really Indian.' Ironically, local Indian communities are more likely to take Indian strangers for Ladinos, especially if they speak different Maya languages and have to communicate in Spanish (Colby and van den Berghe 1969, 172). Despite a categorical distinction by descent between Indians and Ladinos, a mutual, if inverse, default presumption of difference can leave Ladino newcomers 'really Indian' to known Ladinos and Indian strangers Ladinos to local Indians. Being *ladino* ultimately turns on attribution of *ladino* identity by one's own kind, whether Ladino or Indian. Conversely, a suspected 'ladinized' Indian becomes 'a marginal man' (Stavenhagen 1968, 53) to both sides for playing each false in inverse ways.

Third, Pitt-Rivers' first and last observations reveal the power inherent in being *ladino*. More than simply acting civilized, being an accepted Ladino also means politically being able to say who else will pass as *ladino* in Austin's (1975, 5–6) sense of 'performatives' as enabling utterances: Ladinos endorse fellow Ladinos but dismiss as 'really Indian' anyone else they can, no matter how *ladino* these others may feel. This kind of competitive exclusion exemplifies Foucault's (1982) notion of power as actions that act upon the actions of others because it forces all Ladinos to exclude as many 'Indians' below them as they can to forestall corresponding exclusion from other Ladinos above them. A sensitivity for respect results, not just at the top, but all the way down, as Ladinos in between emulate the very discriminations that may deny them acceptance at the top as 'European' – but also keep them from falling to the bottom as Indians. Unable to compel acceptance from above, self-respecting Ladinos must continually distance themselves from any would-be Ladino pretenders from below.

For their part, Indians counter Ladino self-promotion with their own value orientation of moral solidarity, if not superiority (Bricker 1973, 161–166; Stavenhagen 1968; Warren 1989). They substantiate this most often through reciprocal obligations with neighbors, rights to work local community lands, participation in community labor service, and the cultural knowledge, moral sensibilities, and fluency in the local Maya language needed to enact such claims properly (Watanabe 1992). Since these practices by definition exclude Ladinos as outsiders, Indians who act otherwise get disparaged as *ladino*, but they only become Ladinos by going elsewhere – and Ladinos never aspire to be seen as Indians anywhere.

Semantically, *ladino* thus serves as both noun and adjective. It distinguishes Ladinos from Indians even as it makes some Ladinos more *ladino* than others depending on who is speaking to whom about where others – and by implication, the speakers themselves – rightfully belong. This kind of relative, situational attribution of descent and social standing raises two analytical points and a pair of historical questions. First, analytically, if *ladino* entails descent, it is important to distinguish descent from race. Despite common metaphors of parentage and blood, descent differs from race in using parentage to identify individuals as such by filiation (parent–child links), whereas race and racism project universal, conventionally naturalized categories onto often unrelated individuals according to their actual or imagined resemblance in appearance, behavior, or perceived worth. Descent identifies individuals, race defines groups; race implies descent but is not defined by it.

Second, given the contested nature of who qualifies as *ladino*, Ladinos may all claim 'European,' specifically Spanish, descent, but this implies neither common ancestry nor acceptance of each others' assertions of identity or affinity. *Ladino* expresses an ideology of descent, not a genealogical identity. It resembles Fredrik Barth's (1969) definition of ethnicity as a complex interplay of self-ascription and identification by others, but as Rappaport (2014, 12) rightly cautions, a 'mestizo' term like *ladino* never delimits a homogeneous, much less unified, ethnic group. An ideological claim to Spanish descent contrasts Ladinos as such from Indians, but it associates them not with each other but with more privileged others above them, even if Spaniards themselves reject such claims. Thus, neither race nor ethnicity really apply: *ladino* expresses a descent ideology as a collective noun that works like an adjective to identify individuals, not define their common identity (cf. Guzmán-Böckler 1970).

The two historical questions that *ladino* raises involve how this particular descent ideology emerged in colonial Guatemala, and why only there. Answering the first question requires delineating the Foucauldian genealogy that links *ladino* as a descent ideology to the colonial status hierarchy it at once affirms yet subverts. Not surprisingly, vagaries inherent in genealogical reckoning play a central role in understanding this ideology and hierarchy. The second question of why *ladino* emerged only in colonial Guatemala demands broader comparisons beyond the scope of this paper, but I would argue that it relates importantly to the precarious position of Spanish colonial elites both within Guatemala relative to a persistently large native population, and within colonial Spanish America as a whole. In either case, explanation begins with the way conquest became the leitmotif of Guatemalan society institutionalized in the enduring 'republics' of Spaniards and Indians. Attention then turns to preoccupations with descent that for Guatemalan colonial elites defined their predominance – and thus dictated to those below them how best to protest their own worth within this postconquest society.

Institutionalizing conquest in Guatemala

To belabor the obvious, colonial Guatemala began with the military defeat and political subjugation of native polities by Spanish forces under Pedro de Alvarado beginning in 1524 (Kelly [1932] 1971, 121–174). Reflecting on the long-term consequences of this, anthropologist Richard Adams (1989) identified a 'conquest tradition' in Guatemala. By this, he meant not some timeless triumph or trauma but the ongoing, institutionalized violence that even today still discriminates against Indians as Indians, despite centuries of indigenous cultural and political economic coadaptation within Guatemalan society (cf. Bricker 1981, 6; Farriss 1984, 113–114; Stavenhagen 1968). Adams rooted this conquest tradition in the occupation of Guatemala by vastly outnumbered Spanish conquistadors abetted by native allies from central Mexico. Intent on extracting tribute and labor from a large, diverse native population, Spanish abuses fueled both native enmity and Spanish fears of native revolt that together intensified preemptive violence from the top down and instilled in both the terror that for Adams defines a conquest tradition. Even after colonial society stabilized, the decimation of Indian *pueblos* by disease and violence and the influx of peninsular Spaniards from Spain kept demands on native tributaries high (MacLeod 1973; Martínez Peláez [1970] 1979). Conquest lived on in the terror of a predatory tributary economy.

To institutionalize the exactions of conqueror over conquered, the Spanish Crown dictated that Spaniards and Indians live separately, although this began with Crown efforts to regulate Spanish settlement, not dispossess Indians. As early as 1513, the Crown had issued procedures for founding Spanish cities and towns in the New World (Mundigo and Crouch 1977, 248). Instructions for resettling Indians into Spanish-style *pueblos* to Christianize and civilize them only began later, in the 1540s (Lovell 1983, 1990; MacLeod 1973, 120–142; *Recopilación de leyes* 1841, II, 228–232). Decrees forbade 'Spaniards, blacks, mulattoes, or mestizos' from living in Indian *pueblos* and charged Indian officials with keeping order, even to jailing disruptive 'blacks or mestizos' for later judgment by Spanish authorities (*Recopilación de leyes* 1841, II, 230–231). These ordinances established the dual *repúblicas* of Spanish towns and Indian *pueblos* that inscribed conquest on the landscape, since Indian *pueblos* owed tribute and labor, and Spanish towns did not.

Spanish towns, however, faced their own constraints. They could only be founded with a royal license granted to a proprietary settler (*poblador principal*) who had a set period in which to recruit at least 30 Spanish residents (*vecinos*) with requisite livestock, find a priest to minister to the community, appoint town officials, and occupy an appropriate site at least five leagues (not quite 28 km in 16th-century Spanish *leguas*) from other Spanish towns. Indian workers and artisans could join the settlement as long as they did so willingly without compromising the labor or tribute obligations of other settlements. Settlers had to lay out the town's central plaza and gridded streets; set aside common pasture lands (*ejidos*) and town rental property (*propios*); demarcate and divide by lottery individual fields, a quarter for the proprietary settler, five times as much for gentry as commoners; plant crops; and build church and houses. In the absence of a proprietary settler, ten married *vecinos* could together obtain license for a new settlement (*Recopilación de leyes* 1841, II, 102–103, 105–108).

Cities and towns were Spanish, founded as centers of power and privilege 'by Spaniards for Spaniards' (Luján Muñoz 1976a, 57). Accordingly, the ordinances for new Spanish towns (*villas de españoles*), as opposed to Indian *pueblos*, conferred on the successful resident founder and his descendants the status of *hijos-dalgo*, 'children of substance,' endowed with 'noble lineage and known origin [*solar conocido*]' (*Recopilación de leyes* 1841, II, 104). In contrast, as late as the 1780s in Guatemala, the Council of the Indies could still deny the formal status of a Spanish *villa* or even Indian *pueblo* to resettled 'mulattoes, whom they commonly call Ladinos, and some who want to be taken for Spaniards' (see below), because only the king could authorize new towns or *pueblos*. Instead, the new populations would remain *pagos o aldeas* (districts or hamlets) (Luján Muñoz 1976b, 53). By so decreeing, the Council did more than defend a royal prerogative: it also ensured that no Ladino – much less mulatto – living in these settlements could presume to claim the privileges of a Spanish settler. Even after 250 years, the colonial order continued to defend the two republics of Spaniards and Indians and the prerogatives of conquest these signified.

Despite such enduring, institutionalized differences, any attempt at categorical distinctions between conqueror and conquered, Spaniards and Indians, immediately foundered on at least three concerns, even without admixture between the two. First, what standing were native rulers to have if deposing them could challenge the King's own standing as a 'natural lord' (Chamberlain 1939, 132–134)? Second, what consideration did native allies deserve who assisted in the military incursions and subsequent colonial administration of subjugated native populations (Lutz 1994, 24–25, 28, 39–40, 72; Sherman 1979, 22)? Third, where would Creoles as the New World-born descendants of Spanish conquerors fit relative to newly arrived Spanish immigrants born in Spain (Martínez Peláez [1970] 1979)? These ambiguities immediately problematized any categorical opposition between conqueror and conquered, Old World and New, newcomer and native. To understand how Ladinos emerged from the resulting tensions, I will start in the middle and work down, then up.

From *ladino* to Ladinos

Regarding what to do with native allies and brokers, the Spanish dealt with at least some of them by calling them *ladino*. Indeed, anthropologists and historians have long known, if not always remembered, that *ladino* originated in Spain to describe culturally assimi-lated 'barbarians' in Roman times who spoke Latin, then Jews, Muslims, and Africans during the reconquest who mastered Spanish (Taracena Arriola 1982, 89–90; Tax 1941, 27). As an adjective, not a noun, applied to subordinated peoples who learned the conqueror's language, *ladino* in the New World first referred (incongruously to present ears) to *indios ladinos*, 'astute or well-schooled Indians,' who had come to speak Spanish 'perfectly.' Service as intermediaries for conquistadors, missionaries, and, eventually, royal officials often exempted these *indios ladinos* from tribute and forced labor (Taracena Arriola 1982, 89–91). Such privilege undoubtedly provoked resentment from other natives less inclined (or adept) at collaborating with their new overlords. Spaniards too came to suspect their Indian brokers, if only because the more willing and indis-pensable they became, the more self-serving they could appear – and act. Perhaps not surprisingly, by the mid-16th century, *ladino* in Central American Spanish had come to mean 'cunning,' 'wily,' or 'shrewd' as much as 'astute' or 'smart' (Sherman 1979, 187).

In the early 17th century, *ladino* still referred to Spanish-speaking Indians, but it had also come to include black slaves who had adopted 'Spanish [speech] and European customs' (Taracena Arriola 1982, 93–98). As the century progressed, the term extended to a broader group 'of very diverse social stripes [*matices*]' (93). In the city of Santiago de Guatemala, *ladino* became almost synonymous with 'mestizo.' 'Because *ladino* was a secular term deemed inappropriate for Santiago's registers,' however, Ladinos did not begin to appear as such in parish baptismal records until the 18th century (Lutz 1994, 163–164). This would suggest that the term first gained common usage independent of, if not contrary to, official estimations of *casta* and only later became officially recog-nized – *casta* here referring not to 'caste' in the English sense of closed, ranked hereditary groups but to a person's good lineage and breeding (Martínez 2008, 162; Pitt-Rivers 1971; Rappaport 2014, 17, 37–38, 208). Equally significant, once acceptable, *ladino* did not displace other designations because well into the 19th century, parish records continued to register *mestizos, mulatos, pardos* (coloreds), *castizos* (mestizo–Spanish mixes), *sambos* (Afro-Indians), Indians, and Spaniards – including 'European,' 'American,' and even 'Indian' or 'Ladino' Spaniards (Little-Siebold 2001, 114; cf.; Chance 1979, 161).

These increasingly baroque 'complex composite identities' (Little-Siebold 2001, 115) emerged during the 17th century as *ladino* came to include not only mestizos in the cities, but also 'Spaniards, mestizos, mulattoes, and blacks' who lived dispersed across the Guatemalan countryside in haciendas, *valles* (unauthorized rural settlements), and Indian *pueblos*. Although unclear whether *ladino* applied to all or only poor rural Spaniards, the term kept its original meaning of Spanish speaker, as opposed to 'Indians who only speak their maternal tongue' (Fuentes and Guzmán, cited in Taracena Arriola 1982, 93). Apparently, however, having mixed – much less indetermi-nate – ancestry had little to do with being *ladino*, since rural Spaniards, acculturated blacks, and *indios ladinos* presumably had no mixed blood at all. Even mestizos, by virtue of their Spanish antecedents, approximated Spaniards – indeed, equaled many New World-born Spanish Creoles (see below) – in appearance and their 'use of Spanish and regard for certain European customs' (96). Most importantly, mestizos had never been enslaved like blacks or mulattoes or made to pay tribute like Indians (Lutz 1994, 99). If neither Spanish nor Creole, these mestizo Ladinos still outranked Indians and slaves in

THE POLITICS AND PERFORMANCE OF MESTIZAJE IN LATIN AMERICA

their freedom of residence, movement, and work, as well as exemption from tribute or labor obligations (Martínez Peláez [1970] 1979, 285; cf.; Rappaport 2014, 208).

Besides speaking Spanish, what united this increasingly diverse population of Ladinos lay not in their muddied distinctions of blood, but in their common 'economic and social position [that corresponded] neither to that of the mass of subservient Indians, nor to that of Spanish and Creole landlords and merchants, nor to that of black slaves' (Taracena Arriola 1982, 97). That is, *ladino* had come to signify anomalies in the two republics of Spaniards and Indians and African slavery. Despite their other differences, Ladinos fit none of these: poor Spaniards were anomalous for not living up to their station; Spanish-speaking Indians for trying to escape theirs as tributaries and forced laborers; free blacks and mulattoes for no longer being slaves; and mestizos for being none of the above. United by their anomalous condition, however diversely defined, Ladinos of whatever stripe belied the paradigmatic colonial distinctions between Spanish tribute takers, Indian tributaries, and black slaves.

The most surprising of these 17th-century extensions of *ladino*, but perhaps the most decisive, involved the inclusion of rural Spaniards, poor or otherwise. From the late 16th century, Spaniards with declining *encomiendas* (grants of Indian tributaries) had drifted to the Guatemalan countryside (MacLeod 1973, 133, 291), even though this imperiled their family's social standing. They must have taken great pains never to be mistaken for mestizos, much less held liable for tribute (cf. Megged 1992, 438). Similarly, aspiring Ladinos had little reason to challenge their claims as Spaniards because, however poor or marginal (and at times no doubt overbearing), self-identified Spaniards on rural haciendas or in illicit Ladino *valles* or Indian *pueblos* provided other Ladinos living or working there the possibility of claiming by association – and over time perhaps by intermarriage and parentage – a Spaniard's insistently non-Indian, non-tributary identity. Indeed, according to *casta* stipulations, mestizos who married back into Spanish stock for three generations technically became Spaniards again (Martínez 2008, 233).

Conversely, colonial authorities had good reason to oppose any such expansion of Spaniardized Ladinos exempt from tribute obligations. In 1724, the Dominican friar in San Miguel Petapa (near present-day Guatemala City) complained that his Indian parishioners were claiming service as 'soldiers' – that is, militiamen – to abandon his parish for another, 'of Ladinos who are Spaniards, mulattoes, and blacks,' where

> their children and descendants are considered non-tribute-paying mestizos [along with] others called vagabonds who include non-tribute-paying half-mulattoes and mestizos, all children of Indian tributaries who by law should pay tribute by the common rule that the child should follow the derivation [*naturaleza*] of the mother, all of them being Indians and thus subject to paying tribute. (quoted in Taracena Arriola 1982, 94)

The priest decried all these delinquent tributaries as 'prejudicial to the royal treasury' – and not coincidentally, to his own parish income.

This passage suggests three things about Ladino identity in the 18th century. First, the priest labeled as Ladinos only the most obvious non-Indians – Spaniards, mulattoes, blacks – in contrast to the 'half-mulattoes and mestizos' with Indian mothers whom he saw as tribute-owing Indians. What defined Ladinos for him was their non-Indian non-tributary status, not indeterminate ancestry. Second, he specified that only the 'children and descendants' of fugitive *indios ladinos*, not *indios ladinos* themselves, might pass as non-tributary mestizos in Ladino towns, confirming the importance of local estimation in defining, if only from the bottom up, who belonged where. Third, he invoked the 'law of the womb' (Lokken 2001, 178 n. 14; Lutz 1994, 56) to denounce as delinquent tributaries anyone in *ladino* towns who could conceivably have an Indian mother, insisting from the top down that Indian parentage – and thus legal status as tributary – should trump any claim of being *ladino* by vagabond pretenders. By such reasoning, even mestizos could become tributaries. Ladinos thus had every reason to elide any terminological attributions of mixed descent – much less any blanket categorization – that might lump them with Indians, even as they hoped Spaniards and Creoles would accept their children.

At first glance, the priest's distinction between 'mulatto and black' Ladinos and 'half-mulattoes' with Indian mothers might suggest 'Ladino' meant having no Indian blood at all. 'Mulatto' in colonial rural Guatemala, however, evidently applied as easily to Afro-Indians as Afro-Europeans (Lutz 1994, 46; cf.; Martínez 2008, 157). However few in absolute terms, Spanish-speaking people of African descent may have in fact made up a plurality of non-Indians in late 17th-century rural Guatemala (Lokken 2001, 184). More black slaves lived on rural Spanish properties than Spaniards (Megged 1992, 434–436), and these mostly male slaves often sought to marry free Indian or mulatta women so that their children would be both legitimate and freeborn (Sherman 1979, 315). After slave imports into Guatemala fell during the mid-17th century (Lokken 2001, 184), admixture between mulattoes and Indians continued, although Spaniards came to call anyone of even the slightest African appearance a mulatto regardless of actual parentage (Lutz 1994, 94–95). While this inflated mulatto numbers, by the 18th century, lighter skinned mulattoes, especially women, had also begun to pass as non-tributary mestizos (95) or even poor Spaniards (Taracena Arriola 1982, 96).

To counter any loss of tributaries on whom their status and well-being depended, Spaniards tended to attribute wherever possible Indian or Afro-Indian descent. Conversely, to finesse suspicions of having Indian mothers, mulattoes and *indios ladinos* hoping to pass as non-tributary Ladinos emphasized their Spanish language, Catholic religion, legitimacy of birth (if not actual parentage), militia service and colonial loyalties, and mestizo or even poor Creole spouses (if they could find them) (cf. Little-Siebold 2001). 'Real' Ladinos in turn could only try to dissociate themselves from these pretenders, most immediately by identifying with anomalous rural Spaniards classified as Ladinos by the Spaniards and Creoles above them. Indeed, whatever its other liabilities, the term *ladino* made no explicit reference to mixed descent. In this fraught process, the presence of even a scattering of poorer Spaniards in rural Guatemala, however disparaged by urban Spaniards as déclassé Ladinos, may have proven decisive for Ladinos of all other stripes in distancing themselves from Indian tributaries and black slaves.

In this sense, during the 18th century, non-tributary status, not necessarily Spanish speech or identity, may well have become the salient marker for Ladinos. This would explain why Archbishop Cortés Y Larraz (2001, 370, 371) could observe in 1770 that despite 'some, but very few' Ladinos in the provincial capital of Huehuetenango, 'the native language … is not needed in the *cabecera*, or even in the [nearby] *pueblo* of San Lorenzo, because everyone speaks Spanish perfectly.' In contrast, he found Ladinos in the outlying town of Cuilco to be 'of the same inclinations as the Indians, of the same stupidity [*estolidez*] and customs, the same language, and they have married with them'

(388). If fluency in Spanish no longer made Indians in Huehuetenango Ladinos, neither did the Indian behavior, speech, or spouses of Ladinos in Cuilco make them Indians. Instead, what continued to separate the two – despite linguistic and social convergences – was that Indians had to pay tribute and render services, Ladinos (and of course Spaniards and Creoles) did not.

Paying tribute to the Crown became so normalized that Indians would cite their tributary status as 'one of the most important signs of being a pure Indian,' whether as native lords hoping to validate rights to patrimonial lands and privileges or as commoners wanting to be heard before special native courts instead of the Inquisition (Martínez 2008, 103–104). Conversely, Indian *naborías*, servants working for Spaniards and no longer on the tribute rolls of an Indian *pueblo*, 'appear to have been viewed as something other than fully "Indian," and were in fact frequently lumped together with the *non*-Indian population … "Indianness" and tribute status were closely linked' (Lokken 2001, 180–181, original emphasis; cf.; Gasco 1991, 306; Rappaport 2014, 8). Freedom from tribute remained a key distinction for Ladinos throughout the colonial period.

If Ladinos came to differ from Indians as Spanish-speaking non-tributaries, it remains to explain why this political economic distinction became associated with descent, not class or race. This demands closer inquiry into the identity of Spaniards and Creoles in colonial Guatemala that Ladinos sought so closely to emulate in speech, act, and pretention.

Creole genealogies

As already noted, the increase in Spaniards born in the New World raised questions about the status of these Creoles relative to Spaniards born in Spain. Caught between a stagnant tributary economy (MacLeod 1973) and the continual influx of peninsular Spaniards from Spain, Creoles in Guatemala – especially descendants of the first conquistadors – became 'dissatisfied and vexsome [*quisquillosos*] participants in the colonial system of exploitation' (Martínez Peláez [1970] 1979, 38). Forever invoking their proprietary rights of first conquest, however distantly won (Martínez Peláez [1970] 1979; Pagden 1987, 58–62), old Creole families expected respect from their betters and obedience from their inferiors.

Spaniards in turn disparaged Creoles for not having been born in Spain, but the dearth of Spanish women in early colonial Guatemala also left the oldest Creole families forever suspect of having non-Christian Indian (if not African) ancestry that made their *casta* less reputable than peninsular Spaniards' (Casaus Arzú 1993, 30–49; Martínez 2008, 138–139; Megged 1992). Many 16th-century first-generation mestizos had indeed passed for Spaniards (Mörner 1967, 27), especially if their Indian mother's nobility, dowry, but above all religious conversion to Christianity, had led to actual marriage, or a prominent conquistador father had formally recognized them as heirs (Martínez 2008, 119–120, 144–145; Sherman 1979, 317–319). By mid-century, however, the arrival of more Spanish-Christian women and the growing number of illegitimate children by poorer Spaniards and commoner Indian women had made 'mestizo' and 'bastard' almost synonymous (Sherman 1979, 319).

Having to disavow any such disrepute in their own ancestry only hardened Creoles toward mestizos, to say nothing of *indios ladinos*, but it also fueled their resentment against peninsular Spaniards, whom Creoles viewed as *advenedizos*, 'upstarts' bent on dispossessing them of the Indian lands and tribute bequeathed them by their conquistador fathers (Casaus Arzú 1993, 36; Martínez Peláez [1970] 1979, 23–38). Despite the ambivalence, however, Creoles recognized that it was their Spanish blood that distinguished them from *gente ordinaria* (non-Indian commoners). Indeed, Creoles in colonial Guatemala seldom referred to themselves as *criollos*, and all who plausibly could called themselves 'Spaniards' (Lutz 1994, 163). This came in no small part because *criollo* had first applied to slaves born and raised outside Africa (as opposed to *bozales*, 'African-born slaves'), and when used for Spaniards born outside Spain, its demeaning associations lingered (Martínez 2008, 135–136). Only in the 17th century would Spanish Creoles in the New World begin to adopt the term to express their growing disaffection with Spaniards, if not Spain (Pagden 1987, 79).

Spanish blood, however, carried its own vulnerabilities, evidenced in colonial preoccupations with *limpieza de sangre* (purity of blood). Derived from the Christian reconquest of Muslim Spain, purity of blood involved not race, as the term immediately conjures up today, but a descent ideology of having Christian parentage going back ideally to before the Muslim conquest of Spain that certified claimants as religiously orthodox, politically trustworthy, and socially deserving. Certifications of *limpieza de sangre* originated in the 15th century, when 'Old Christian' families who presumed to have always been Christian began to question the orthodoxy of converted Jewish and Muslim 'New Christians' (cf. Martínez 2008, 71, 77–78; Poole 1999, 365). Debate ensued over how many generations – if any – had to pass to secure converts' faith. By the 16th century, the Inquisition had minimally defined as pure those whose parents and grandparents had all been legitimately born to Christian families, at least insofar as existing public records and memory in the person's Iberian place of origin could establish (Martínez 2008, 49–50, 62–70). This soon escalated into an infinite regression of having to demonstrate exclusive Christian lineage indefinitely back in time. Seventeenth-century genealogists became expert at tracing Old Christian families back countless generations to 'Gothic' regions of northern Spain never conquered by Muslims (70–80).

Conceptually, purity of blood equated Christian faith and practice with legitimate birth to a reputable Old Christian family. Whether this presumed some already essentialized *naturaleza* (nature) linked to individual character and quality of birthplace (Martínez 2008, 177), or simply the 'spiritual virtues' imbibed with one's mother's milk in a family known always to have been Christian (Rappaport 2014, 19, 38), the ideal of *limpieza* proved powerful yet ever problematic (Little-Siebold 2001; Martínez 2008, 83–84). 'Blood,' however, pertained to family and religious upbringing, not race or biology.

Hoping to create an Old Christian utopia in the New World, the Crown officially – if ineffectively (Silverblatt 2000) – prohibited New Christian emigration (Martínez 2008, 128–129). Debate in the Indies centered on whether Indians qualified as 'gentiles' free of Jewish or Muslim blood who could then become Old Christians after two generations as Catholics – the official legal view – or whether as inveterately backsliding idolaters they belonged with Jews, Muslims, and Africans as perpetually suspect New Christians – the view of many Creoles anxious to keep Indians subservient (96–98, 201–214). Either way, purity of Indian – not just Spanish – blood could theoretically qualify Indians as Old Christians, especially Indian nobles who could show their family's early – and willing – conversion to Catholicism and generations of loyalty to faith and Crown, if not always intermarriage with 'pure' Spaniards (120, 153–154).

Conversely, poor colonial records and fading memories of grandparents in Spain made it ever harder for even 16th-century Creoles to validate their purity of blood. By the next century, many would argue that their native roots lay in the New World, not Spain, and their purity needed to be assessed accordingly (Martínez 2008, 175–177, 195–196), although *limpieza* petitions persisted in Guatemala into the early 19th century (Little-Siebold 2001). Ironically, Iberian standards of Christian purity intended to exclude Jews and Muslims enabled New World Indians potentially to become Old Christians precisely because they were not Iberian, even as distance from Spain and the passage of time disadvantaged Spanish Creoles needing to prove their religious purity because they were Iberian.

Doubly beset genealogically, Guatemalan Creoles bolstered their claims as Spaniards by having their children marry newly arrived Spaniards of 'known origin' as Old Christians. Such unions affirmed Creole worthiness while admitting peninsular new-comers to local society, offices, and power (Lutz 1994, 108). Such mutual accommodation produced densely interwoven elite networks that the Creole children of these marriages did well to reproduce (Casaus Arzú 1993). Marrying Spaniards validated and extended elite Creole circles, even as it closed their ranks to those below (Martínez 2008, 191). Less advantaged Creoles – to say nothing of aspiring Ladinos – had to marry into lesser families and live in provincial towns or rural holdings that could increasingly jeopardize their standing as Spaniards (Lutz 1994, 103–109). The more marginalized they became, the more insistent humbler Creoles grew about distinguishing themselves from mestizos, mulattoes, and *indios ladinos*, even as these others strove to identify with (or marry) them to improve their own chances of being taken for Spaniards – or at least not Indians or descendants of slaves (139–140).

What to present day sensibilities looks like racial prejudice and whitening reflected Creole concerns with family legitimacy and religious, not racial, purity (cf. Rappaport 2014). The ideological primacy of descent over race found clear expression in the continual displacement of successive generations of Spaniards downward (cf. Martínez Peláez [1970] 1979, 106–117). Peninsular Spaniards by definition became Creoles in the next generation and had to marry Spaniards to retain their preeminence. Creoles without peninsular connections fell in esteem, their continued consideration as Spaniards increasingly dependent on distancing themselves from the mestizos, mulattoes, and *indios ladinos* below them. This mirrored Ladino descent ideology, but Creoles religiously sanctioned social and political respectability from above, while *ladino* language, religion, and proper marriage expiated problematic parentage and liability for tribute from below. Each contested, if inversely, the same vagaries of genealogical descent inherent in the inevitable passing of generations. Both excluded everyone they could.

In the end, despite the ambiguities of *limpieza*, imperial authorities ruled that the ongoing 'wretched' condition of untutored Indians justified treating them not unlike Jewish and Muslim New Christians as perennial 'recent converts' best left to the watchful paternalism – and not coincidentally, worldly benefit – of Church and Crown (Martínez 2008, 102–104). Creoles saw Indians more straightforwardly as 'the worker of the land …

obliged to work and pay tribute …. That had been [the Indian's] reason for being from the moment – always present in the consciousness of the Creole – that the land had been won' (Martínez Peláez [1970] 1979, 255). However much colonial distinctions and passing generations had unmoored Creoles and Indians from their precolonial origins, an abiding conquest tradition (Adams 1989) continued to privilege conqueror over conquered. The dilemma Creoles faced involved how to articulate an identity in their new native land that would give them precedence over Spaniards from Spain without debasing their own privileged position as Spanish conquerors over the natives they still expected to serve them (cf. Martínez Peláez [1970] 1979).

In seeking to nativize their identity, Creoles in Mexico and Peru had the advantage of mythologizing the past glories of Aztec and Inca civilizations as autochthonous, imperial traditions associated with the land itself that they could then appropriate by virtue of their birth there. At the very least, they could appeal to their forebears' legitimacy (and prowess) in supplanting these empires and having a Christianized native nobility acknowledge their rule, if more grudgingly in Peru than Mexico (Pagden 1987; cf. Martínez 2008, 128, 196–197). Mexican Creoles could also appeal to the Virgin of Guadalupe as divine proof of their exceptionalism (Poole 1996; Taylor 1987). Guatemalan Creoles had no such native imperium to invoke, nor imperial native nobility to endorse them, only the piecemeal defeat of less spectacular warring polities than those in Mexico or Peru (Carmack 1981; Lovell 1992). Their claim to distinction depended instead on their stewardship as Spanish gentry of the lands and peoples won by their conquistador fathers (Martínez Peláez [1970] 1979). Any infringement of such privilege – except perhaps marriage with 'pure' Spaniards – diminished their interests as well as entitlements.

Guatemalan Creoles' self-portrayal as pure Spaniards, however refracted by time and distance from Spain and the mythopoeic limitations of the native societies they had dispossessed, closed their ranks to anyone of questionable Catholic birth or heritage. Those with Indian or African blood became politically and morally suspect, however, not by race but by parentage and religion. Ladino appeals to Spanish heritage and legitimate birth thus begin to make sense given the Creole ideal of *limpieza de sangre* to which they had to aspire. Indeed, this Creole descent ideology of Spanish purity may have pushed the less privileged in colonial Guatemala to reappropriate for themselves the original meaning of *ladino* as Spanish-speaking other, if only because the term elided mixed descent while foregrounding Spanish Catholic affiliations and loyalties, regardless of birth.

Conclusion

This paper has argued that the term *ladino* from the old colonial Kingdom of Guatemala raises questions about *mestizaje*, not as the admixture of Amerindian, European, African, and Asian populations in Latin America, but as a contemporary nationalist-cum-postcolonialist ideology that we must only cautiously project back into a world before modern notions of nation, state, race, or culture. Even in 20th-century Chiapas and Guatemala, close attention to the use of *ladino* reveals, not a homogeneously hybridized race concept, but a descent ideology of competitive exclusion by which Ladinos accept or reject each other to validate their own 'civilized' status. Historically, *ladino* as a descent ideology emerged during the 17th century, not as the residuum of racial distinctions collapsing under rampant miscegenation, but as the identity of anomalous others caught between the two republics of Spaniards and Indians and African slaves. To rationalize their respectability, Ladinos appealed to Creole ideals of *limpieza de sangre*, but it was a purity of blood signifying legitimate birth to an Old Christian family, not race, that obliged Ladinos to perpetuate the very postconquest society that had disadvantaged them in the first place.

Conceptually, the distinction between descent and race is key. Although both invoke the inalienable substance of 'blood,' descent personalizes where race generalizes. While both socially legitimize, race naturalizes collective attributions in individuals where descent sanctifies in anthropologist Roy Rappaport's (1999, 281) sense of posing an 'unverifiable yet unfalsifiable' ideal that validates adherents. In kinship, sanctification genealogically unites individuals and groups in the idealized founding ancestor. In *limpieza de sangre*, Christian ancestry then enabled living Christians to claim a purely Christian mythic past to 'make unquestionable' their own religious purity – and social acceptability – in the present. Genealogies, however, also work collaterally through marriage to produce ever widening alternate – and potentially delegitimizing – lines of descent. Descent remains problematic in ways the overgeneralizations of race erase.

Attention to descent over race complements Joanne Rappaport's study of 'the disappearing mestizo' in colonial Colombia that belies *mestizaje* as always and only about race as presently conceived. She reminds us that *casta* – and *raza* – in the 16th century related to proper descent, not wholesale categories of inclusion or exclusion, and we should focus instead on less reified 'circumstances of *identification*' (Rappaport 2014, 232). In similarly emphasizing descent, I have tried to show that one circumstance of identification for Ladinos – if not also for New Granada's *libres de todos colores* (free people of color) (208), Peru's *cholos* (almost Indians) (De La Cadena 1998), Yucatán's Maya *mestizos* (Eiss, this volume) and *vecinos de color* (residents of color) (Eiss 2010, 25, 33) – lay in the slippage inherent in *limpieza de sangre* as a descent ideology by which each passing generation attenuated Spanish Christian genealogies while establishing Indian and mulatto Christian ones. Identity remained a matter of who belonged where, not where each group ranked.

A limiting case would involve race explicitly. Significantly, Robin Sheriff's (2004) work on color terminology in Brazil parallels the dynamics of descent ideologies outlined here. She argues that what first appear as relativizing color terms actually privilege whiteness. To be white means seeing oneself – and being seen by others – as not having color and thus untroubled by race or racism. Conversely, in the inverse of the United States where one drop of black blood makes someone black, color terminology in Brazil presumes that one drop of white blood makes someone not black, whether out of courtesy or self-promotion, and the less black the better. Whites, however, always see anyone of whatever color as categorically black and act accordingly. That the same competitive exclusion from the top all the way down can be found among Brazilians of color and Guatemalan Ladinos suggests a shared Foucauldian genealogy related not to race, but to racing to the top entangled by countervailing genealogies.

This does not mean we should replace a general presumption of racialized *mestizaje* with one of descent. Systematic comparison of local histories remains crucial to explaining why the idiom of descent varies from parentage and practice to race and color, and to what effect. By the 17th century, generational time had opened sufficient space in Spanish, Indian, and mulatto genealogies for maneuver in between. By the 18th century, whether Indian *pueblos* declined, as in Colombia (Rappaport 2014, 218–220), or remained large, as in Guatemala (Adams 1989), the relatively few Spaniards in both places had reason to tolerate those in between – in Colombia as proxies for disappearing Indians and needed *vecinos* in respectable trades, in Guatemala as illicit buffers against an indigenous majority. Conversely, an oversized *república* of imperial Spaniards and Creole descendants in central Mexico may have precipitated the elaboration of *casta* categories as racing to the top became more fraught and thus more self-consciously calibrated.

More generally, the asymmetrical dynamics of Creole and Ladino descent ideologies in Guatemala may also suggest why ideological distinctions between top and bottom persist despite *mestizaje* in between. Ladinos need local places 'Indian' (or Ladino) enough not to challenge their 'Spanish' credentials, however they broker this (or not) into wider respectability – and Creoles need the emulation of Ladinos (if not the enmity of Indians) to satisfy the respect they require. More broadly still, if post-Reconquest religious purity, trans-Atlantic imperial conquests, and African slavery comprise key colonial nodes in the Foucauldian genealogy of *mestizaje*, then subsequent postcolonial nodes of 19th-century Liberal state building, biologized discrimination, and multicultural activism descend from previous articulations of inequality and power that do not simply recapitulate a timeless racism. Nonetheless, the inalienability yet indeterminacy inherent in descent ideologies may well have prefigured, if not motivated, the turn to more overtly racist ideologies later in the 19th century.

Despite such racialization, descent ideologies still demand that 'mestizos' play their part. More outspokenly than most, Archbishop Cortés y Larraz decried in 1768 where dissembling Indians learned their *ladino* roles:

> If they have learned anything from Spaniards, it is this trick of changing names and pretending to be from somewhere else, because here [in Guatemala] the Aragonese is Andalusian, the Castilian Galician, and Pedro Fernández don Miguel Antonio Sálazar Guzmán de Córdoba, Spanish gentleman born in the court of Madrid, one vagabond lending his services to another and mutually supporting each other as witnesses in declarations that affirm their freedom and nobility. (2001, 149)

This being the case at the top, why would any self-respecting Ladino ever think to do otherwise?

Acknowledgments

I thank Paul Eiss for generously inviting me to contribute to this collection; the Nelson A. Rockefeller Center and Claire Garber Goodman Fund, both of Dartmouth College, the National Humanities Center, the National Endowment for the Humanities, and the Dean of Faculty of Dartmouth College for long and generous support as the ideas presented here gestated. Todd Little-Siebold, Chris Lutz, and George Lovell have been knowing, steadfast guides for an ethnographer too long writing his way out of 19th-century Huehuetenango.

Funding

This work was supported by the Nelson A. Rockefeller Center for Public Policy and the Social Sciences, Dartmouth College; the Claire Garber Goodman Fund in the Department of Anthropology at Dartmouth College; the National Humanities Center, Research Triangle Park, NC; the National Endowment for the Humanities; and Dean of Faculty of Dartmouth College.

References

Adams, R. N. 1988. "Conclusions: What Can We Know About the Harvest of Violence?" In *The Harvest of Violence: The Maya Indians and the Guatemalan Crisis*, edited by R. M. Carmack, 274–291. Norman: University of Oklahoma Press.
Adams, R. N. 1989. "The Conquest Tradition of Mesoamerica." *The Americas* 46 (2): 119–136. doi:10.2307/1007079.
Austin, J. L. 1975. *How to Do Things with Words*. 2nd ed. Edited by J. O. Urmson and M. Sbisà. Cambridge, MA: Harvard University Press.
Barth, F. 1969. "Introduction." In *Ethnic Groups and Boundaries: The Social Organization of Culture Difference*, edited by F. Barth, 9–25. Boston: Little, Brown.
Bricker, V. R. 1973. *Ritual Humor in Highland Chiapas*. Austin: University of Texas Press.
Bricker, V. R. 1981. *The Indian Christ, the Indian King: The Historical Substrate of Maya Myth and Ritual*. Austin: University of Texas Press.
Brintnall, D. E. 1979. "Race Relations in the Southeastern Highlands of Mesoamerica." *American Ethnologist* 6 (4): 638–652. doi:10.1525/ae.1979.6.4.02a00020.
Carmack, R. M. 1981. *The Quiché Mayas of Utatlán: The Evolution of a Highland Guatemalan Kingdom*. Norman: University of Oklahoma Press.
Casaus Arzú, M. 1993. *Guatemala: Linaje y racismo*. San José: Facultad Latinoamericana de Ciencias Sociales.
Chamberlain, R. S. 1939. "The Concept of the *Señor Natural* as Revealed by Castilian Law and Administrative Documents." *The Hispanic American Historical Review* 19 (2): 130–137. doi:10.2307/2507437.
Chance, J. K. 1979. "On the Mexican Mestizo." *Latin American Research Review* 14 (3): 153–168.
Colby, B. N. 1966. *Ethnic Relations in the Chiapas Highlands*. Santa Fe: Museum of New Mexico Press.
Colby, B. N., and P. L. van den Berghe. 1969. *Ixil Country: A Plural Society in Highland Guatemala*. Berkeley: University of California Press.
Cortés Y Larraz, P. 2001. *Descripción geográfico-moral de la Diócesis de Goathemala hecha por su arzobispo el ilmo. Sr. don Pedro Cortés y Larraz*, edited by J. M. Blasco and J. M. García Añoveros. Madrid: Consejo Superior de Investigaciones Científicas.
De La Cadena, M. 1998. "Silent Racism and Intellectual Superiority in Peru." *Bulletin of Latin American Research* 17 (2): 143–164. doi:10.1111/j.1470-9856.1998.tb00169.x.
Eiss, P. K. 2010. *In the Name of El Pueblo: Place, Community, and the Politics of History in Yucatán*. Durham, NC: Duke University Press.
Euraque, D. A. 2004. *Conversaciones históricas con el mestizaje y su identidad nacional en Honduras*. San Pedro Sula: Centro Editorial.
Euraque, D. A., J. L. Gould, and C. R. Hale, eds. 2004. *Memorias del mestizaje: Cultura política en Centroamérica de 1920 al presente*. La Antigua Guatemala: Centro de Investigaciones Regionales de Mesoamérica.
Farriss, N. M. 1984. *Maya Society Under Colonial Rule: The Collective Enterprise of Survival*. Princeton, NJ: Princeton University Press.
Foucault, M. 1980. "Two Lectures." In *Power/Knowledge: Selected Interviews and Other Writings, 1972–1977*, edited by C. Gordon. Translated by C. Gordon, L. Marshall, J. Mepham, and K. Soper, 78–108. New York, NY: Pantheon Books.
Foucault, M. 1982. "The Subject and Power." *Critical Inquiry* 8 (4): 777–795. doi:10.1086/448181.

Gasco, J. 1991. "Indian Survival and Ladinoization in Colonial Soconusco." In *Columbian Consequences*, edited by D. H. Thomas, 301–318. Vol. 3. Washington, DC: Smithsonian Institution Press.

Gould, J. L. 1993. "'¡Vana ilusión!' The Highlands Indians and the Myth of Nicaragua Mestiza, 1880-1925." *The Hispanic American Historical Review* 73 (3): 393–429. doi:10.2307/2517696.

Gould, J. L. 1998. *To Die in This Way: Nicaraguan Indians and the Myth of Mestizaje, 1880–1965.* Durham, NC: Duke University Press.

Guzmán-Böckler, C. 1970. "El ladino: Un ser ficticio." In *Guatemala: Una interpretación histórico-social*, edited by C. Guzmán-Böckler and J.-L. Herbert, 101–121. Mexico City: Siglo Veintiuno Editores.

Kelly, J. E. [1932] 1971. *Pedro de Alvarado, Conquistador.* Port Washington, NY: Kennikat Press.

Lauria-Santiago, A. A. 1999. "Land, Community, and Revolt in Late-Nineteenth-Century Indian Izalco, El Salvador." *The Hispanic American Historical Review* 79 (3): 495–543.

Little-Siebold, T. 2001. "'Where Have All the Spaniards Gone?' Independent Identities: Ethnicities, Class, and the Emergent National State." *Journal of Latin American Anthropology* 6 (2): 106–133. doi:10.1525/jlca.2001.6.2.106.

Lokken, P. 2001. "Marriage as Slave Emancipation in 17th Century Guatemala." *The Americas* 58 (2): 175–200. doi:10.1353/tam.2001.0106.

Lovell, W. G. 1983. "Settlement Change in Spanish America: The Dynamics of *Congregación* in the Cuchumatán Highlands of Guatemala, 1541–1821." *Canadian Geographer* 27 (2): 163–174. doi:10.1111/cag.1983.27.issue-2.

Lovell, W. G. 1990. "Mayans, Missionaries, Evidence and Truth: The Polemics of Native Resettlement in Sixteenth-Century Guatemala." *Journal of Historical Geography* 16 (3): 277–294. doi:10.1016/0305-7488(90)90043-B.

Lovell, W. G. 1992. *Conquest and Survival in Colonial Guatemala: A Historical Demography of the Cuchumatán Highlands, 1500–1821.* Revised ed. Kingston: McGill-Queen's University Press.

Luján Muñoz, J. 1976a. "Fundación de villas de ladinos en Guatemala en el ultimo tercio del siglo XVIII." *Revista de Indias* 36 (145–146): 51–82.

Luján Muñoz, J. 1976b. "Reducción y fundación de Salcajá y Sijá (Guatemala) en 1776." *Anales de la Sociedad de Geografía é Historia de Guatemala* 49: 45–57.

Lutz, C. H. 1994. *Santiago de Guatemala, 1541–1773: City, Caste, and the Colonial Experience.* Norman: University of Oklahoma Press.

Lutz, C. H. 1995. "Evolución demográfica de la población ladina." In *Historia general de Guatemala, tomo III: Siglo XVIII hasta la Independencia*, edited by C. Zilbermann De Luján and J. L. Muñoz, 119–134. Guatemala City: Asociación de Amigos del País and Fundación para la Cultura y el Desarrollo.

MacLeod, M. J. 1973. *Spanish Central America: A Socioeconomic History, 1520–1720.* Berkeley: University of California Press.

Martínez, M. E. 2008. *Genealogical Fictions: Limpieza de Sangre, Religion, and Gender in Colonial Mexico.* Stanford: Stanford University Press.

Martínez Peláez, S. [1970] 1979. *La patria del criollo: Ensayo de interpretación de la realidad colonial guatemalteca.* 6th ed. San José: Editorial Universitaria Centroamericana.

Megged, A. 1992. "The Rise of Creole Identity in Early Colonial Guatemala: Differential Patterns in Town and Countryside." *Social History* 17 (3): 421–440. doi:10.1080/03071029208567848.

Mörner, M. 1967. *Race Mixture in the History of Latin America.* Boston: Little, Brown and Company.

Mundigo, A. I., and D. P. Crouch. 1977. "The City Planning Ordinances of the Laws of the Indies Revisited: Part I: Their Philosophy and Implications." *The Town Planning Review* 48 (3): 247–268. doi:10.3828/tpr.48.3.g58m031x54655ll5.

Pagden, A. 1987. "Identity Formation in Spanish America." In *Colonial Identity in the Atlantic World, 1500–1800*, edited by N. Canny and A. Pagden, 51–93. Princeton, NJ: Princeton University Press.

Pitt-Rivers, J. 1967. "Words and Deeds: The Ladinos of Chiapas." *Man* 2 (1): 71–86. doi:10.2307/2798655.

Pitt-Rivers, J. 1969. "Mestizo or Ladino?" *Race & Class* 10 (4): 463–477. doi:10.1177/030639686901000404.

Pitt-Rivers, J. 1971. "On the Word 'Caste'." In *The Translation of Culture: Essays to E. E. Evans-Pritchard*, edited by T. O. Beidelman, 231–254. London: Tavistock Publications.

Poole, S. 1996. *Our Lady of Guadalupe: The Origins and Sources of a Mexican National Symbol, 1531-1797*. Tucson: University of Arizona Press.

Poole, S. 1999. "The Politics of Limpieza de Sangre: Juan de Ovando and his Circle in the Reign of Philip II." *The Americas* 55 (3): 359–389. doi:10.2307/1007647.

Rappaport, J. 2014. *The Disappearing Mestizo: Configuring Difference in the Colonial New Kingdom of Granada*. Durham, NC: Duke University Press.

Rappaport, R. A. 1999. *Ritual and Religion in the Making of Humanity*. New York, NY: Cambridge University Press.

Recopilación de leyes de los reinos de las indias. 4 vols., 5th ed. 1841. Madrid: Boix.

Sheriff, R. E. 2004. *Dreaming Equality: Color, Race, and Racism in Urban Brazil*. New Brunswick, NJ: Rutgers University Press.

Sherman, W. L. 1979. *Forced Native Labor in Sixteenth Century Central America*. Lincoln: University of Nebraska Press.

Silverblatt, I. 2000. "New Christians and New World Fears in Seventeenth-Century Peru." *Comparative Studies in Society and History* 42 (3): 524–546. doi:10.1017/S0010417500002929.

Silverblatt, I. M. 2004. *Modern Inquisitions: Peru and the Colonial Origins of the Civilized World*. Durham, NC: Duke University Press.

Smith, C. A. 1995. "Race-Class-Gender Ideology in Guatemala: Modern and Anti-Modern Forms." *Comparative Studies in Society and History* 37 (4): 723–749. doi:10.1017/S0010417500019939.

Stavenhagen, R. 1968. "Classes, Colonialism, and Acculturation." In *Comparative Perspectives on Stratification: Mexico, Great Britain, Japan*, edited by J. A. Kahl, 31–63. Boston: Little, Brown, and Company.

Sullivan, P. 2000. "The Yucatec Maya." In *Supplement to the Handbook of Middle American Indians: Ethnology*, edited by J. D. Monaghan, 207–223. Vol. 6. Austin: University of Texas Press.

Taracena Arriola, A. 1982. "Contribución al estudio del vocablo 'ladino' en Guatemala (s. XVI-XIX)." In *Historia y antropología de Guatemala: Ensayos en honor de J. Daniel Contreras R.*, edited by J. Luján Muñoz, 89–104. Guatemala: Facultad de Humanidades, Universidad de San Carlos de Guatemala.

Tax, S. 1941. "World View and Social Relations in Guatemala." *American Anthropologist* 43 (1): 27–42. doi:10.1525/aa.1941.43.issue-1.

Taylor, W. B. 1987. "The Virgin of Guadalupe in New Spain: An Inquiry into the Social History of Marian Devotion." *American Ethnologist* 14 (1): 9–33. doi:10.1525/ae.1987.14.1.02a00020.

Warren, K. B. 1989. *The Symbolism of Subordination: Indian Identity in a Guatemalan Town*, with a new introduction. Austin: University of Texas Press.

Watanabe, J. M. 1992. *Maya Saints and Souls in a Changing World*. Austin: University of Texas Press.

Weber, M. [1968] 1978. *Economy and Society: An Outline of Interpretive Sociology*. Vol. 1. Edited by G. Roth and C. Wittich. Berkeley: University of California Press.

Mestizaje, multiculturalism, liberalism, and violence

Peter Wade ⓘ

ABSTRACT

Mestizaje has been theorized as a racial–cultural process of nationalist homogenization, as a mode of subaltern contestation or inconformity, and as a practice that simultaneously combines both inclusion and exclusion. This exclusive inclusion is characteristic of liberalism generally, and may involve violence. The core meanings of mestizaje are rooted in sex and reproduction, which allow ideas of inclusion (family, kinship) to gain traction. These ideas mask the violence of mestizaje (rape, coercion, enforced assimilation, elimination). In Colombia, the long-standing tension between democracy and violence has recently articulated in a particular way with mestizaje as this has become reconfigured as inclusive multiculturalism, coinciding with the explosive spread of extreme violence to once peaceful 'black regions' of the country. This violence should not be understood as inherently racial – for example, as purposely targeting black populations. But in placing mestizaje in relation to multiculturalism through a common dynamic of inclusion and exclusion that characterizes liberal social orders in general, I highlight the racialized connections between mestizaje and violence in the Colombian context.

Introduction

In this essay, I explore the tensions between processes of inclusion and exclusion that are characteristic of liberalism and *mestizaje*, and the role of violence in their operation. I analyze how the liberal tension between inclusion and exclusion works in relation to racialized difference in regimes of mestizaje and, more recently, multiculturalism in Colombia; and how racialized difference has become recently more clearly articulated to violence in that country, even though most of the violence has little explicit racial dimension to it. As racialized difference has become enshrined in multiculturalist law, the violence that is constitutive of liberal social orders ensnares that difference in more overt ways.

Liberalism and mestizaje are not concepts of exactly equivalent order. The former is a mode of political organization. The latter describes acts understood to 'mix' different bio-cultural categories to create forms that bear the marks of the originary categories, while being distinctively new. But mestizaje also describes political arrangements of citizenship, which have a dual character: certain bio-cultural categories of people are

111

politically superior, while others are subordinate; and/or everyone is (or will be) a mestizo and equally a citizen. Mestizaje describes a process of nation-state formation based on the idea of race – an inherently political concept – which defines who can properly govern (Appelbaum, Macpherson, and Rosemblatt 2003). Mestizaje is about acts of sex and kinship – the symbolics and passage of blood (Smith 1997) – and this makes it intensely political, whether we consider the genealogical governance of honor and property in colonial Latin America, or the regulation of sexual behavior (especially female) in the name of public morality and social hygiene in the region in the early 20th century (Caulfield 2000; Martínez 2008; Noguera 2003; Stepan 1991; Twinam 1999; Wade 2009).

I look first at the tensions within liberalism, and how violence figures in them. I then look at the way violence and racialized difference figured in Latin American regimes of citizenship. Turning to Colombia, I explore inclusion, exclusion, and violence in mid-20th-century ideologies of mestizaje, before examining the post-1990 turn to multi-culturalism. Although this turn is not a radical rupture with mestizaje, I argue that racialized difference is now more clearly articulated to violence than it was before, even if the connection remains ambiguous.

Liberalism, inclusion, and exclusion

Liberal rule – including its neoliberal variants – is characterized by fundamental tensions. It is beset by the constitutive conflict between the democratic inclusion demanded by ideologies of liberty and equality, and the political and economic exclusions demanded by the need to govern 'properly' and the need of governing elites to preserve the hierarchies of economic stratification in which they hold a dominant position. The dictates regarding the proper ways of governance and who can properly be a governor vary over time. For example, there have been long-term shifts toward a Foucauldian concept of the bio-political, in which the regulation and maximization of life force become the key principles of governance. There have been recent shifts toward a neoliberal variant of liberalism, in which decentralization and the individualization of citizenly responsibility for self-governance are core values (Rose and Miller 2008; Wacquant 2012).

Liberalism was originally an ideology 'born out of the struggles of the [European] bourgeoisie against the abuses of royal authority,' which, in order to 'destroy corporate privilege…made freedom, equality before the law, and the right to property universal rights of men' (Viotti da Costa 2000, 54). When liberals faced the challenge of translating theory into practice, 'everywhere in this process liberalism lost its revolutionary mean-ing' (55). Liberal ideology invokes the image of universal citizenship, of equal rights and sameness vis-à-vis the state; it denies the relevance of difference to the question of rights.

Liberalism must also deal with particularity and difference, and it does so first by consigning them to the 'private' sphere: differences (of race, gender, culture, religion, etc.) exist, but they are deemed irrelevant to the 'public' sphere of rights. However, the laboriously constructed divide attempting to separate public and private as pure domains is constantly made porous as the differences of the 'private' domain are integral to the functioning of the liberal project in the public domain: the feminist slogan 'the personal is political' points at a general truth. Liberalism constitutes difference as relevant to rights by means of moral judgments made about who is fit to be a citizen, what a good citizen is, and who is in a position to make such judgments. Such judgments are necessary to maintain a political and economic division of labor. Liberalism constitutes difference as hierarchy, even if hierarchy is rhetorically denied in assertions about being 'different but equal' (Baumeister 2000; Mehta 1997, 93). Sometimes liberalism attempts to eradicate some forms of difference – genocide, ethnocide, forcible assimilation – but ultimately it needs difference.

As a mode of governance, liberalism moves between sameness and difference or universalism and particularism in a strategic fashion, emphasizing one or the other, in order to regulate change and maintain hegemony. Universalist and public claims that everyone is equal before the state and the law coexist with particularist and public discriminations on the basis of difference. The differences understood to be relevant in determining the ability or right to rule or be included in citizenly rights can be diverse: gender, age, race, class status, national origin, etc. While it is not clear that racial difference, in particular, is *necessary* to liberal regimes, there is little question that racial discrimination has been historically constitutive of them, as liberal modernity's darker side (Goldberg 1993; Mignolo 2011). Holt contends that historical evidence from the 19th-century Atlantic world 'suggests that "racism" was embedded in the very premises of a presumably nonracist liberalism' (1992, xx). It seems unlikely that hierarchical difference can ever be ironed out of liberal rule – despite the progress made in some areas of the world in terms of antisexist and antiracist public policy – and differences such as sex and race are likely to continue to provide ways of organizing and justifying liberal hierarchies, especially when seen on a global scale (Goldberg 2008; Stokes and Meléndez 2003).

Those who suffer discrimination because of their perceived difference may protest at the resulting inequality, invoking the principles of liberal equality that are supposed to govern public life. Such protests provoke reassertions of the universalist principle, which states that to highlight difference in the domain defined as public – even when done in protest at the failure of the principle itself – is to challenge the basis of equality and to introduce division where it does not belong. Examples of this, in relation to racial difference, can be seen in the violent backlash against black antiracist political organization in Cuba in 1908–1912, in recent critiques made of racial quota policies in Brazil, and in the reluctance in much of postwar Europe to allow the language of racial difference to enter the public policy domain. These challenges to racial inequality have all been criticized for reinforcing racial division. Another example is the critiques of multiculturalism that object to its universalization of the right to *public* difference, and restate the liberal principle that racial and ethnic differences – all glossed as cultural difference – should be confined to the private sphere (Fry et al. 2007; Helg 1995; Lentin 2004). A bone of contention here is the difference between equality of outcome and equality of opportunity: some insist that racial–ethnic inequalities of outcome in the public sphere, when long term and collective, must indicate failures in equality of opportunity, which necessitate direct attention to differences of race and ethnicity for reparative purposes; others contend that paying such attention may itself undermine equality of opportunity and reinforce hierarchy. Equality is a common value, but it contains different elements that may be incommensurable (Baumeister 2000, 179).

The difference-making, hierarchy, and exclusion that are constitutive of liberal rule, rather than aberrations of it, may involve violence of various types, from everyday discriminations and exclusions, to structural segregation, forcible displacement, and killing. I will expand on this below.

Mestizaje, difference, citizenship, and violence in Latin America

After independence in Latin America, political elites attempted to dismantle the colonial regimes that had institutionalized racialized difference; they adhered to a liberal emphasis on universalism and the creation of equal citizens (Larson 2004; Lasso 2007; Viotti da Costa 2000). However, as usual in liberal regimes, there were major limits to equality. Women were excluded from suffrage, as they were in many liberal regimes worldwide.[1] In Brazil, when the first constitutional charter, dated 1824, 'defined freedom and equality as inalienable rights of men, millions of blacks continued to be enslaved' (Viotti da Costa 2000, 57). Indigenous and free black people were not usually explicitly excluded, although indigenous people were more likely to be named in this respect. This was the case in Brazil, where in addition to being legally defined as wards or orphans of state, the 1916 Civil Code classified *silvícolas* (translated as 'savages' in the English version) as 'relatively incapable,' and thus not fit to vote, along with married women and prodigal sons (Ramos 1998, 18, 157). More usually, however, literacy requirements – which persisted in Colombia until 1932 and in Brazil until 1988 – were used to exclude them from suffrage, along with many other poor people (Agudelo 2005, 108, note 112; Engerman and Sokoloff 2005, 913; Sanders 2004, 128, 191; Yashar 2005, 141, 156, 227). In short, 'converging race-class correlations … cemented modern forms of social inequality and marginality under liberalizing "republics without citizens"' (Alberto Flores Galindo, cited in Larson 2004, 247).

Racialized difference – and inequality – persisted, but this was not simply a delay in progressively ironing out the kinks in a universalist policy of citizenship. Two processes were at work. On the one hand, citizens who felt themselves to be excluded made efforts at inclusion, which raised issues of racial difference in varying ways. On the other hand, elites actively produced difference in their discourse and practice. In this sense, differences were simultaneously produced – indeed coproduced – from below and above. Everyone agreed on the value of equality and freedom for all, but everyone also kept producing difference – and, in some cases, hierarchy. In rural Rio de Janeiro, the appearance of color terms in legal and bureaucratic documents declined from the 1860s, except in relation to slaves: increasingly, *negro* became a synonym for slave. The ex-slaves, especially immediately after abolition in 1888, avoided the category *negro*, wanting to distance themselves from slavery and be accepted as free; to some extent, official processes reflected this universalization of citizenship by being silent about color. Everyone converged on the values of freedom and silence about color. Nevertheless, everyone also produced difference. In the 1890s, documents often still labeled recently freed slaves (and indeed their children) as *negros*, and the categories of *blanco, pardo* (brown), and *negro* persisted in official usage. Meanwhile, among the plebeian classes, *negro* was used as an insult, which could provoke free blacks to take legal action (Mattos de Castro 1995). For these freedmen, participation in freedom meant excluding *negros*, as elites also did.

An example of producing difference from below is Colombia during and immediately after independence, when the *pardos* (free blacks and mixed-race people) of the Caribbean coastal region fought for the equality promised by revolution. However, Simón Bolívar himself denied that South America was suited to full liberal democracy, as the participation of the (nonwhite) popular classes would, he said, 'lead to Colombia's ruin' (cited in Lasso 2007, 3). Although by the 1820s, with the active participation of *pardos*, Colombia had 'developed a nationalist ideology that proclaimed the equality and harmony of its people of European, African, and indigenous descent,' many among the new elite, while they adhered to the idea of equality, also shared Bolívar's views (153). It is not surprising that, although some *pardos* were admitted into political office and they enjoyed formal legal equality, they were aware of the racial exclusion of dark-skinned people. They occasionally complained about this, effectively highlighting their own difference, even though they sought only an equal society. Such grievances, especially when expressed by *pardos* in positions of authority, provoked accusations that they were undermining the nation's hard-won racial harmony with their unpatriotic 'racial enmity' and were threatening to provoke a 'race war' (107, 155).

Another example is of indigenous communities in the Cauca region of Southwestern Colombia, whose members in the mid- to late 19th century made claims to be treated as full citizens, especially in relation to land rights (Sanders 2004). The claims invoked the argument that they were *indios*: they were poor, weak, defenseless, and stupid – contemporary stereotypes about indigenous people – and thus needed special help. They claimed to be citizens and also highlighted their status as *indios* – the same as others and yet different.

In Brazil and in Cuba, some black people organized in the early decades of the 20th century – in the short-lived Cuban Partido Independiente de Color or the black São Paulo press – claiming equality of citizenship, but in the process pointing up racial difference. This caused critics to accuse them of being 'racist,' that is, focusing on race in a society that aspired to, or claimed it had already achieved, race-blindness in the public political sphere (Andrews 1991; Helg 1995). In sum, blacks and indigenous people sought equality and participated in the production of a society of liberal values, which nevertheless excluded them in practice.

In the second mode of difference production, elites actively produced difference as part of national ideologies based on foundation narratives of mestizaje, the mixture of Europeans, native Americans, and Africans – or more accurately white *men* and indigenous and black *women* – to form new mestizo people and societies. In keeping with the tensions that beset the modern liberalism to which they aspired, elites equivocated between the democratic inclusion and the racist exclusion of black and indigenous populations, deemed by contemporary science to be inherently inferior. Mestizaje is, at one level, all about sameness and inclusion: everyone is mestizo, everyone is the product of a cultural–biological fusion, no one is pure; people may look and act differently, but they all share in mixture; racial difference is overwhelmed by shared mixedness and cannot operate as criterion of discrimination. But mestizaje is simultaneously about exclusion: people classified as black and indigenous belong to the past and to the margins; they are seen as inferior and backward. Racial difference motivates exclusionary discrimination. In order to become full citizens, these people must discard such identities – by leaving behind dress, languages, and habits seen as indigenous and black, by leaving communities that seem ethnically endogamous – and integrate into mestizo society, where they can become educated and break the ties of kinship to their communities.

Mestizaje has thus been seen by some as the forcible eradication of difference, often involving extreme violence that operated apparently outside the boundaries of the law. Examples include the massacres of Afro-Cubans in the 1912 'Guerrita del 12,' which demolished the racial mobilization of the Partido Independiente de Color (Helg 1995); the 'Conquest of the Desert' in late 19th-century Argentina, in which mass executions of indigenous people took place (Andermann 2000); the massacres of Matagalpa people by the Nicaraguan state repressing an 1881 rebellion (Gould 1998); and the extreme abuses practiced by rubber companies in the Colombian Amazon in the early 20th century, which created a 'space of terror' (Taussig 1987).

In this view of mestizaje as ethnocide, inclusion would be seen as linked to cultural 'improvement,' coming within the compass of the law and achieving proper citizenship; while exclusion would be linked to noncitizenship (in practice, if not in the letter of the law) and to violence directed against racialized people seen as belonging to the realm of nature and animality. But there is more to it than this: the balance between inclusion and exclusion is more subtle.

As an ideology in practice, mestizaje is not just about the definition of noncitizens and their assimilation or violent eradication but is also about the active production and continued management of difference (Wade 2005). In the 1850s, for example, the newly formed government of New Granada (effectively Colombia) sent out a Chorographic Commission to map the country's people and resources and the country's possibilities for progress. Driven by a project of national integration and modernization, the Commission *produced* difference as it documented the country's regional and racialized variety in text and watercolor paintings (Restrepo 1984). A century later, in the 1950s and after, Colombian school textbooks unfailingly mentioned the mixture of African, Spanish, and indigenous people that is the foundational story of the nation; they reproduced thumbnail sketches, in text and pictures, of the three 'original' components of the mix – and ranged them hierarchically, with blacks and indigenous people in clearly subordinate positions (Wade 2000, 34–36). Such diversity was not only located in the past: the textbooks also always referred to the variety and diversity of the contemporary national population, usually in regional and/or racial terms. In Colombia, regional diversity is strongly racialized (Wade 1993) and, as I will discuss below, the difference enshrined in politics by the new multiculturalist constitution of 1991, which focused on black and indigenous minorities, was not a radical departure from these representations.

Difference has long been constitutive of the nation in ways more complex than merely being subject to eradication – multiculturalist legislation is only a recent and explicit variation on this theme. In this history, difference has always constituted the hierarchy at the apex of which the elites placed themselves: continual, managed difference has always been needed in order to reproduce the distinction elites claimed for themselves, even under multiculturalism.

Hierarchical exclusions often entail violence, but this may take diverse forms. Mestizaje can involve one or more of a range of processes: the symbolic violence of denial, invisibilization, and forced assimilation; the structural violence of exclusion and impoverishment (leading, for example, to high rates to morbidity and mortality); and the violence of extirpation, which can take the form of administrative dislocation and/or physical extermination. Collins (2015), for example, in his account of the conversion of the traditionally black Pelourinho zone of Salvador (Brazil) into a heritage site, a representation of Afro-Brazilian history and culture as part of the national (and international) patrimony, documents the displacement of the majority of the local black population. This involved a combination of local state administrative interventions, with social scientists who collected and archived data, officials who counted and measured, and then evicted (and sometimes relocated or compensated) the locals, and policemen who harassed and killed them.

I focus mainly on overt violence – killing, displacement, terror, physical fights – and explore how they have figured in regimes of mestizaje and, more recently, multiculturalism. The management of difference in regimes of mestizaje not only could organize or even generate violence against racialized categories of subordinated people but also could ameliorate racialized violence, because these categories were simultaneously included as well as excluded, following the logic of liberalism. In Colombia, the idea of mestizaje made it possible to say 'you are black, therefore you are not mestizo citizens,' and thus subject to exclusion; and *simultaneously*, 'OK, you are black, but you are also (kind of mestizo) citizens' – a claim also made by black people themselves. With the advent of multiculturalism, alongside the intensification of neoliberalized development, the dynamic of inclusion and exclusion alters. The differences evoked by the narrative of mestizaje become *institutionalized* as categories of governance that are targeted for inclusion, while those defined by those same categories become – and come to be seen as – particular victims of the violence that affects society as a whole.

Mestizaje and violence in mid-20th-century Colombia

Colombia has been wracked by episodes of violence characterized by extraordinary levels of atrocity and impunity, in which the state and its proxies have been involved, such as the Liberal–Conservative conflicts of the Guerra de los Mil Días (War of a Thousand Days, 1899–1902); La Violencia (The Violence, 1948–1958); and the more recent decades of guerrilla, paramilitary, state, and drug-fueled violence (Bushnell 1993; Sanford 2003, 2004; Taussig 2005; Uribe 2004). Colombia's citizens have long been caught between the apparatus of a liberal democratic state system, in one of Latin America's most durable democracies, and very high levels of violence and abuse of citizens' rights. The role of race in these conflicts has been ambiguous and equivocal; although my argument is that it has recently become rather less so.

Historically, black people and the regions where they have concentrated – mainly the Pacific and Caribbean coastal regions and some areas of the Cauca Valley in the southwest of the country (such as Northern Cauca province) – have been staunchly Liberal. The Liberals ushered in abolition in 1851 and have generally been associated with populist challenges to the Conservative and clerical oligarchy, although of course a section of the elite was Liberal and Liberalism was a heterogeneous political current, with more and less radical versions (Green 2000; Pisano 2012, 112–125). In the 19th century, black- and brown-skinned people formed the bulk of the plebeian classes in much of the country, and many of those living in urban areas participated in Colombia's *sociedades democráticas de artesanos* (democratic societies of artisans), which represented the liberal aspirations (and Liberal loyalties) of an emerging middle stratum (Agudelo 2005, 105; Green 2000). But there was no straightforward correlation between race and political affiliation and the Liberal–Conservative conflicts of the Guerra de los Mil Días and La Violencia by no means followed clear racialized lines.

A case in point is Jorge Eliécer Gaitán, the left-leaning populist Liberal leader, whose assassination in 1948 sparked La Violencia. On the one hand, 'There is no question that Gaitanismo was a "dark" movement. The terms "pueblo," "plebeyo," "chusma" ("rabble") and even "país nacional" all had strong race as well as class connotations' (Green 2000, 120). Gaitán himself was nicknamed El Negro Gaitán and El Indio Gaitán – disparagingly by the white oligarchy and proudly by the urban working classes – and Gaitán used his mestizo appearance for populist appeal. He also gained the support of many black and brown intellectuals (Urrea Giraldo, Viáfara López, and Viveros Vigoya 2014, 89). Yet 'Gaitanista mobilization never mustered overtly along color lines' (Green 2000, 121) and the ensuing conflict did not target categories of people identified in racialized terms: the key divide was between Liberals and Conservatives, at least in theory (Uribe 2004, 87).

The regional distribution of violence in the province of Antioquia during this period shows that racial connotations were in play, but ambiguously so. Roldán (2002) argues that racial difference was a factor influencing the pattern in which the Antioquian municipalities with the highest rates of violence in 1949–1953 were 'peripheral' to the central, highland coffee-growing zones of the province. Her argument is that, compared to the central zones, these peripheral municipalities were all lower altitude, more tropical, less stable in terms of landownership, and subject to rapacious colonization by capitalist interests from the highland zones or overseas, which exploited cattle-ranching, forest resources (timber), and minerals (gold, oil), rather than coffee. At the same time, the province's central zones were populated by people who had developed a self-image – a mythology – based on the idea of a *raza antioqueña*, reputed to be dynamic, entrepreneurial, adventurous, colonizing, hard-working, devoutly Catholic – and rather white. The people of the peripheral zones were seen by these highlanders as morally and religiously lax, backward, and lazy – and, in the peripheral areas close to the Caribbean coastal region, *moreno* (brown) or *negro*. In addition, these areas were often Liberal strongholds. Violence was then a complex product of partisan loyalties operating through a dynamic of internal colonialism with its attendant economic interests and its moral judgments about cultural and racial differences.

Roldán is one of the only scholars to explicitly link race to La Violencia, but her material shows that racial difference was not articulated in a clear or simple way with patterns of violence. To start with, she focuses only on Antioquia, with its arguably quite particular regional mythology and racialized configuration; extending the analysis to the whole country would be difficult. Second, within Antioquia itself, some peripheral zones (Urrao, Medio Magdalena) were not 'black,' even in the highland imaginary, compared to others (Bajo Cauca, Urabá), which bordered the Caribbean province of Bolívar. Third, the peripheral areas with the highest incidence of violence were actually the least black: 'western Antioquia,' for example, was a buffer zone between the highlands and Urabá (which was Antioquia's corridor to the Caribbean coast, and was very dark-skinned and Liberal); it was a contested zone where the struggle between Liberal guerrilla forces and

Conservative paramilitaries – and the terrorizing of the civilian population by the latter – had the most drastic effect. Fourth, complex local scenarios emerged. In Urabá, for example, the soldiers were brought in not from distant highland Antioquia, but from nearby Caribbean coastal provinces; they were dark-skinned Liberals, as were the local policemen and other local residents. Another contingent of police was brought in from the more indigenous provinces around Bogotá (Boyacá, Cundinamarca): they were Conservatives and little liked by the locals or by the army; the same went for the customs officers who came from the highlands of Antioquia. In other words, what might be seen as agents of colonization of a peripheral area – the army, the police – were themselves divided by race and partisan loyalty (Roldán 2002, 177, 197).

La Violencia shows that serious conflict might have some racial connotations, but that these were diffuse and were crosscut by other forms of social identification. An example of how racial difference was more explicitly articulated comes from a period slightly before La Violencia and does not deal with such overt violence. Indeed, black intellectuals' ideas about racial difference at the time, while challenging in some respects the view of mestizo Colombia as racially harmonious, took a nonconflictive stance and tried to avoid actual violence – not always with complete success. These intellectuals generally came from a minority of black families, based in the urban areas of the Pacific and Caribbean coastal regions and the south-western provinces of Cauca and Valle, which, from about the 1920s, had been able to give their offspring a university education, usually in the white-mestizo cities of the Andean interior, such as Bogotá and Medellín. Being a tiny minority of blacks in nonblack cities, they often experienced everyday racism in the form of stares, insults, being stereotyped, and feeling excluded from certain social contexts (e.g. as potential boyfriends – most of the immigrants were men – of local young women) (see Wade 2000, 125–138, 188–191). At the same time, some of them knew about the Black Renaissances in Harlem and Chicago; they had heard of Négritude and other such black diaspora phenomena.

On 20 June 1943 in Bogotá, a small group of resident blacks organized El Día del Negro, which involved 'invading' the Music Room of the National Library, where they persuaded the staff to play records by black US artists, after which they gave some public speeches in local cafés and below the statue of Simón Bolívar in the city's main Plaza. Here, some passersby objected to what they saw as an insult to the memory of the great 'Liberator': violence threatened to erupt and the police had to intervene, taking Natanael Díaz, Marino Viveros, Adolfo Mina Balanta, and Delia and Manuel Zapata Olivella to the police station for the night (Pisano 2012, 67). In the face of an overt assertion of racial difference, which was at the same time a claim to equality, public reaction was negative – the local press accused the event of introducing racial division into Colombia, where, according to the journalists, it did not exist (68) – and there emerged a threat of physical violence, which was defused by police intervention. Apparently, the black people were the only ones arrested.

These individuals and others, such as the politician Diego Luis Córdoba – several of them local and national political figures – soon founded the short-lived Club Negro in Bogotá. The public statements of this organization show the equivocal and ambiguous role assigned to race and the desire to avoid conflict, above all by these black intellectuals aspiring to middle-class status in a mainly white-mestizo city. The Club's propaganda secretary, Natanael Díaz, claimed racism did not exist in Colombia – in contrast to the

United States – and said the country's mixed national identity ensured a basic racial equality. Yet, he claimed that the contribution made by '*la raza negra*' to the nation – their martyrdom – had been ignored and that they lived in particularly poor conditions, which demanded reparation. Díaz and his colleagues were reticent about racial discrimination when addressing a national audience – for example, in Congress – and emphasized an encompassing Colombianness. However, when in their regions of origin, addressing audiences who were generally darker skinned, they challenged the image of racial equality more openly (Pisano 2012, 227). An explicit assertion of racial difference was combined with the invocation – hovering between the present and future tenses – of equality and integration, in which such difference would no longer have significance. Almost no claim was made for cultural distinctiveness.

In 1947, some members of the Club Negro founded the short-lived Centro de Estudios Afrocolombianos (Pisano 2012, 103–107). Seeking to emulate the state-funded Instituto Etnológico Nacional (IEN), which was founded in 1941 by the French anthropologist Paul Rivet and focused exclusively on indigenous groups, the spokesman of the Center, the writer and folklorist Manuel Zapata Olivella, defined an anthropological agenda, proposing studies of black people's contributions to Colombian history and culture, and of black culture itself. At a time when the term *afrocolombiano* was little used, the Center's name adduced the idea of African origins. The Center's stance challenged the homogeneity of Colombian mestizo culture, yet the basic tension between difference and equality evident in the Club Negro's formulations remained. Black people were different and were treated unequally; they deserved to be treated equally, but this formal equality was associated in these statements – and arguably in many of the later writings of Zapata Olivella – with an attachment to the positively valued idea of Colombian mestizaje as a unifying force, albeit heterogeneous and, in Zapata Olivella's work, able to represent subaltern as well as dominant stances.[2] Mestizaje would avoid the kind of racial violence and hatred that was seen as afflicting the United States, to which these activists routinely opposed Colombia, and which Zapata Olivella knew at first hand through his travels.

The discourse of the black intellectuals actively produced racial difference and racial mixture as simultaneous processes that existed in an irresolvable tension: in mestizaje, mixture never produces complete homogeneity, and difference never exists without mixture blurring its boundaries. In the vision of the black intellectuals in Bogotá, mestizaje made blackness invisible. This symbolic form of violence, with material entailments in terms of everyday racism, was both highlighted when talking with regional audiences, and denied when they addressed a national forum and inclusiveness was being rhetorically emphasized, along with the speaker's adherence to such ideals. Mestizaje was also valued because it was seen to prevent racial violence from emerging or to defuse a particular context if it did so. The critique and valuing of mestizaje are not opposed tendencies, but rather express the constitutive tension between inclusion and exclusion. For the black leaders, mestizaje could indeed invisibilize blackness but could also include black people as ordinary citizens, although the leaders equivocated on whether their blackness would be accepted as normal or viewed with disdain. Racialized violence was thus contained by the equivocations of mestizaje; despite the devastating impact of violence on the country, the racial dimensions of that violence were blurred by the constant potential of mestizaje to appear inclusive as well as exclusive – and black leaders themselves participated in the production of that blurring.

This unstable balance has changed in recent decades, especially with the rise of official multiculturalist policies – although these do not represent a radical break with ideologies of mestizaje.

Multicultural reform and racialized violence

From the 1960s, indigenous and, slightly later, Afro-descendant social movements began to organize politically in Latin America. These movements built on long-term indigenous and black resistance to domination, and formed part of a broader worldwide trend toward ethnic minority organization and recognition politics. In the 1990s, many Latin American states enacted political and legal reforms that defined the nation as multi-cultural and pluriethnic, and recognized indigenous (and to a lesser extent, black) minorities as culturally specific and often as the holders of particular sets of rights (e.g. in relation to land holding) (Postero 2007; Rahier 2012; Sieder 2002; Van Cott 2000; Wade 2006). Some critics see these shifts as linked to neoliberal decentralization and globalization agendas, which seek to open up new areas – often inhabited by indigenous and black communities – to capitalist exploitation, while giving limited rights to these communities and meshing their self-organization processes with the techniques and mechanisms of state governance (Hale 2002; Speed 2005; Wade 2002).

Colombia was a front-runner in these reforms, which began with the 1991 Constitution and continued with numerous laws and decrees relating to indigenous and Afro-Colombian communities. By 2013, legally constituted indigenous *resguardos* (land reserves) numbered 715, with an area of about 32 million hectares, representing 30 per cent of the national territory; although about 80 per cent of this reserve area is home to a mere 5 per cent of reserve-dwelling indigenous people.[3] Indigenous reserves receive fiscal transfers from the state under a scheme called Participación en los Ingresos Corrientes de la Nación (participation in the current income of the nation). In 1993, Law 70 created new rights for 'black communities,' including the possibility of collective land titles, which in 2013 numbered 181, encompassing over 5 million hectares or about 4 per cent of the national territory (Salinas Abdala 2014). Over 95 per cent of these lands are located in the country's Pacific coastal region, an underdeveloped area, the popula-tion of which is about 80 per cent black. This law and subsequent decrees have created arguably the most comprehensive legal framework for the recognition of black people in Latin America (with the possible exception of Brazil's affirmative action policies).

These measures represent new forms of legal inclusion and citizenship for black and indigenous minorities in Colombia. Such official multiculturalism is often understood as representing a radical break with regimes of mestizaje, seen as simply creating a mestizo homogeneity. My view is that multiculturalism reconfigures the previous ways in which difference was actively produced and managed in ideologies and practices of mestizaje. Difference now becomes a basis on which to claim special rights and establish or reinforce ethnic communities, which can be portrayed as representing modern political democracy, rather than being an obstacle to it. But the image of the mestizo nation remains powerful: it coexists easily alongside multiculturalist representations of differ-ence, because difference was always already present in the idea of the mestizo nation. This much is evident from recent genetic studies of the Colombian population – and their reporting in popular media – which rehearse the familiar script of three original source 'populations' (rather than 'races') mixing together to form a majority mestizo population, whose DNA is heterogeneous but nevertheless the norm, compared to the DNA of indigenous and black populations, treated as distinctive bio-cultural samples. Strikingly, such studies manage to combine elements of both mestizaje discourse (the mestizo is the norm) and multicultural discourse (black and indigenous people are separate and distinctive) (Olarte Sierra and Díaz del Castillo Hernández 2014; Wade et al. 2014).

The continuities linking mestizaje and multiculturalism are evident in the simultaneous existence of racialized inclusion and exclusion. The liberal tension between inclusion and exclusion that shaped mestizaje remains evident in a multiculturalism shaped by neoliberal policies that recognize ethnic minority rights, while facilitating capitalist exploitation of ethnic group territories. However, the exclusion of racialized minorities now operates more powerfully through violence and displacement. As noted above, violence has occasionally targeted such minorities in the past in Latin America. In Colombia, black and indigenous groups were caught up in the cross fire of state, guerrilla, and paramilitary violence before the 1991 reforms, and some of them made specific efforts to distance themselves from these conflicts. In the mid-1980s, anthropologist Jaime Arocha Rodríguez (1987) argued that the way violence affected ethnic minorities was being widely ignored, especially in relation to Afro-Colombians, in keeping with the tendency pre-1991 of public policy to sidestep ethnic difference and particularly blackness. His analysis traced a continuous pattern of violence from colonial times, enacted through racial discrimination and segregation, and operating in the mid-20th century in terms of discrimination, encroachment by colonists, and capitalist interests on lands held by Afro-Colombian and indigenous groups, and interethnic frictions (including those between indigenous and Afro-Colombian groups over lands, which resulted in part from the greater recognition of indigenous land claims by the state) (Arocha Rodríguez 1987, 1989, 1998; see also Chomsky 2007; Pulido Londoño 2010).

On the other hand, Arocha and others noted that La Violencia of the 1950s had been mainly confined to the Andean center of the country, although with important impacts on the plains to the east of the Andes, known as Los Llanos. Afro-Colombian communities had generally escaped this violence: in the Pacific coastal region, for example, although violence spilled over from Antioquia into the Northern Chocó province of the region, when the army pursued Liberal guerrillas who took refuge there (Almario 2004, 82), it is also true that local Conservative leaders had turned away the *chulavitas*, the Conservative 'police' militias sent from the interior of the country to terrorize and kill Liberals (Agudelo 2005, 127; Castillo 2007, 323). Arocha characterized areas of the Pacific coastal region as a 'haven of peace' that, at least until the early 1990s, was relatively immune from the conflicts wracking central areas of the country, and able to resolve local disagreements without resorting to violence (1999, 116).

During the 1990s and 2000s, however, violence spread into areas of the Caribbean coastal region, which had largely escaped the violence of the 1950s, and where significant black and indigenous populations live. In particular, violence spread into the Pacific coastal region, with its predominant Afro-Colombian population as well as significant indigenous populations. The region became a target for guerrilla activity and soon after for military incursions. Most damaging of all, paramilitary forces, using tactics of terror and coercion, displaced large numbers of people, which severely under-mined many of the newly gained collective land titles (Wouters 2001) and converted the whole region into a 'strategic space' for conflicts between the state, the guerrilla, and the paramilitaries (Almario 2004, 86), imposing a 'geography of terror' replete with 'landscapes of fear' (Oslender 2004, 40, 2007). Sanford (2004) sees displacement as a key strategy of the war, rather than its side effect (cf. Escobar 2003). Challenging these destructive forces, black communities and organizations such as the Proceso de Comunidades Negras (PCN) have devised tactics of resistance, showing great resilience and creating some spaces for autonomous action and alternative life projects (Asher 2009; Escobar 2008; Oslender 2016).[4]

The violence affecting the Pacific region is part of a war with goals that are not only political but also economic, facilitated by the state's neoliberal openness to global capital. As local people have been displaced, capitalist economic interests that had a foothold in the region have expanded their range of operations in African palm-oil plantations, industrial shrimp-farming, mining, and so on (Escobar 2003, 2008). In effect, the displacement of local people by tactics of terror opened the way for economic interests to take over the recently 'cleansed' landscape – *limpieza* (cleansing) is a common term for campaigns of forced displacement and killing. In short, although violence in Colombia is long established and endemic, indigenous and especially black regions and people have recently been included into its ambit in unprecedented ways.

Data on displacement reinforce this picture. *Desplazados* (displaced people) are flood-ing towns and cities all over Colombia. The Consultoría para los Derechos Humanos y el Desplazamiento (CODHES) estimates 4.1 million Colombians were forced from their homes between 1999 and 2012 (CODHES 2012). Of these people, it was estimated in 2009 that 24 per cent belonged to some ethnic group, with 17 per cent being Afro-Colombians and 6.5 per cent indigenous.[5] The 2005 census showed that, of the total population, Afro-Colombians were 10.5 per cent and indigenous people were 3.4 per cent. These categories are heavily overrepresented among the displaced. The circulation of these statistics is part of a public recognition – by the state, the media, and ethnic social movements – that the violence now has noteworthy racial–ethnic dimensions.

The link between the extension of new rights to Afro-Colombian communities and the extension of pitiless violence into the areas where key dimensions of those rights (collective land titles) are being exercised obeys the perverse logic of a Colombian society in which violence and impunity coexist with a comprehensive system of legal and constitutional protections. On the one hand, there is inclusion, not just as a fiction, but in terms of land titles given to black communities, resguardos assigned to indigen-ous people, and fiscal transfers made to them. There is also the *tutela* mechanism,[6] used by individual black people to challenge everyday racial discrimination (Meertens 2009) and, in one case, used by a black NGO to force a local city council to recognize the existence of a 'black community' in the city – effectively reshaping that category as enshrined in Law 70, which restricted eligibility to rural black communities in the Pacific region (Wade 2002). The state has recognized the 'victim' status of many Afro-Colombian and indigenous people and the 2011 Victims Law, designed to restore land and make reparation to the victims of internal conflict and displacement, includes ethnically 'differentialist' policies (Cárdenas 2012; Jaramillo Salazar 2014; Salinas Abdala 2014).

On the other hand, there is continued and very violent exclusion, by means of the displacement and assassination of Afro-Colombian and indigenous people, at a level disproportionate to their presence in the population. Much of this violence is carried out by forces that, while they have important connections to the state, are not the state but rather operate outside the law and with widespread impunity.

Official multiculturalism actively produces and manages blackness and indigenous-ness, playing a new variation on previous ideas of mestizaje, but with significant continuities. In line with neoliberal agendas of community self-management, it brings ethnic communities into direct relationship with the state (e.g. via the land reform agency and other state departments, such as those for justice, planning, statistics, culture, etc.), bureaucratizing them and instituting them as collective citizens, charged with administering themselves under the aegis of the state. As various authors have commented, there is not a necessary contradiction between neoliberal projects of governance and the creation of collective subjects of citizenship: on the contrary, collective citizens can fit well into neoliberal governance and can extend the reach of the state into peripheral areas where it had little presence (Hale 2002, 2005; Postero 2007; Speed 2005). As well, subaltern minorities use the spaces created – or rather retooled – for them by official multiculturalism and its legislation as a vehicle for their claims (with good reason, as struggles to promote these claims were a significant spur to multiculturalist reform in the first place). In this sense, Afro-Colombian mobilization around a black identity connects, at some points, with official recognition of 'black communities' as legitimate interlocutors with the state. Inclusion is a common ideal; the state and the minorities approach it with rather different perspectives.

At the same time, violence and displacement tend to produce the kind of erosive effects associated with mestizaje-as-ethnocide or simply as imposed assimilation: significant numbers of Afro-Colombians and indigenous people are killed and others are recruited into guerrilla and paramilitary armies (sometimes forcibly). Many more end up in cities, both as *desplazados* and as 'voluntary' urban migrants.

Although, for Afro-Colombians at least, ethnic nuclei form in the cities, reproducing difference in urban spaces, and cities are places for ethnic–racial organization and resistance (Barbary and Urrea 2004; Wade 1993, 1999), there are also powerful forces of structural violence and urban assimilation in the longer term. Urbanization has long been seen as a motor of mestizaje, and it involves both inclusion and exclusion, but violent displacement results a more agonistic version of this dynamic as large numbers of vulnerable black and indigenous people are thrust into an urban environment. For black people in Cali, life expectancy and mortality rates are a reflection of the direct violence of homicide and the structural violence of poverty and environmental stresses (including racism) that cause illness, early death, and a suicide rate that is double that for nonblacks. Rates of homicide are twice those for nonblacks; Afro-Colombians' life expectancy is 8 years lower in poor areas of the city and 5 years lower even in middle-class areas; for black males aged 10–24 years, mortality rates are about double those of nonblack peers (Urrea Giraldo 2012, 154–156). These patterns are of course related to class position, but this does not alter the fact that violence, both immediate and structural, powerfully shapes the experience of urbanization for many black people.

At the same time, the areas that are 'cleansed' – such as parts of the Pacific coastal region – are the object of intense interest from the state and capitalists, for whom it is a key site of developmentalist and geopolitical importance: a gateway onto the Pacific basin, seen as the hub of global development for the 21st century; a repository of resources, ranging from traditional primary products (minerals, etc.) to chemical and genetic products, perhaps as yet uncharted, stored in the region's famed biodiversity and exploitable within new conservationist regimes of the capitalist management of life itself (Escobar 1997, 2008). Thus, as black and indigenous people are displaced from these archaic seeming, but actually intensely modern peripheries, they leave spaces open for colonization of a more industrial kind, which assimilates the region into the national project of modernization, progress, and neoliberal opening to global capital. Of course, progress was part of the older regime of mestizaje, which was not just about assimilating individuals but also integrating and modernizing nations. But now progress takes on a more racially violent face.

Conclusion: mestizaje, multiculturalism, and violence

I have argued that mestizaje and multiculturalism are connected through a common dynamic of inclusion and exclusion, which characterizes liberal social orders in general. Both regimes aspire to be inclusive – one by declaring difference to be irrelevant in the public sphere, even as everyone actively reproduces it; the other by making difference a reason for inclusion. Both also effect the exclusions necessary to maintain political hierarchy and an economic division of labor.

But there is a difference between the way racial exclusions work in each regime. Before multiculturalism, the possibilities of racial inclusion and exclusion were mediated through mestizaje, which contained both processes within itself in a relationship of mutual constitution, and thus blurred the racialization of violence; this was not just imposed from above but also attracted some support from below. With the declaration of official multiculturalism, although there are strong continuities with ideologies of mestizaje insofar as they too produced difference, a distance opens up between the means of inclusion, which are increasingly channeled through multiculturalist legislation and mobilization around racial–ethnic identities, and the means of exclusion, which are effected most glaringly by murder, terrorization, and displacement. This undermines mestizaje's ability to equivocate between inclusion and exclusion.

The distance between racial inclusion and exclusion is now more evident than it was, both because the violence affecting ethnic minorities has become more intense and pervasive, and because mestizaje is less able to operate as an ambiguous equivocator in a multiculturalist context. Previously, the inclusions and exclusions of mestizaje did not align closely with the inclusions and exclusions of state and civil violence: there were some overlaps, as I showed, but these were partial. With the advent of multiculturalism, the two dynamics of racial inclusion/exclusion and violence have become more closely integrated and aligned, laying bare the ethnic and racial dimensions of violent exclusion. The more explicit recognition of black and indigenous minorities, as special classes of citizen to be included on the basis of their difference, generates both the more intense practice and the more public recognition of the violent exclusions they experience.

Processes of inclusion and exclusion in Colombia also – indeed mainly – operate in nonethnic ways. Violence has ethnic dimensions, but it is not primarily about ethnicity and race. But the recent intensification of violence affecting black and indigenous communities is not just a difference-blind accident: there is a structural coincidence between the regional location of these communities – peripheral, vulnerable, colonizable – and the kinds of places targeted both by armed actors and neoliberal capitalist colonization. The inclusions and exclusions that affect racial and ethnic minorities have larger repercussions, because mestizaje and multiculturalism act as a definition of the nation as a whole. They speak to the fate of the nation, and the partial dethroning of mestizaje as an official sign of the nation – however much it continues to operate as an everyday ideology of nationhood – makes more evident the racialized exclusions that characterize Colombian society.

Parallels can be drawn with contexts in Brazil. Above, I referred to Collins' study of Pelourinho, in Salvador, to illustrate the diversity of forms of violence deployed by the city authorities, ranging from interventions for data collection on the local populace, through physical displacement, to murder. Collins (2015, 281) notes that 'the attempt [by the local state] to extinguish violently the residents … is fairly new;' it is a recent development linked to the post-1990 program of patrimonialization and reification of blackness, which is part of Brazil's multicultural reforms. According to Collins, the attempt 'exemplifies and reproduces the blurry boundaries between extirpation and care that are so essential to the heritage-based management of the life of an Afro-Bahian populace in the Pelourinho' (Collins 2015). The state not only intervenes, now with greater violence, to remove locals but it also retains some locals considered suitable to represent Afro-Bahian heritage in an officially multicultural Brazil, and, in collaboration with NGOs, delivers health-care projects to the residents. Thus, the 'systematic war' waged on the area's residents by the local state was balanced with the authorities' assurances that it was caring for them (210).

This ambivalent relation between extirpation and care is linked to ideologies of *mestiçagem* insofar as Pelourinho has long served both as a symbol of African roots (i.e. an original source for mestiçagem) and as a site of an Afro-Bahian version of race mixture, in which elite and middle-class white men came, until recently, to consort with black women in the brothels and taverns of the zone's red-light district. These sexual exchanges parallel the ones understood to have founded Brazil's mestizo population and thus function as 'a path for passage from interior spaces like brothels … to the public life of the nation' (Collins 2015, 162). Pelourinho's mixture is 'a space for constructing inclusionary and exclusionary impetuses that lie at the core of the production of national history and community' (161). Collins does not make a specific argument about changes and continuities that occur when multiculturalism retools mestizaje, but I am struck by his identification of 'extirpation' and 'systematic war,' alongside rhetorics and practices of care, as post-1990 phenomena linked to the reification of Brazilian blackness.

Making exclusion more evident is arguably a useful thing. Mestizaje has the power to equivocate and make ambiguous, but in so doing it masks the oppression that exists alongside integration and makes it more difficult to contest. Multiculturalist legislation, which has added to, rather than superseded mestizaje in Colombia and elsewhere, has provided Afro-Colombian and indigenous people with new legal tools and political spaces with which to challenge discrimination and claim rights. This is part of the increasing 'judicialization' of ethnic politics, which may occur particularly in the transnational arena of multilateral bodies such as the ILO (International Labor Organization), creating opportunities for indigenous people to formalize their claims and take them to court (Sieder, Angell, and Schjolden 2005). The increasing entry of indigenous and Afro-descendant actors into the political arena, which has been a corollary of official multi-culturalism and ethnic mobilization, has provided new means by which ethnic and racial minorities can claim rights and defend livelihoods. The price they have to pay is, however, increased violent attacks on precisely those rights and livelihoods.

Notes

1. Women gained the vote between 1929 (Ecuador) and 1961 (Paraguay).
2. The subtitle to Zapata Olivella's autobiographical novel, ¡Levántate, mulato! (rise up, mulato!) is the phrase 'Por mi raza hablará el espíritu' (the spirit will speak for/through my race), the motto of the Universidad Autónoma Nacional de México, coined in 1921 by its rector, José Vasconcelos. The motto referred to Vasconcelos' vision of the Latin American mestizo as the positive future for humanity (Vasconcelos [1925] 1997). Zapata Olivella distanced himself from the homogenizing overtones of Vasconcelos' romantic idealism, but he still valued the notion of the hybrid (de Luca 2001).
3. These resguardos do not all date from 1991, as reserves existed as a legal institution from colonial times.
4. Sanford (2004) describes the 'Peace Communities,' formed in the Pacific coastal region by returnees from violent displacement, which act as spaces that refuse all armed actors. They draw on state administrative and juridical agencies, as well as the church and international entities, to sustain themselves (see also Castillo 2007, 334–338).
5. These 2009 figures are given by the Comisión de Seguimiento a la Política Pública Sobre Desplazamiento Forzado (2009, 145). Figures for 2002 estimated 38 per cent of displaced people belonged to an ethnic group, of which 33 per cent were Afro-Colombian; see CODHES bulletin 44, Destierro y repoblamiento, April 2003, http://www.codhes.org/index.php?option=com_si&type=4. Castillo (2007, 330) cites official statistics for the early 2000s, indicating 43 per cent of displaced people were Afro-Colombians. The 2008 figures cited by Rodríguez Garavito, Alfonso Sierra, and Cavelier Adarve (2009) are lower.
6. The tutela is a writ for the protection of constitutional rights, found in many Latin American judicial systems, and widely used by individuals in Colombia to protect their everyday rights.

ORCID

Peter Wade ⓘ http://orcid.org/0000-0003-4070-4187

References

Agudelo, C. E. 2005. *Retos del multiculturalismo en Colombia: política y poblaciones negras*. Medellín: La Carreta Editores, Institut de recherche pour le développment, Universidad Nacional de Colombia, Instituto Colombiano de Antropología e Historia.

Almario, O. 2004. "Dinámica y consecuencias del conflicto armado colombiano en el Pacífico: limpieza étnica y desterritorialización de afrocolombianos e indígenas y 'multiculturalismo' de estado e indolencia nacional." In *Conflicto e (in)visibilidad: retos en los estudios de la gente negra en Colombia*, edited by E. Restrepo and A. Rojas, 73–120. Popayán: Editorial Universidad del Cauca.

Andermann, J. 2000. "Argentine Literature and the 'Conquest of the Desert', 1872–1896." Iberoamerican Museum of Visual Culture, Birkbeck College. Accessed May 9, 2009. http://www.bbk.ac.uk/ibamuseum/texts/Andermann02.htm.

Andrews, G. R. 1991. *Blacks and Whites in São Paulo, Brazil, 1888–1988*. Madison: University of Wisconsin Press.

Appelbaum, N. P., A. S. Macpherson, and K. A. Rosemblatt, eds. 2003. *Race and Nation in Modern Latin America*. Chapel Hill: University of North Carolina Press.

Arocha Rodríguez, J. 1987. "Violencia contra minorías étnicas en Colombia." In *Colombia: violencia y democracia*, edited by Comisión de Estudios sobre la Violencia en Colombia, 105–133. Bogotá: Universidad Nacional.

Arocha Rodríguez, J. 1989. "Aniquilamiento en traje de tolerancia: El Plan Nacional de Rehabilitacion en Colombia." *América Indígena* 49 (1): 171–192.

Arocha Rodríguez, J. 1998. "Etnia y guerra: relación ausente en los estudios sobre las violencias colombianas." In *Las violencias: inclusión creciente*, edited by J. Arocha, F. Cubides, and M. Jimeno, 205–235. Bogotá: Centro de Estudios Sociales, Universidad Nacional de Colombia.

Arocha Rodríguez, J. 1999. *Ombligados de Ananse: hilos ancestrales y modernos en el Pacífico colombiano*. Bogotá: Centro de Estudios Sociales, Facultad de Ciencias Humanas, Universidad Nacional de Colombia.

Asher, K. 2009. *Black and Green: Afro-Colombians, Development, and Nature in the Pacific Lowlands*. Durham: Duke University Press.

Barbary, O., and F. Urrea, eds. 2004. *Gente negra en Colombia, dinámicas sociopolíticas en Cali y el Pacífico*. Cali: CIDSE/Univalle, IRD, Colciencias.

Baumeister, A. 2000. *Liberalism and the 'Politics of Difference'*. Edinburgh: Edinburgh University Press.

Bushnell, D. 1993. *The Making of Modern Colombia: A Nation in Spite of Itself*. Berkeley: University of California Press.

Cárdenas, R. 2012. "Multicultural Politics for Afro-Colombians: An Articulation 'Without Guarantees'." In *Black Social Movements in Latin America: From Monocultural Mestizaje to Multiculturalism*, edited by J. M. Rahier, 113–134. New York: Palgrave Macmillan.

Castillo, L. C. 2007. *Etnicidad y nación: el desafío de la diversidad en Colombia*. Cali: Editorial Universidad del Valle.

Caulfield, S. 2000. *In Defense of Honor: Sexual Morality, Modernity, and Nation in Early-Twentieth-Century Brazil*. Durham: Duke University Press.

Chomsky, A. 2007. "The Logic of Displacment: Afro-Colombans and the War in Colombia." In *Beyond Salvery: The Multlayered Legacy of Aficans in Latin America and the Caribbean*, edited by D. J. David, 171–198. Lanham: Rowman and Littlefield.

CODHES (Consultoría para los Derechos Humanos y el Desplazamiento). 2012. "Estadísticas históricas de desplazamiento." Consultoría para los Derechos Humanos y el Desplazamiento. Accessed January 5, 2015. http://www.codhes.org/index.php?option=com_si&type=1.

Collins, J. 2015. *Revolt of the Saints: Memory and Redemption in the Twilight of Brazilian 'Racial Democracy'*. Durham: Duke University Press.

Comisión de Seguimiento a la Política Pública Sobre Desplazamiento Forzado. 2009. *El reto ante la tragedia humanitaria del desplazamiento forzado*. Vol. 3. Superar la exclusión social de la población desplazada. Bogotá: Comisión de Seguimiento a la Política Pública Sobre Desplazamiento Forzado.

de Luca, D. 2001. "La práctica autobiográfica de Manuel Zapata Olivella en ¡Levántate mulato! 'Por mi raza hablará el espíritu'." *Afro-Hispanic Review* 20 (1): 43–54. doi:10.2307/23054509.

Engerman, S. L., and K. L. Sokoloff. 2005. "The Evolution of Suffrage Institutions in the New World." *The Journal of Economic History* 65 (4): 891–921. doi:10.1017/S0022050705000343.

Escobar, A. 1997. "Cultural Politics and Biological Diversity: State, Capital and Social Movements in the Pacific Coast of Colombia." In *Between Resistance and Revolution: Cultural Politics and Social Protest*, edited by R. G. Fox and O. Starn, 40–64. New Brunswick: Rutgers University Press.

Escobar, A. 2003. "Displacement, Development, and Modernity in the Colombian Pacific." *International Social Science Journal* 55 (175): 157–167. doi:10.1111/issj.2003.55.issue-175.

Escobar, A. 2008. *Territories of Difference: Place, Movements, Life, Redes.* Durham: Duke University Press.

Fry, P., Y. Maggie, M. C. Maio, S. Monteiro, and R. V. Santos, eds. 2007. *Divisões perigosas: políticas raciais no Brasil contemporâneo.* Rio de Janeiro: Civilização Brasileira.

Goldberg, D. T. 1993. *Racist Culture: Philosophy and the Politics of Meaning.* Oxford: Blackwell.

Goldberg, D. T. 2008. *The Threat of Race: Reflections on Racial Neoliberalism.* Malden: Wiley-Blackwell.

Gould, J. L. 1998. *To Die in This Way: Nicaraguan Indians and the Myth of Mestizaje, 1880–1965.* Durham: Duke University Press.

Green, W. J. 2000. "Left Liberalism and Race in the Evolution of Colombian Popular National Identity." *The Americas* 57 (1): 95–124. doi:10.1017/S0003161500030224.

Hale, C. R. 2002. "Does Multiculturalism Menace? Governance, Cultural Rights, and the Politics of Identity in Guatemala." *Journal of Latin American Studies* 34: 485–524. doi:10.1017/S0022216X02006521.

Hale, C. R. 2005. "Neoliberal Multiculturalism: The Remaking of Cultural Rights and Racial Dominance in Central America." *PoLAR: Political and Legal Anthropology Review* 28 (1): 10–28. doi:10.1525/pol.2005.28.1.10.

Helg, A. 1995. *Our Rightful Share: The Afro-Cuban Struggle for Equality, 1886–1912.* Chapel Hill: University of North Carolina Press.

Holt, T. C. 1992. *The Problem of Freedom: Race, Labor, and Politics in Jamaica and Britain, 1832–1938.* Baltimore: Johns Hopkins University Press.

Jaramillo Salazar, P. 2014. *Etnicidad y victimización. Genealogías de la violencia y la indigenidad en el norte de Colombia.* Bogotá: Ediciones Uniandes.

Larson, B. 2004. *Trials of Nation Making: Liberalism, Race, and Ethnicity in the Andes, 1810–1910.* Cambridge: Cambridge University Press.

Lasso, M. 2007. *Myths of Harmony: Race and Republicanism during the Age of Revolution, Colombia 1795–1831.* Pittsburgh: University of Pittsburgh Press.

Lentin, A. 2004. *Racism and Anti-Racism in Europe.* London: Pluto.

Martínez, M. E. 2008. *Genealogical Fictions: Limpieza de Sangre, Religion, and Gender in Colonial Mexico.* Stanford: Stanford University Press.

Mattos de Castro, H. M. 1995. "El color inexistente. Relaciones raciales y trabajo rural en Rio de Janeiro tras la abolición de la esclavitud." *Historia Social* 22: 83–100.

Meertens, D. 2009. "Discriminación racial, desplazamiento y género en las sentencias de la Corte Constitucional. El racismo cotidiano en el banquillo." *Universitas Humanística* 66: 83–106.

Mehta, U. S. 1997. "Liberal Strategies of Exclusion." In *Tensions of Empire: Colonial Cultures in a Bourgeois World*, edited by F. Cooper and A. L. Stoler, 59–86. Berkeley: University of California Press.

Mignolo, W. 2011. *The Darker Side of Western Modernity: Global Futures, Decolonial Options.* Durham: Duke University Press.

Noguera, C. E. 2003. *Medicina y política: discurso médico y prácticas higiénicas durante la primera mitad del siglo XX en Colombia.* Medellín: Fondo Editorial Universidad EAFIT.

Olarte Sierra, M. F., and A. Díaz del Castillo Hernández. 2014. "'We Are All the Same, We All Are Mestizos': Imagined Populations and Nations in Genetics Research in Colombia." *Science as Culture* 23 (2): 226–252. doi:10.1080/09505431.2013.838214.

Oslender, U. 2004. "Geografías de terror y desplazamiento forzado en el Pacífico colombiano: conceptualizando el problema y buscando respuestas." In *Conflicto e (in)visibilidad: retos en los estudios de la gente negra en Colombia*, edited by E. Restrepo and A. Rojas, 35–52. Popayán: Editorial Universidad del Cauca.

Oslender, U. 2007. "Violence in Development: The Logic of Forced Displacement on Colombia's Pacific Coast." *Development in Practice* 17 (6): 752–764. doi:10.1080/09614520701628147.

Oslender, U. 2016. *The Geographies of Social Movements: Afro-Colombian Mobilization and the Aquatic Space*. Durham: Duke University Press.

Pisano, P. 2012. *Liderazgo político 'negro' en Colombia, 1943–1964*. Bogotá: Universidad Nacional de Colombia.

Postero, N. G. 2007. *Now We Are Citizens: Indigenous Politics in Postmulticultural Bolivia*. Stanford: Stanford University Press.

Pulido Londoño, H. A. 2010. "Violencia y asimetrías étnicas. Multiculturalismo, debate antropológico y etnicidad de los afrocolombianos (1980–1990)." *Antípoda, Revista de Antropología y Arqueología* 11: 259–280. doi:10.7440/antipoda11.2010.13.

Rahier, J., ed. 2012. *Black Social Movements in Latin America: From Monocultural Mestizaje to Multiculturalism*. New York: Palgrave Macmillan.

Ramos, A. 1998. *Indigenism: Ethnic Politics in Brazil*. Madison: University of Wisconsin Press.

Restrepo, O. 1984. "La Comisión Corográfica y las ciencias sociales." In *Un siglo de investigación social: la antropología en Colombia*, edited by J. Arocha and N. de Friedemann, 131–158. Bogotá: Etno.

Rodríguez Garavito, C., T. Alfonso Sierra, and I. Cavelier Adarve. 2009. *Raza y derechos humanos en Colombia: informe sobre discriminación racial y derechos de la población afrocolombiana*. Bogotá: Universidad de los Andes, Facultad de Derecho, Centro de Investigaciones Sociojurídicas (CIJUS), Observatorio de Discriminación Racial, Ediciones Uniandes.

Roldán, M. 2002. *Blood and Fire: La Violencia in Antioquia, Colombia, 1946–1953*. Durham: Duke University Press.

Rose, N., and P. Miller. 2008. *Governing the Present: Administering Economic, Social, and Personal Life*. Cambridge: Polity.

Salinas Abdala, Y. 2014. "Los derechos territoriales de los grupos étnicos: ¿un compromiso social, una obligación constitucional o una tarea hecha a medias?" *Punto de Encuentro* 67: 1–39.

Sanders, J. 2004. *Contentious Republicans: Popular Politics, Race, and Class in Nineteenth-Century Colombia*. Durham: Duke University Press.

Sanford, V. 2003. "Learning to Kill by Proxy: Colombian Paramilitaries and the Legacy of Central American Death Squads, Contras, and Civil Patrols." *Journal of Social Justice* 30 (3): 63–81.

Sanford, V. 2004. "Contesting Displacement in Colombia: Citizenship and State Sovereignty at the Margins." In *Anthropology in the Margins of the State*, edited by V. Das and D. Poole, 253–277. Santa Fe: School of American Research.

Sieder, R., ed. 2002. *Multiculturalism in Latin America: Indigenous Rights, Diversity and Democracy*. Basingstoke: Palgrave Macmillan.

Sieder, R., A. Angell, and L. Schjolden, eds. 2005. *The Judicialization of Politics in Latin America*. Basingstoke: Palgrave Macmillan.

Smith, C. A. 1997. "The Symbolics of Blood: Mestizaje in the Americas." *Identities: Global Studies in Power and Culture* 3 (4): 495–521. doi:10.1080/1070289X.1997.9962576.

Speed, S. 2005. "Dangerous Discourses: Human Rights and Multiculturalism in Neoliberal Mexico." *PoLAR: Political and Legal Anthropology Review* 28 (1): 29–51. doi:10.1525/pol.2005.28.1.29.

Stepan, N. L. 1991. *"The Hour of Eugenics:" Race, Gender and Nation in Latin America*. Ithaca: Cornell University Press.

Stokes, C., and T. Meléndez, eds. 2003. *Racial Liberalism and the Politics of Urban America*. East Lansing: Michigan State University Press.

Taussig, M. 1987. *Shamanism, Colonialism, and the Wild Man: A Study in Terror and Healing*. Chicago: Chicago University Press.

Taussig, M. 2005. *Law in a Lawless Land: Diary of a 'Limpieza' in Colombia*. Chicago: University of Chicago Press.

Twinam, A. 1999. *Public Lives, Private Secrets: Gender, Honor, Sexuality and Illegitimacy in Colonial Spanish America*. Stanford: Stanford University Press.

Uribe, M. V. 2004. "Dismembering and Expelling: Semantics of Political Terror in Colombia." *Public Culture* 16 (1): 79–96. doi:10.1215/08992363-16-1-79.

Urrea Giraldo, F. 2012. "Race, Ethnicity, Crime, and Criminal Justice in Colombia." In *Race, Ethnicity, Crime, and Criminal Justice in the Americas*, edited by A. Kalunta-Crumpton, 133–168. New York: Palgrave Macmillan.

Urrea Giraldo, F., C. A. Viáfara López, and M. Viveros Vigoya. 2014. "From Whitened Miscegenation to Tri-Ethnic Multiculturalism." In *Pigmentocracies: Ethnicity, Race, and Color in Latin America*, edited by E. E. Telles and Project on Ethnicity and Race in Latin America, 81–125. Chapel Hill: University of North Carolina Press.

Van Cott, D. L. 2000. *The Friendly Liquidation of the Past: The Politics of Diversity in Latin America*. Pittsburgh: University of Pittsburgh Press.

Vasconcelos, J. [1925] 1997. *The Cosmic Race: A Bilingual Edition*. Translated by D. T. Jaén. Baltimore: Johns Hopkins University Press.

Viotti da Costa, E. 2000. *The Brazilian Empire: Myths and Histories*. 2nd ed. Chapel Hill: University of North Carolina Press.

Wacquant, L. 2012. "Three Steps to a Historical Anthropology of Actually Existing Neoliberalism." *Social Anthropology* 20 (1): 66–79. doi:10.1111/j.1469-8676.2011.00189.x.

Wade, P. 1993. *Blackness and Race Mixture: The Dynamics of Racial Identity in Colombia*. Baltimore: Johns Hopkins University Press.

Wade, P. 1999. "Working Culture: Making Cultural Identities in Cali, Colombia." *Current Anthropology* 40 (4): 449–471.

Wade, P. 2000. *Music, Race and Nation: Música Tropical in Colombia*. Chicago: University of Chicago Press.

Wade, P. 2002. "The Colombian Pacific in Perspective." *Journal of Latin American Anthropology* 7 (2): 2–33. doi:10.1525/jlca.2002.7.2.2.

Wade, P. 2005. "Rethinking Mestizaje: Ideology and Lived Experience." *Journal of Latin American Studies* 37: 239–257. doi:10.1017/S0022216X05008990.

Wade, P. 2006. "Afro-Latin Studies: Reflections on the Field." *Latin American and Caribbean Ethnic Studies* 1 (1): 105–124. doi:10.1080/17486830500509960.

Wade, P. 2009. *Race and Sex in Latin America*. London: Pluto Press.

Wade, P., C. López Beltrán, E. Restrepo, and R. V. Santos, eds. 2014. *Mestizo Genomics: Race Mixture, Nation, and Science in Latin America*. Durham: Duke University Press.

Wouters, M. 2001. "Ethnic Rights under Threat: The Black Peasant Movement against Armed Groups' Pressure in the Chocó, Colombia." *Bulletin of Latin American Research* 20 (4): 498–519. doi:10.1111/1470-9856.00027.

Yashar, D. 2005. *Contesting Citizenship in Latin America: The Rise of Indigenous Movements and the Postliberal Challenge*. Cambridge: Cambridge University Press.

Index

INDEX